DISABILITY DISRUPTIONS

DISABILITY HISTORIES

Series editors: Stefanie Hunt-Kennedy, Kim Nielsen, and Michael Rembis

Disability Histories seeks scholarship that explores the lived experiences of individuals and groups from a broad range of societies, cultures, time periods, and geographic locations, who either identified as disabled or were considered by the dominant culture to be disabled.

We conceive of disability and disabled experiences broadly and seek to include scholarship that spans a range of embodiments, including the emerging field of mad studies. We are especially interested in scholarship that not only employs innovative approaches to using disability—in constant interaction with systems of race, class, gender, and sexuality—as an analytical tool to deepen our understanding of larger power relations, ideologies, and institutions, but also engages in meaningful dialogue with other subdisciplines within history, such as legal and political histories, social histories, histories of technology, science, and medicine, histories of the body and sexuality, and histories of the development of capitalism and imperialism. We welcome submissions from a variety of geopolitical locations, especially those that situate disability history outside European and North American contexts, including regions or nations that would become identified as the "global South." We are interested in scholarship that moves beyond traditional disability frameworks and offers methodologies and approaches to disability history that are rooted in decolonial, transnational, and transimperial perspectives.

For a list of books in the series, please see our website at www.press.uillinois.edu.

DISABILITY DISRUPTIONS

Gender, Family, and Care in Post-1989 Poland

NATALIA PAMUŁA

UNIVERSITY OF ILLINOIS PRESS
Urbana, Chicago, and Springfield

1 2 3 4 5 C P 5 4 3 2 1
♾ This book is printed on acid-free paper.

Cataloging data available from the Library of Congress

ISBN 978-0-252-04990-3 (hardcover)
ISBN 978-0-252-08956-5 (paperback)
ISBN 978-0-252-04906-4 (ebook)

The manufacturer's authorized representative in
the EU for product safety is Mare Nostrum Group
B.V, Doelen 72, 4831 GR Breda, The Netherlands.
Email: gpsr@mare-nostrum.co.uk

CONTENTS

ACKNOWLEDGMENTS

I am deeply indebted to many activists with disabilities and caregivers who have publically shared their stories and fought for their rights in Poland for many years. This book would have not been written if it was not for their resilience, strength, and courage. Their experiences, stories, and confessions have shaped my thinking about disability and caregiving. I would like to thank a no-longer-existing activist group, Art. 6, which welcomed me when I returned to Poland in 2018 after six years in the United States and taught me a lot about disability, ableism, and, in particular, solidarity and allyship.

I am also indebted to many people who have read and commented on earlier versions of this book. I would like to thank my friends and colleagues from the Gender and Sexuality Research Group at the University of Warsaw: Jędrzej Burszta, Ludmiła Janion, Aleksandra Kamińska, Agnieszka Kotwasińska, Karolina Krasuska, Anna Kurowicka, Joanna Mąkowska, and Marta Usiekniewicz, who offered valuable feedback at different stages of this project and energized my writing. I also want to thank the doctoral students working with us in the Gender and Sexuality Research Group: Olga Gajek, Joanna Kaniewska, Maria Łusakowska, Aleksandra Malinowska, Zuzanna Mazzoll, Julia Płaczkiewicz, Joanna Szymaniak, and Anna Temel. I am extremely lucky to have worked at the American Studies Center at the University of Warsaw, which provided me with institutional support. In particular, I would like to thank Tomasz Basiuk, Paweł Frelik, Grzegorz Kość, and Anna Kurowicka for their encouragement, kindness, and professional advice. I would also like to thank Agnieszka Kościańska for her mentoring and unwavering belief in my project and scholarship. Krystyna Mazur was the first mentor I met in my academic life and nothing—neither this book nor, earlier, my PhD—would have been possible without her. I have benefited tremendously from the professional advice, kindness, and support I received from Cynthia Wu. Ewa Płonowska Ziarek and Michael Rembis were the best supervisors and mentors I could have imagined.

Thank you to Małgorzata Rajtar, Michael Rembis, Robert Stock, and Magdalena Zdrodowska for inviting me to share my ideas when they were not quite in shape. I am grateful for my Friday evening Zoom disability studies in eastern Europe gang: Maria Bucur, Frances Bernstein, Evgenia Davidova, Maria Cristina Galmarini, Kateřina Kolářová, Sarah Phillips, Magdalena Zdrodowska who read and commented on earlier versions of this project and helped me articulate my ideas. I also want to thank Ada Arendt for her support, warmth, and generosity when commenting on the first ideas for this book. In 2023, Katarzyna Ojrzyńska organized a panel, "Polish Dis-stories: from the Nazi Extermination to the 1989 Transformation," for a conference in Liverpool, and I am very grateful to her for putting together in conversation her work, Marcin Stasiak's work, and mine. I am excited to be a part of a growing Polish disability studies research and very happy to work and be in dialogue with Kamila Albin, Katarzyna Bierzanowska, Monika Dubiel, Wojciech Figiel, Zbigniew Głąb, Ewelina Godlewska-Byliniak, Angelika Greniuk, Magdalena Kocejko, Agnieszka Król, Iwona Leonowicz-Bukała, Justyna Lipko-Konieczna, Monika Ładoń, Paweł Kubicki, Dorota Krzemińska, Monika Kwaśniewska-Mikuła, Sławomir Łotysz, Marek Mackiewicz-Ziccardi, Klaudia Muca-Małek, Katarzyna Ojrzyńska, Sabina Pawlik, Anna Piniewska, Mateusz Płatos, Patrycja Polczyk, Maria Reimann, Jolanta Rzeźnicka-Krupa, Marta Sałkowska, Marcin Stasiak, Monika Struck-Peregończyk, Magda Szarota, Monika Świerkosz, Milena Trojanowska-Ludwin, Alicja Wang, Justyna Wielgus, Agnieszka Wołowicz, Izabela Zawadzka, Magdalena Zdrodowska, and Katarzyna Żeglicka. I am sorry to all of those I might have omitted here, and I hope that Polish disability studies keeps growing and developing.

I am grateful that the University of Illinois Press team saw the potential in this project, and it was a huge pleasure to work with editor Alison Syring. Alison, Megan Donnan, and Leah Ann Cowan made the publishing process smooth and understandable. The anonymous reviewers provided invaluable feedback, and these acknowledgments are not going to adequately express my gratitude for the close reading they did of the manuscript. The series editors, Stefanie Hunt-Kennedy, Michael Rembis, and Kim Nielsen, were very helpful in asking questions and bringing up topics, which helped me shape this project. I also want to thank Michael Rembis who has continued to support and guide me long after my graduation, for which I am extremely grateful. I hope to find a novel as good as *Easy Reading* again!

Over the years, I have benefited tremendously from the wisdom, humor, and generosity shared with me by Agnieszka Król. I cannot imagine doing disability studies without talking about it with Magda Szarota. I am in awe of her deep commitment to disability activism, disability justice, and human rights. I am grateful for all the conversations and her support: It carried me forward. I am extremely fortunate to have Selma Siew Li Bidlingmaier as a friend who cares and cheers for me. I have learned a lot from the way she expresses and teaches care. And she is always able to find the best vegan restaurant in town!

I want to thank Ela Krawczyk, Mateusz Płaziński, Roman Dmowski, Tomasz Kaznocha, Kasia Kiełtyka, Paweł Jasik, and Arek Tomaszewski for being great friends and family, with whom time passes by always too quickly and who remind me that there are other things in life than working and writing.

I cannot express how lucky and happy I am that my Buffalo community Guðrún Elsa Bragadóttir, Shayani Bhattacharya, Karolina Kulicka, and Doruk Tatar have remained a part of my life. Their friendship has sustained and nurtured me. Doruk, I cannot wait for the trip in Turkey! Elsa, our Zoom meetings and trips in Iceland and Poland are a great source of joy, pleasure, and comfort for me. And your movie recommendations are always the best, most funny, and smart. Shayani, I remember with great affection our talks in coffee shops and restaurants, and I look forward to many more in the future (in Calcutta!). Our talks of the pains and pleasures of academic life and life in general keep me going. Karolina, I am so happy you contacted me all these years back in January, and that what started as a tragedy (or farce) ended as a friendship. I admire your courage, curiosity, and passion for learning new things and not being afraid of new challenges.

I do not know how to thank Anna Kurowicka. She not only read every page of this book at least twice, but was always happy to talk about all my doubts and concerns. I am deeply grateful for her friendship and support.

Lastly, I thank my mother, Jolanta Pamuła, and my sister, Aleksandra Pamuła, for their unwavering support and cheering me on. Words cannot express my gratitude for the love, support, joy, and support they give me. I am so grateful to Justyna Pelaska, my partner, who has made my life so much fuller and richer.

The work on this book has been funded by a National Science Centre grant (2020/39/D/HS2/01223).

DISABILITY DISRUPTIONS

INTRODUCTION

In April 2024, the daily news platform OKO.press published an interview with Joanna Marnik, the mother of a twenty-one-year-old disabled son, Bruno. In it, Marnik discussed the complex network of the state, family, welfare system, and "ordinariness of abandonment" she has experienced living alone with her child, like many other mothers raising disabled children in Poland.[1] The title of the interview encapsulates the mother–child relationship in these circumstances: "Bruno and I are connected vessels. A mother of a disabled child asks that euthanasia be extended to her son."[2] Despite touching upon such difficult and controversial topics as euthanasia and state indifference toward the disabled population, thereby directly contradicting the claims of politicians promising support to families raising disabled children, this interview did not provoke any public discussion.

As the state has withdrawn from the sphere of care and assistance, this mother is the only person tasked with caring for her disabled child and with organizing their lives. State benefits for disabled families are vastly inadequate, and, given the lack of a personal assistance act in Poland and the high cost of hiring care assistants, most disabled people have no choice but to depend on family members: They are tied together not only by biological kinship, love, and intimacy, but also by a lack of other options.

Death, which is frequently depicted as the only possible future in the Polish novels about disability that I analyze in this book, features prominently in the lives of disabled subjects and their families. In other words, the depiction of disability in these novels is, to a certain extent, reflective of reality. For mothers, there is the ever-present concern of what will happen to their children when they are gone. According to Marnik, the state leaves no other possibility than a combined death: "We have to be granted the right to extended euthanasia. Bruno and I are connected vessels and when either of us is unable to function, we simply both end our lives and that's it."[3] For the mother of a disabled child, how and when to die are crucial decisions that also raise questions about the agency of people with disabilities. However, as euthanasia is illegal in Poland, dying, as much as living, is almost impossible. The state neither offers support while mother and child are alive, nor lets them die on their own (at least on the mother's) terms. Life is privatized and must be sustained by her: Death cannot be legally self-generated.

When asked by the interviewer what social policies she would like to see introduced, Marnik opted for a voucher that she and her son could spend on services as they wished, "because if the state starts organizing, it won't be good."[4] This brief comment might be read in two ways: First, intentionally or otherwise, it echoes the capitalist critique that the state inadequately distributes resources and should intervene in individual lives as little as possible; second, it displays an utter lack of trust in the state. This lack of trust is grounded in the fact that the Polish state provides no life scripts for people with disabilities: Although Bruno has the right to attend school until he is twenty-five, he will then be unable to take employment, and the state offers no other options.

When asked what the future holds, Marnik replied, "There is nothing."[5] In the public imagination, family signifies a future, yet a family raising a disabled child is not vested with the same symbolism. Thus, as the state has abdicated from designing potential life trajectories for part of its population, a disabled person's future must not only be managed within the family, but must also be imagined within the family. By withdrawing educational and social opportunities for the disabled population, the state engages in the construction of "people with no ties to the world."[6] Instead of expanding community and social ties, the state orchestrates a shrinking world for disabled people and their families, reducing their networks to sporadic medical and social services, and a "step by step" social death.[7] This abandonment of the disabled population and their caregivers does "not appear on any city map" and is therefore invisibilized.[8] As a result, the family home becomes the site of abandonment.

Marnik has not been on vacation since Bruno was born. When asked if she hoped to do so one day, she discussed her financial difficulties and the inaccessibility of public spaces and concluded that, as her house has been adapted to Bruno's needs through her own efforts and resources, "home is the best for me."[9] Going on vacation with Bruno is unimaginable: Given the time and effort it takes to dress her adult son, put him in a wheelchair, and then navigate an inaccessible urban space, Marnik compared going for a short walk to scaling the mountains of Himalaya.

Adapting their home was an act of radical DIY accessibility and survival. In *Vita: Life in the Zone of Social Abandonment*, Brazilian American scholar Joao Biehl describes the secluded areas on the outskirts of Brazilian cities in which poor and marginalized populations, abandoned by society and the authorities, are left to die. Although not pushed beyond city limits, the situation in Poland does have a clear spatial character; it is dispersed, normalized, and, being confined to the domestic sphere, may appear to be a "humane" alternative to indefinite institutionalization. As a result, this invisibilized population, cut off from educational and social opportunities, also becomes "unknowable."[10]

Bruno is Marnik's third and youngest child. Her two older children live elsewhere but visit and support their mother. Marnik believes that the families of people with disabilities, including siblings, should receive psychological care from the state.[11] Without going into detail, she described her middle child suffering from mental problems but, not wanting to "burden his mother," keeping these to himself. Like his younger brother, he is now certified as disabled and requires regular psychiatric treatment. It appears that, in Poland, abandonment is the "social destiny" of all those living with disability, and that the appearance of a disability within a family can trigger other disabilities as well.[12]

Unsurprisingly, the Polish state disregards the needs of Marnik's middle child, as it does Bruno's. More than disability itself, it is this social abandonment that refigures kinship. While Marnik has managed to hold on to her job as a polytechnic lecturer and leads an NGO that advocates for disability issues in the city of Rzeszów, where she lives, her life is devoted to and determined by her youngest son. She is primarily a mother and caretaker. A lack of social support and disability policies destructures the family and refigures kinship: The older siblings are socially imagined as future caretakers of their disabled brother. Agnieszka Szpila, a writer and mother of three daughters, two of whom are disabled, has stated that "when I die, my place is to be taken by the nondisabled siblings who also have to give up their lives."[13] In Poland, care work is the maternal legacy for nondisabled children.

* * *

In *Disability Disruptions*, I explore how disability narratives challenge conventional accounts of post-socialist family and society in Poland. I analyze both popular and lesser-known examples in light of the cultural, political, and economic backdrop of Poland between 1989, the beginning of democratic capitalism, and 2022, a year in which caregivers of children with disabilities staged demonstrations. By examining the conflicts engendered by disability within conventional narratives of family life in Poland, and the social and political transformation in 1989, I demonstrate how disability narratives disrupt the cultural and social status quo. My primary materials include literary and cultural artifacts, such as disability memoirs, novels, journalistic articles, and statements made during the protests or posted on social media and republished in print and online media. (A study of the reception of the texts and novels I examine is not provided.)

I approach disruptions created by disability in a twofold manner: as an analytic tool and as a lived reality. The disability disruptions analyzed in chapter 1 are mostly epistemic: I show how disability as an analytic tool allows us to rewrite Polish history of the events of 1989 and the early period of the transformation. Chapters 2 and 3 (and, to a certain extent, chapter 4) discuss the ways in which disability as a lived reality triggers disruptions. These disruptions restructure families and kinship, generate new narratives, and thus reconfigure both private and public spheres. Abandoned by the Polish state, caregivers are burdened by care work; in turn, the family often inflicts violence on the disabled subjects in their care. Within the reconfiguration of the public that followed the protests, disabled subjects emerge and stake claims to public recognition. They and their caregivers endeavor to become "known" in society, to fight alienation and social abandonment, and to rewrite recent Polish history from a disability perspective. In the book's conclusion, I return to the idea of disability as an epistemic disruption and show how disabled people's experiences contradict the mainstream stories of the COVID-19 pandemic as a break in "normal" life.

Focusing on disruptions does not eliminate discussion about continuities, however. While acknowledging that disability knowledge challenges mainstream beliefs about the 1989 transformation and the COVID-19 pandemic, chapter 1 highlights what has persisted since the socialist era—namely, the state's abandonment of its disabled population, the resulting poverty, and the violence to which disabled people are subjected. Chapter 2 illustrates disruptions that disability causes to the family, as it is imagined and lived, but reminds us of the state's continued withdrawal, which makes state abandonment into a stable experience. Chapter 3 moves disruption from the private to the public sphere, identifying continuity in the desire of disabled people and their caregivers to be heard. In its discussion of autism narratives, chapter 4 continues the analysis of autistic subjects' efforts of self-presentation while showing how autism disrupts families.

Disability Disruptions is a work of excavation. The voices of disabled people and their caregivers in Poland—persistently overlooked, forgotten, ignored, or actively silenced—do not always correspond, but, when read together, they complicate what we have come to believe about family, the state, and the transition from state socialism to democracy and capitalism. My amplification of formerly silenced voices and perspectives is not only an academic exploration but also an activist and ethical endeavor: an attempt to ameliorate the systematic erasure of disabled people and their caregivers and thereby expand our knowledge and understanding of history, family, and society in post-1989 Poland. To that end, and in a spirit of advocacy and accessibility, I refrain as much as possible from erecting a barrier of academic terminology and instead rely on clear and plain language.

The archive I have assembled does not correspond to the traditional understanding of archive. Jennifer Douglas writes that "archival theory rests on the notion that archives result from the activities of a creator, it has, historically, characterized the accretion of archives as a fairly passive process: an archives develops over time as a natural by-product of activity, not through the deliberate efforts."[14] The archive I present in this book is a result of my deliberate effort to look for disability in Poland's recent history and culture: It is a subjectively curated repository that aims to break the pattern of writing about post-socialist Polish culture and history without thinking with or about disability. Archives, as institutions and collections of documents, "have always been about power. . . . Archives have the power to privilege and marginalize," and *Disability Disruptions* is written with this idea in mind.[15]

Although the archive I present is directed against the silencing of people with disability in post-1989 Poland, the book does not offer an exhaustive retelling of disability experiences in this period. Instead, it focuses on family, care politics, and state abandonment, which is why many topics are not covered. I mainly focus on written materials, including the recorded statements of caretakers and disabled people, and I did not use social media as primary sources, despite the strong presence there of caregivers as well as disabled activists who post about family, accessibility, and social benefits as well as comment on topics not directly related to disability issues. For methodological reasons, I have not included these materials: I believe they deserve a separate, in-depth examination that I am not able to provide.

Family in the Polish Cultural Imaginary

The archive I have collected reveals that while disability experiences are forged within a family in post-1989 Poland, they are not always created through choices made by disabled people, or even by their family members. Those raising disabled children or living with disabled family members are often abandoned by the Polish state, a situation legalized and normalized through government policy and a dominant ableist culture. Put simply, the post-socialist period has witnessed a violent familialization and privatization of disability in Poland. However, as I discuss below and in chapter 1, this privatization did not start in 1989: The transition to democratic capitalism only strengthened an existing relegation of disability to the domestic sphere.

Although *Disability Disruptions* prioritizes the voices of people with disabilities, it recognizes that caregivers remain the leading advocates for disability rights in Poland and actively shape disability discourses in the post-socialist period. The 2024 interview that opened this introduction illustrates how the relationship between disability and family operates in Poland and exemplifies the entanglement of disability, gender, care work, and state neglect that are at the center of this book. I call the family dynamics that Marnik describes "violent intimacy" (which I explore in detail in chapter 2). Marnik's use of the phrase "connected vessels" bespeaks this kind of intimacy: a connection that starts on a biological and material level yet extends into the social and political. Violent intimacy determines both the course of life for mother and child and, as the interview's subtitle suggests, the end of life. Violent intimacy disrupts a Polish cultural imaginary and political discourse in which family is afforded the utmost value.

In 2023, during reelection campaigning, the then-minister of family, labor, and social policy Marlena Maląg professed that "support for families is not a favor, but a duty of the state." She went on to add that "Poland has a beginning in Polish families, and it is in them that everything begins. Without families and the children born in them, there can be no future—bright or otherwise."[16] A few months later, a post on her official Facebook account declared family to be "one of the greatest desires, so it is at the center of our activities. Poland is becoming a community of fulfilled dreams in which every person is equally important."[17] During his 2020 reelection campaign, the then-president of Poland, Andrzej Duda, published a "family charter" that opened by declaring the family to be "the smallest community in which we grow up and mature, it is the foundation of our identity. The Polish state must do everything to support and protect the family economically and socially."[18] These examples of family fetishization by Poland's most prominent politicians are by no means isolated.

The family imagined here is resolutely heterosexual; the intent of the family charter was to glorify heteronormativity over queerness and queer families. It was during the same presidential campaign that Duda infamously stated: "They are trying to make people believe that LGBT are people. But they are not people; it is an ideology."[19] As seen in his comments, queerness has been publicly posited in Poland as a threat to the family, which is imagined as antithetical to queerness.

Popular culture elevates and valorizes the idea that a certain type of cisgendered hetero-patriarchal family is the most valued form of sociality in Poland. In 1995, the popular Polish music band Bayer Full released a song entitled "All Poles" with the following chorus: "Because all Poles are one family / Whether young or old, boy or girl." Still popular, the song—expressing the notion that Poles only vary in gender and age—can regularly be heard during football matches, family picnics, celebrations, and summer festivals, as well as on TV or the radio. The phrase "boy or girl" echoes the homophobic chant "boy, girl, normal family" often heard in Poland from counterprotesters during Pride marches or conservative demonstrators promoting "family values." Mainstream discourses of family in Poland are inextricably heteronormative and homophobic.[20] It is perhaps for this reason that an intersection between queerness and disability rarely appears in the material I cover in this book, with the relatively recent exception of autistic subjects who identify themselves as queer or lesbian.

By emphasizing this particular song, I wish to underline the public fetishization of family and confront it with the words of Joanna Marnik, who considers herself abandoned by the state and asks for euthanasia for herself and her child.[21] While families without disabled members are unlikely to share her desire, it seems to me that the public fetishization of the family is intricately connected with the abandonment and abuse made known through this family's experience, and that enables or conceals the violent intimacy analyzed in this book.

Consequently, the Polish post-socialist archive I present largely consists of family stories shared in the form of memoirs, nonfiction and journalistic articles, protest statements, and interviews. Each chapter presents a story, from various vantage points, about family disruptions, struggles, reconfigurations, and protests. Some of these stories denounce family, which, as I will demonstrate, can be a site of authorized state violence, including violent intimacy. In chapter 4, I examine how family constitutes a legitimated site of violence toward disabled subjects, and resistance to this form of violence by autistic writers. The family both experiences violence and is complicit in exercising it; the family is disrupted but also disrupts.

The Privatization of Disability Under State Socialism

Because a detailed and comprehensive survey of disability under state socialism is beyond the scope of this book, I focus on the familial and particularly the maternal management of disability under state socialism in Poland. As stated earlier (and discussed in more detail in chapter 1), the 1989 transition to democratic capitalism did not entail a sudden familialization of disability, but rather continued and strengthened what had long been established. This familialization of disability was mobilized in other places, such as socialist Hungary and the German Democratic Republic (GDR), as shown by Monika Baár and Pia Schmüser, respectively. But, in a country shaped by dominant Polish values—with the family as the "basic social unit," the nineteenth-century cultural ideal of a sacrificial "Polish Mother," and the relentless grip of Catholicism on Polish society throughout the socialist period—its presence was uniquely secure.[22]

This privatization was also enabled by the failure to emancipate women under socialism. During the Stalinist period after World War II, Polish women forced from home were allowed to seek employment and imagine themselves beyond the conventional notions of womanhood, as Malgorzata Fidelis has discussed.[23] However, traditional values returned after 1956,[24] and the Soviet pledge to rearrange the gender order was seen as "a violation of Polish national identity."[25] Consequently, masculine jobs were afforded superior status to familial tasks.

Another potential reason for the privatization of disability was a lack of medical infrastructure and staff during the postwar period. According to Marcin Stasiak, the funding and development of rehabilitation professionals and services were prompted not by the needs of the many Polish people left disabled, traumatized, and ill as a result of World War II, but by an outbreak of polio in 1951 and the threat it posed to the most innocent segment of the population—children.[26] Institutions, clinics, and wards for both children and adults were opened between 1951 and 1953, initially for patients with polio, but later for those with other diseases and disabilities. Stasiak has identified these institutions as the "foundation of the Polish rehabilitation system," intended primarily to help patients internalize the goals and methods of rehabilitation, restore them to fitness, and ensure their future employability and productivity.[27] It bears emphasizing that this network of institutions was never as developed in Poland as in other countries in socialist Eastern Europe. In her groundbreaking book *Disability and Mobile Citizenship in Postsocialist Ukraine*, American scholar Sarah Phillips has described the placing of disabled citizens in specialized residential institutions—with material and practical support, "home-like" living conditions, organized medical and social care, and vocational rehabilitation—as common practice in Soviet Ukraine.[28] As the infrastructure required to provide the necessary expertise for such endeavors was never developed in socialist Poland, it was the domestic space that was transformed into a facility for care and rehabilitation.

In a 1951 medical brochure, *Kalekie dziecko* (*The Impaired Child*), Wiktor Dega, one of the most important orthopedists in postwar Poland, stated that it was a mother's responsibility to rehabilitate her child: Having been instructed by a doctor, if she "patiently and persistently applies the prescribed treatments, in many cases she can remove the defect through this simple route."[29] As I have noted elsewhere, in 1984—over thirty years after the publication of Dega's brochure—experts on disability from the Polish Academy of Sciences expressed the same sentiment directly stating that parents were obligated to rehabilitate their disabled children.[30]

This cultural pressure to provide care within the home has been echoed by some disabled people as well. In her 1967 memoir, *Białe niebo* (*White Heaven*), Eugenia Siemaszkiewicz criticizes her parents, who did not want to take care of their disabled child and left her in an institution.[31] Maria Dzięgielewska, author of the 1972 disability memoir *Losowi na przekór* (*Against Fate*), describes the future of disabled people as "in the hands of you, our mothers."[32] Although the history of Polish socialism is rife with turbulent upheavals and conflict between the state and citizens (as I will discuss in chapter 1), the privatization of disability was never fiercely opposed under socialism. Only during the many protests and Parliament occupations of the 2010s were frustrations at the overburdening of families with care work openly articulated.

Disability writing during the socialist era, particularly memoirs by mothers of children with disabilities, confirm the *maternalization* of care work and rehabilitation. In *Syn! Będzie szczęśliwa* (*Son! She Will Be Happy*), published in the 1980s, Eugenia Chajęcka presents the minutiae of her day-to-day life during the 1950s and 1960s with a nondisabled daughter and a son unable to walk due to polio. She describes her attempts to secure a decent wheelchair and ensure that her son can attend school, and her efforts to locate a doctor in West Germany for high-quality medical care. In other words, this memoir depicts the transformation of a mother into a social, medical, and rehabilitative worker.

Because rehabilitation primarily operated as a tool of social and physical normalization in socialist countries, including Poland, it was not free from ideological underpinnings. In *Los w rękach twoich* (*Your Destiny Is in Your Hands*), Anna Domańska describes the hours she spent in the 1970s teaching her deaf son how to read lips and to speak, in the hope of the societal inclusion promised by this oral method of communication. As Kateřina Kolářová and Martina Winkler have stated, the goal of rehabilitation in this context was to "achieve one's most optimal usefulness for the purposes of socialist society"—in other words, to transform disabled bodies into laboring bodies.[33] Participation in the workforce was proof that disabled people had overcome their "defects."[34] It is perhaps this prioritizing of productivity by both socialism and capitalism that ensured the muted effect of the Polish transition on the disabled population and their caregivers. Kolářová and Winkler have emphasized the extent to which "*visions* of futurity" in socialist Eastern Europe relied on able-bodiedness,[35] and both disability memoirs and fiction about disability abound with images of disabled children vigorously exercising at home, driven by the hope of achieving this condition.[36] In Poland, responsibility for ensuring that a disabled person could approximate able-bodiedness fell upon the family.

Despite such prioritization of home-based care and rehabilitation, Polish parents of disabled people have attempted to establish connections within the wider community. In 1960, parents of mentally disabled children founded Komitet i Koła Pomocy Dzieciom Specjalnej Troski (Committee for Assistance to Children with Special Needs).[37] Initially part of a larger organization, the Children's Friends Society, from which it separated after the 1989 transition, the committee became the Polish Association for People with Mental Impairment in 1991. It continues to be a parent-led organization and is now the largest NGO working for the rights of mentally disabled children in Poland. A decade later, parents of mentally disabled children who established a similar organization in socialist Hungary encountered problems their Polish peers had not: government claims that no disabled population existed.[38] As the founding of the Polish organization has not been subjected to the same in-depth research that Monika Baár has conducted on the situation in Hungary, it is difficult to assess whether the Polish government had similar convictions. However, this brief comparison does demonstrate that two socialist states in which disability was largely privatized did adopt distinct approaches to disability.

Despite commonly held beliefs about the inhumanity of the few institutions available in Poland, some disabled people have preferred this option to life at home. Irena Kowalczyk, who published her memoir, *Poza granicą skargi* (*Beyond the Possibility of Grievance*) in the 1970s, spent time in hospitals and sanatoriums during the 1950s and yearned to live permanently in an institution that would meet and respect her needs. Yet there were simply not enough places in state institutions for disabled people, not to mention the intended residents with polio, and any facilities for disabled people were usually bestowed on "the retarded or the elderly." Kowalczyk declared: "If you have been sick as many years as I have, there is no rescue." Born into rural poverty with a mother too sick to provide care, Kowalczyk deemed the state responsible for "what to do with people like me." She concluded: "Let them poison us."[39] Testifying to the fact that many disabled people in socialist Poland received only temporary treatment in hospitals or sanatoriums, her memoir speaks to the social abandonment of some people with disabilities and complicates the conventional understanding of institutionalization as a final, undesired resort.[40] In an article on the privatization of disability in the GDR, Pia Schmüsser has claimed that ongoing economic and infrastructural constraints prevented the state from ever achieving comprehensive institutional care.[41] The Polish socialist state, it appears, may have encountered the same obstacles.

As Kowalczyk's words illustrate, living at home was not synonymous with living in a community. While home can be a place of love, nourishment, and care, it can also be a site of abuse. Even in the best of circumstances, disabled people living at home experience isolation, due to the absence of social and architectural infrastructure that would support their presence in public. Practical issues in socialist Poland, including a lack of accessible housing and transportation, reinforced the invisibility of disabled people. In the early 1980s, the Polish sociologist Magdalena Sokołowska claimed that "almost half of Polish society has no contact with disabled people," which she attributed to a "separatist" model that left disabled people "barely visible in our society."[42] From this perspective, there was little difference between life in an institution or at home: Both made people with disabilities "unknown" to society.

In chapter 1, I continue my discussion of disabled people's lives under and after socialism in Poland. The memoirs by disabled women I analyze document both a lack of change and a multiplicity of (hi)stories of the events in 1989: As we are reminded by the Polish gender studies scholar Magdalena Grabowska, "There is no single true story, but there is a story told from the perspective of different social groups whose experience is mediated by material living conditions and position in the hierarchy of power."[43]

Thus, there is no one story about family, gender, and care in post-1989 Poland. In writing this book, my hope is to complicate, nuance, and excavate both disability narratives in Poland and narratives on Poland, and to investigate an assemblage of—at times—contradictory and polyphonic narratives about disruptive historical episodes, the disavowal and embrace of disability, and the disruptive potential of disability. My primary goal is to illuminate what has been silenced or overlooked in the post-socialist period, including violent intimacy and the enforced location of disability experiences within the domestic sphere. Crucially, this is not a complete chronicle of post-socialist disability disruptions, but, rather, the beginning of one.

Methodology

While Eastern European histories, representations, and policies governing disability in the twentieth and twenty-first centuries disrupt anglophone disability theories, they are not central to my analysis. I write this book with and alongside these potential disruptions rather than in pursuit of them. Where I can, I name and attempt to redefine some anglophone notions of disability but direct my efforts toward thinking with and through Polish disability disruptions. By choosing the specificity of local disability narratives over references to anglophone narratives and secondary sources, I wish to highlight the importance of investigating that which has been deemed marginal and peripheral to the imperial sites of knowledge production.

As my focus is the disabled people of Poland, I do not review disability narratives from other Eastern European countries, thus pushing against the idea that a book about a single marginal Eastern European location is not legible. The Soviet Union and Russia have dominated the few discussions of disability in this part of the world, and I wish to give priority to an area that is rarely placed center stage.[44] I do provide additional information on how disability operates in other post-socialist settings whenever this relates to my argument, but Eastern Europe is an ill-defined, heterogeneous territory, shaped by distinct histories, cultures, and religions.[45] My refusal to include multiple Eastern European disability histories draws on a recognition that "Eastern European societies did not constitute a homogeneous socialist 'bloc.'"[46] Neither do they constitute a unified political or cultural region today.

My research also challenges conventional chronology: As I discuss throughout the book (particularly in chapter 1), the usual periodization of Polish history, with 1989 marking the transition from state socialism to democratic capitalism, does not capture disabled experiences. Consequently, I emphasize continuities rather than ruptures. Moreover, the temporalities of change and transition from state socialism to democracy in Eastern Europe do not overlap: Socialism in Eastern Europe did not uniformly end in 1989, and, as noted by Israeli historian Sharon Rotbard, the relationship between history and geography is "direct and a necessary one."[47] Therefore, rather than taking an overarching perspective, I choose to seek and amplify that which is often deemed insignificant. In this way, I challenge both the content and the construction of global disability history.

Although I pay significant attention to disability knowledges, I do not use the American neologism "cripistemology" to refer to their making and unmaking.[48] As Jess Whatcott has stated, cripistemology is a form of counterknowledge, an oppositional knowledge, and this is indeed my focus.[49] However, Whatcott, like other anglophone scholars, situates cripistemology within a contemporary context of "neoliberal governance."[50] While acknowledging the importance of considering political economy, I do not engage with neoliberalism in the same way. One of my central arguments is that the disability narratives I analyze problematize the neat division between socialism and capitalism: Post-socialist disability knowledge in Poland refuses to sustain this political distinction. Many disabled people in this part of the world have lived through the continuum of these two systems and experienced an ableist demand for productivity under both. Plus, if we subscribe to the materialist belief that knowledge production is a dialectical process situated within particular economic and political regimes, then Polish disability knowledges originated under different conditions and do not easily align with American cripistemologies.

Despite these reservations, I do mobilize wider developments stemming from crip theory in my analysis of autism narratives and in ongoing reflections on its employment and utility for theorizing disability in Eastern Europe. As this book demonstrates, theorizing disability in a non-anglophone setting is both enriched and undermined by abundant and easily available anglophone disability studies scholarship. *Disability Disruptions* documents a self-reflexive pursuit for language and theories that can respond to disability on the ground while remaining legible to both anglophone and Eastern European audiences. While this book may at times appear to be awash in apparent contradictions, these reveal not only my own uncertainties, but also the fissures and tensions that emerge when establishing disability studies beyond the increasingly well-worn paths of the Anglophone canon.

The disruptions I explore, presented in more or less chronological order, create a *longue durée* of disability within Polish history. Emphasizing the multidirectionality of these disruptions I show how disability narratives challenge the dominant narratives on history, family dynamics, and social organization that in turn complicate disabled lives. By attending to various disruptions and drawing from diverse cultural artifacts, the chapters in this book are mutually illuminative. As a whole, these disruptions preclude a teleological chronology of Polish history and thus require us to think anew not only about care, family, and intimacy, but also the accepted account of historical change in post-socialist Poland. To this end, rather comprehensively renarrating Polish post-socialist culture and history via disability, *Disability Disruptions* organizes itself around thematic tropes, sometimes forgotten and misrepresented episodes and sites of friction, and the tensions produced by and because of disability.

The Road Map

As these chapter summaries demonstrate, the disruptions I explore flow from one to the next rather than stand as distinct episodes. In chapter 1, "Disrupting History," I address the 1989 transition through a 1991 collection of disability memoirs entitled *Cierpieniem pisane: Pamietniki kobiet niepelnosprawnych* (*Written Through Suffering: Disabled Women's Memoirs*). The result of a memoir competition held in 1990, this collection shows that, contrary to the mainstream narrative in Poland, Western Europe, and the United States, 1989 produced no "revolution" for disabled women. The twenty-one memoirs included in the volume question the notion of a teleological linear progression from state socialism to democratic capitalism and, by disavowing the 1989 transition, challenge the mainstream liberal, right-wing, and left-wing presentations of the year as a breakthrough event in Polish history. By engaging with domesticity and focusing on violence and poverty, the collection reveals the ongoing forms of exclusion experienced by disabled women, as well as the continuing familialization of disability and its relegation to the private sphere. Moreover, the texts analyzed in this book destigmatize and center marginalized knowledges that have been afforded no place in the dominant archives of post-socialist Eastern Europe.

In chapter 2, "Violent Intimacy," I privilege the perspective of nondisabled mothers who take on the role of care provider. The rights of disabled people are closely intertwined with those of women in post-socialist Poland, and mothers of disabled children are among the most visible activists fighting for increased state provision for disabled people. Centering on care work between 1995 and 2022, this chapter focuses on domestic rather than public and historical narratives. Driving my analysis is the concept of "violent intimacy": an affective structure that binds a nondisabled mother with her disabled child. Though never identified as such, the violent intimacy present in all the texts I discuss disrupts the mainstream narrative of maternal love and the mother–child relationship. But this is also a story of maternal lives disrupted by their child's disability, of fathers who are rarely interested in providing care, and a state indifferent to the fate of the disabled population and their families. This does not mean that there is no room for love: Intimacy is often forced and violent, but it can also be tender and caring.

In chapter 3, "Disability Confessions," which focuses on the protests that took place in 2014, 2018, 2020, and 2022, I show how disabled communities have made themselves known to the public, what they have demanded from the state and society, and how these protests have changed over time. This is a story of disruptions and reconfigurations of the private and public triggered by the mutual refusal of disabled people and their caregivers to accept violent intimacy and the privatization of disability. Through this chronology of protests, I trace the emergence of what I have termed a "disability confessional culture" in Poland and explore how most of the confessions emphasize the relational and communal aspects of disability. Illustrating both the deeply private and public nature of disability, references to Polish history and the 1989 transition demonstrate how, more than twenty years later, people with disabilities and their allies are both inscribing themselves into and rewriting this history. This is one of the few parts of the book in which I engage race, eugenics, and the intersection of race and disability. While these issues are of huge importance, the Polish population has little racial diversity, and the texts I examine rarely comment on the issue.

Chapter 4, "Autistic Disavowals," investigates family from the perspective of autistic subjects, not care providers. But, unlike chapter 3, it examines examples of disavowals of disability. It analyzes two sets of materials from the 2010s: neurodivergent memoirs published by queer women and nonbinary subjects, and nonfiction and journalism by experts and mothers of autistic children. The memoirs mostly constitute neurodivergent and queer experiences of coming out, and I position them against the Polish reiteration of the well-known narrative of autism as a threat to individuals, families, and society. Most prominently, while disavowing the categories of disability and, to a certain degree, autism, these writers reveal the family to be both the origin of their condition and a site of violence toward autistic subjects. By closely following the primary sources, I explore this double disavowal of disability and family and the way this creates a different style of disruption, while also illuminating an incoherence within the Polish post-socialist archive.

In the epilogue, I revisit the entanglement of family, care work, and intimacy, and the private and public nature of disability in Poland in light of the COVID-19 pandemic. A global movement is attempting to document how disabled populations in different locations lived and died during this historic moment. In and of itself, COVID-19 was globally experienced as a disruption of nondisabled lives, and I show that disabled trajectories underwent little upheaval. Rather, disability policies and practices, including social abandonment and violent intimacy, were reinforced. Yet again, disabled knowledge disrupts nondisabled knowledge of what constitutes radical rupture and change.

* * *

In the interests of integrity and transparency, it is important to present my positionality. Born in the second half of the 1980s, I have no recollection of the year 1989. I first encountered disability studies when doing PhD research in the United States and have worked at the largest Polish university, the University of Warsaw, since 2019. As well as academic research and teaching, I have taken part in disability activist projects and cooperated with a governmental agency on disability research. I translated Rosemarie Garland-Thomson's *Extraordinary Bodies: Figuring Physical Disability in American Culture and Literature* into Polish, and, despite being preoccupied with the question of how to conduct Polish disability studies that respond to the specificity of the Polish and Eastern European cultural, political, and geographical context, I have participated in disseminating knowledge about American disability studies. I am a nondisabled person, and disability is not a part of my lived experience, although I consider myself an ally of people with disabilities. Perhaps not always directly, and certainly not always consciously, my positionality will inevitably have shaped the archiving I conducted to write *Disability Disruptions*, as well as my analysis.

1 DISRUPTING HISTORY

As the focus of this book is the locations and meanings of disability in post-socialist Polish culture, there is no more apt historical moment with which to open than the 1989 transformation from state socialism to capitalist democracy.[1] This peaceful, bloodless, and gradual change of regime lacks the imagery of a spectacular revolution or another grand and legendary gesture.[2] While almost every decade of state socialism in Poland was marked by strikes and social unrest—often bloodstained—the transition to democracy and capitalism resulted from peaceful negotiations between the socialist government and the representatives of (and intellectuals connected with) the Independent Self-Governing Trade Union (Solidarność, or Solidarity).[3] Yet the meaning of the transformation remains contested among scholars, politicians, journalists, and the public. Right-wing politicians claim that the changes initiated that year were left "unfinished," thereby producing the contemporary social and political problems of a country that was never fully "decommunized." Disappointment is also evident among those who hold left-wing beliefs and revile the economic and social inequities they trace to the transition. Only the liberal parties—the views of which represent many segments of present-day Polish society—view the events of 1989 as a complete triumph, and it was their account, their retelling of history, that dominated during the 1990s and early 2000s.

In a 2021 interview, Janusz Lewandowski, the first minister of privatization in the newly elected government of 1989, declared: "I will not apologize for the transformation."[4] Lewandowski was defending the transition in the face of increasing criticism from both left- and right-wing politicians and journalists, who were troubled by the vast social cost of such a rapid shift and implementation of neoliberal reforms.[5] Philosopher, historian of ideas, and leading oppositional thinker during the late socialist era Marcin Król had published a book six years earlier entitled *Byliśmy głupi* (*We Were Stupid*), in which he accepts that there had been negative consequences for many segments of society—consequences that Król believes have been ignored by architects of the transformation. While opinions on the results of 1989 may differ, the fact remains that the majority of analysts view this political and economic transformation as a teleological progression from state socialism to capitalism.

Poland has not been alone in this discursive framing of 1989. Kateřina Kolářová reconstructs the Czech retelling of the transformation as a transition from disfranchisement to freedom, illness to health, socialist "backwardness" to capitalist "civilization."[6] Akin to "overcoming" or "curing" a malady, democratic transitioning in Czechoslovakia acquired moral worth and an affective dimension. With the promise that the country could "catch up with the West," the transition in Poland was understood as "a return" to "the normal path of development": capitalism.[7] Thus, notwithstanding local idiosyncrasies and mutations, the narrative of escape from state socialism in Poland has expanded beyond national borders to pervade the lore of Eastern Europe in general.

Within official discourse and historiography, the transformation timeline is rather unclear. While the start point of 1989 is based on the first semi-free parliamentary elections that took place on June 4 of that year, the end of the transformation is far more difficult to define.[8] Scholars suggest a range of dates from early-to-mid-1990s. In this chapter I conceive of transformation as a temporary period: Although the socialist system had gone by the end of 1989, democracy and capitalism had yet to be fully implemented.

In this chapter, through an analysis of the 1991 collection of memoirs by disabled women, *Cierpieniem pisane: Pamiętniki kobiet niepełnosprawnych* (*Written Through Suffering: Disabled Women's Memoirs*), I present an alternative way of conceptualizing the events of 1989, one that challenges the understandings that dominate among political parties and society as a whole.[9] These memoirs resist official interpretations of the transformation, whether critical, revisionist, or laudatory, and show that the political changes of 1989 had little effect on disabled women, who continued to experience the same exclusion and poverty they had suffered throughout their lives. *Written Through Suffering* reminds us that there is no single definitive history or narrative; disabled women whose lives are determined by their embodiment, material conditions, and relationship with the state and society will experience a different history than other social groups. This framing disrupts public discourse and official historiography, both of which remain invested in positioning 1989 as a breakthrough moment in Polish history. Despite the proclamation by the major liberal newspaper founded the previous month, *Gazeta Wyborcza* (*Electoral Newspaper*), "Nic już nie będzie tak jak dawniej" ("Goodbye old, welcome new"), in June 1989,[10] for the authors of these memoirs the events of that year constituted what American scholar Lauren Berlant has termed a "crisis ordinariness."[11]

If challenging common wisdom about the official "ruptures" of Polish history on the basis of twenty-one memoirs appears rather bold, that raises the question of how many documents and testimonies would be sufficient to do so. Members of marginalized groups do not always leave an abundance of material testifying to their experiences and knowledge: As I will discuss later, they may lack the time and opportunity to produce such documents, and there may be little interest in preserving what they do produce. Given the economic turbulence and "shock therapy" of the early 1990s, which resulted in an unprecedented amount of strikes and rising unemployment, it is inevitable that other disabled and disadvantaged people in Poland at that time experienced the poverty and abandonment described in these memoirs.[12] The cruel effects of capitalist reforms were not limited to Poland: Kolářová has described an "abandonment of lives considered invaluable, ideologically troubling, or too demanding" during the Czechoslovakian transformation as well.[13]

Disabled women were not alone in their experiences of abandonment in Poland post-1989. After a pedestrian was killed by a car driven by a young Roma man in Mława in 1991, up to two hundred young inhabitants of the town vandalized and burned homes belonging to the local Roma population and called for their banishment from Poland.[14] Rather than racism, journalists and academics attributed the violence to the transformation: While the financial situation of the Polish population as a whole had worsened, sociologists claimed that the Roma population had actually benefited from economic reforms.[15] However, as Agnieszka Kościańska and Michał Petryk have discussed, research shows that Roma people were often the first to lose employment, and many felt compelled to emigrate for work.[16] Thus, post-transition abandonment took various forms—for the Roma community, in the lack of both police protection and economic support.[17]

The socialist government in Poland attempted to assimilate the Roma population through "stabilization," "adaptation," and "productivization." They were to accomplish their first objective by persuading the Roma to relinquish nomadism and settle down, offering accommodation in often primitive and unsanitary barracks. However, pogroms against the Roma, who were viewed as undesired, racialized others, occurred in several towns, including Łuków i Kłodawa in 1976 and Konin and Oświęcim in 1981.[18] As the events in Mława illustrate, 1989 had also constituted a "crisis ordinariness" for the Roma. Thus, investigating the transformation from the perspective of marginalized populations not only challenges the dominant narrative of a teleological progression from state socialism to capitalist democracy; it also affords us a better understanding of what socialism was, and what capitalism and democracy are, within the Polish context.

Attending to disabled knowledges disrupts our understanding by allowing access to knowledge that cannot be produced by a dominant population. This is not to say that such knowledge is superior, but that it is required to prevent knowledge created by dominant groups from being taken as universal truth. Accentuating minoritized subjectivities and their meaning-making practices is necessary to disrupt the epistemic status quo.[19]

This is not the first attempt to either privilege minoritized knowledges in recent Eastern European history or to disrupt it via disability. In her 2018 book, Magdalena Grabowska describes Polish feminists of the 1990s turning their back on the legacy of socialist feminism in Poland in order to legitimize their own movement, solidify anticommunist sentiments, and emphasize connections with Western feminism. This not only hindered potential alliances with socialist and Eastern European feminist traditions, but also led to a loss of Polish feminist experiences and achievements within the histories of socialism and feminism in the country.[20] Also in a 2018 book, *Polio Across the Iron Curtain*, Dóra Vargha claims that the history of this disease "disregards the watersheds that are traditionally held as dividing the early history of communist regimes in Eastern Europe, and more visibly overrides decisive moments in Hungarian history."[21] In the same vein, I aim to destabilize recent retellings of Polish history and culture. In particular, I will show how disabled women's life-writing disrupts the framing of the 1989 transformation as a "revolution."

During the 1990s, any claim that the transformation made little difference to certain people would have been met with derision. The end of state socialism brought hope, and the transition period was for many a time of joy and relief. As Kateřina Kolářová has discussed, the official discursive positioning of the transition in Czechoslovakia as "the path to recovery" and "cure" effectively "foreclosed the possibility of crip epistemologies."[22] A similar situation appeared in post-socialist Poland, where politicians described the transformation as a healing process. For example, in a 1994 interview, Jarosław Kaczyński, a prominent opposition leader during the 1980s and one of the most important post-1989 politicians, claimed that it was "impossible to build a democratic society, a new state, on the old totalitarian structure," as that "pathology" could not sustain anything "healthy": The "tumor had to be cut out."[23] State socialism was an illness, a cancer, requiring the surgery of the transition. The phrase "cut out" presupposes a need for drastic, radical measures, rather than gradual reforms that could ease economic hardship. It is clear that Polish politicians were invested in the idea of transformation as a sharp line between systems to which they attached moral meanings, associating socialism with illness, and democratic capitalism with health. Consequently, there was no room for any oppositional knowledge in the early post-socialist period. As I discuss in chapter 3, an acknowledgment of disability knowledge would only become possible later, mostly in the 2010s.

In the next part of this chapter, I provide contextual details about the memoir competition that initiated *Written Through Suffering* and briefly discuss the contents and authors. I then present a close reading of the memoirs and an intersectional analysis focused on gender and disability, and discuss how this intersection shapes the life trajectories of the memoir authors. Moreover, I explore how these texts disrupt official Polish periodization and discuss the ways in which they produce disability knowledge, emphasizing that while we must heed what disabled women tell us about Polish socialist and post-socialist politics, we should also attend to how and under what circumstances this knowledge has been created.

The Memoirs

The collection *Written Through Suffering* was the result of a memoir competition entitled "I Am a Disabled Woman," organized in 1990 by the Maria Curie-Skłodowska University in Lublin and a Polish NGO, Polskie Towarzystwo do Walki z Kalectwem (Polish Society for the Struggle Against Impairment).[24] More than three hundred women from across the country responded, but only half of the material submitted met the competition criteria. The organizers also received requests for help, as well as letters of support for holding the competition, and some of the memoir authors did not provide their names, a competition requirement.[25] Although it is hard to assess the extent to which the collection represents disabled women in Poland as a whole, it is important to keep in mind the size of this response. Also, as I will discuss in the next section, the experiences described by the authors in the collection have been echoed in research produced in both socialist and post-socialist Poland. Unfortunately, the original documents of the three hundred submissions from 1990 are not available. For many years after publication, the editor Maria Chodkowska attempted to find a museum, library, or any other institution that would preserve them and allow public access; having met with no success, she finally threw the collection away a few years before I first contacted her in 2016.

The memoir competition took place a year after the first democratic elections were held in Poland. The call for submission was published in the popular and widely available weekly women's magazine *Przyjaciółka* (*A Best Friend*) and broadcast on TV and radio.[26] Due to the ubiquitous and insidious presence of ableism, *Written Through Suffering* has received little attention since its initial publication. As Susan Wendell has stated, "Disabled people's knowledge is dismissed as trivial, complaining, mundane (or bizarre), *less than* that of a dominant group."[27] It is my hope that this chapter and the book as a whole will challenge this—often unconscious—notion.

Topics in the collection include the manner in which an author's disability came about, with the majority of authors living with acquired rather than congenital disabilities, and the problems they faced relating to poverty, access to education and healthcare services, hunger, and abuse by parents and spouses. There are also stories of motherhood and work. Among the authors are women with physical and sensory disabilities, and, while most directly name their disabilities, some only allude to their condition. Disabilities include visual, aural, neurological, and mobility impairments; some of the women had prostheses. Although a number of the authors refer to depression and anxiety in their works, none identify as mentally disabled: Thus the collection does not address issues of mental, intellectual, and developmental disabilities.

I have been unable to find any information on how memoirs that met the criteria were assessed, or by whom.[28] Via email, Maria Chodkowska informed me that the choice of publisher—the Catholic publishing house PAX—was somewhat random: An acquaintance had put her in touch with one of their editors after receiving little interest from other publishers.[29] With a papal visit to Poland scheduled for the year of publication, the publisher decided to feature on the cover a photograph of the pope talking to, or perhaps blessing, an elderly woman standing beside a wheelchair; the pope was presented with a copy of the book when meeting disabled and ill children in Olsztyn during June 1991.[30] This cover image is particularly significant since, alongside Lech Wałęsa, leader of the Solidarity movement and the first democratically elected president of Poland, John Paul II is commonly seen as one of the principal supporters and symbols of the transition to democratic capitalism.

The framing of *Written Through Suffering* as a gift for John Paul II is made clear in the dedication: "These published memoirs are a gift of disabled women's suffering given to John Paul II. It is an expression of gratitude for his love of those who because of God's will—incomprehensible to humans—are affected by illness or impairment." Presumably composed by the editor, this dedication explicitly frames disability in religious terms. In her introduction, Chodkowska also refers to religion, at one point claiming that faith makes it easier for disabled people "to grasp the meaning" of their suffering.[31] To a certain extent, as I will explore in chapter 2, this reflects a standard understanding of disability during the 1990s. Chodkowska also describes the discrimination, social exclusion, and unequal treatment experienced by disabled women.[32] Although she blends the discourses of religion and social justice, it is clear that for Chodkowska, however, disability remains synonymous with individual tragedy.

Living as Surviving

The entangled dynamic of gender and disability guides my analysis in this section. If, at times, I centralize the issues of gender expectations or the difficulties of living in isolated parts of the country, it cannot be forgotten that these experiences were not separate from the authors' disabled embodiment. Consequently, the argument I make in this section emphasizes the inseparability of gender and disability. I describe and analyze the ways in which disabled women internalized societal values and tried to live up to the expectations of nondisabled society, and how not only gender and disability, but also economic and marital status, as well as access to employment, structured their life trajectories. Consequently, I do not approach either of these identities or experiences as supplementary, nor do I highlight a single identification to the exclusion of others.[33] Instead, I explore the intersection of identifications to reveal the multifaceted ways in which the authors of the memoirs suffered societal exclusion while attempting to negotiate their place within their families and in society.

Almost all (if not all) the accounts originate from working-class women who identify their lives as a struggle for survival. Although the memoirs were written in 1990 and 1991 and include references to the post-1989 situation, they focus mainly on life in pre-1989 Poland, an officially classless society that had pledged to redistribute resources as needed. These disabled women, however, describe living in abject poverty: The socialist state provided services that benefited a few. One author stated that "my achievements, education, and social position were enabled by—so criticized today [in post-1989 Poland]—state benefits and programs. Otherwise, I would not have been able to afford it financially, I was too poor."[34] This is also the only memoir in which the author describes her life under state socialism as "idyllic."[35] Other sources, too, discuss poverty experienced by people with disabilities under state socialism in Poland. A sociological summary of the survey distributed among over two hundred disabled people in the late 1970s in Warsaw notes that "many of these people lived on the brink of poverty and in any case beneath the social minimum."[36] The 1984 report *Sytuacja ludzi niepełnosprawnych i stan rehabilitacji w PRL* (*The Situation of Disabled People and the Condition of Rehabilitation in the Polish People's Republic*) indicates that in 1976 the average state benefit equaled 35.5 percent of the average salary that year.[37] It comes as no surprise, then, that benefits were not enough for most authors, who had to find other ways to make a living.

The 1952 Polish Constitution, revised in 1976, declared that "work shall be the right, the duty, and a matter of honor for every citizen."[38] This promise remained unfulfilled for disabled subjects. The 1984 report emphasized that employment was understood both by the medical services and the government as the most desirable form of rehabilitation for disabled people, yet there were not enough jobs for employees with disabilities.[39] Employment was lacking in the sheltered workshops[40] as well as in the "regular" places.[41] The 1984 report clearly states that "the realization of the right to work for all disabled people is not possible due to the shortage of available jobs."[42] One of the authors included in *Written Through Suffering*, a blind woman who graduated with a high GPA and a master's degree from the History Department at the Adam Mickiewicz University in Poznań and a graduate of the State Institute of Special Education in Warsaw, stated that "neither my grades nor acquired skills made it easier for me to find employment."[43] Disability as a category of analysis enables us to see how Polish socialist law suspended itself in certain situations. Work, in other words, was not—no matter the socialist pledge—accessible to everyone.

Despite their difficulties finding employment, most authors had to work for some time before receiving disability benefits and held poorly paid, often custodial jobs (many that did not match their often-higher qualifications).[44] One author wrote fondly about her experience at a workshop for blind people making her "very happy. The workshop offers me vacations, trips, health care, and only now—nearing the end of my life—I have started to live. I feel that I am needed now . . . and I am not lonely anymore. . . . Better late than never."[45] This quotation underlines the advantages of working in the company of other disabled people. For this woman, work was not only a necessity but also a source of joy and pleasurable interaction. Perhaps this particular workshop offered both employment and rehabilitation services, which would have been rare, since the majority of sheltered workshops required disabled people to work at home without any additional benefits.[46] Not surprisingly, then, this was the only author within the collection who describes her employment in such an environment, indicating how scarce these jobs were and continued to be during the time these memoirs were written. For most of these women, work was both a physical and psychological burden, but, despite advice from doctors to give up their jobs, this was not an option; work was a financial necessity. "Doctors cannot help me anymore," one author writes. "The only solution is to stop working, avoid physical effort and eat nutritional food. But how can I stop working now, when I am waiting for a new apartment [and I need money for it]?"[47] *The Situation of Disabled People and the Condition of Rehabilitation in the Polish People's Republic*—probably the most comprehensive survey of disabled people's situation under state socialism, containing extensive data on issues such as types of disability, employment, living situation, access to medical and social services—stated that because of the narrow legal understanding of disability, some disabled people were not entitled to disability benefits or any other kind of social support.[48] As such benefits were rare and inadequate—an average monthly wage was over two times higher[49]—these women who secured jobs continued to work in hostile environments that often exacerbated health issues and were both difficult to obtain and poorly remunerated.[50]

Disability, in these cases, did not contradict productivity; on the contrary, disability required these women to work. The state provided insufficient work programs and benefits, and disabled women, who often had no one to depend on and had dependents themselves, particularly children, were forced to find jobs. American scholars have argued that in the context of disability, citizenship is grounded in one's work and productivity.[51] *Written Through Suffering* shows that looking through the lens of disability at citizenship and its relationship with work and productivity complicates general understandings of what it means to be a citizen. These Polish disabled women worked and wanted to belong to a working community, yet their participation in the labor force was fraught, since there were not enough jobs and, what is more, employment did not guarantee their belonging to society or the rights of citizenship. In the introduction to their edited collection, *Civil Disabilities: Citizenship, Membership, and Belonging*, Nancy J. Hirschmann and Beth Linker describe citizenship as "a matter of entitlement, obligation, and belonging."[52] The collection by Polish disabled women, *Written Through Suffering*, demonstrates that citizenship is also a matter of disability and gender. The intersection of these two embodied social identities, connected with the state's failure to provide good jobs for disabled subjects (for, as the collection attests, most available jobs were poorly paid and physically taxing and, as such, did not provide one with dignity), resulted in uneven access to citizenship rights and equality.

Article 5 of the 1976 Constitution stated that socialist Poland cared for its citizens' health. The same article claimed that the state worked on erasing the differences between the quality of life in cities and in the countryside. Yet, as the memoirs testify, for disabled women living outside big cities these promises were rarely fulfilled. The anonymous writers from the countryside enumerated problems with accessing health care. One of the authors wrote that in order to get to the doctor's office, she had to walk two kilometers just to get to the nearest town with a bus station. From there, she would catch a bus at 6:12 a.m., and the bus trip took an hour. She said: "I am most afraid to walk in the winter because it is completely dark when I walk to the bus station."[53] She had multiple sclerosis, so, when she finally got to the bus stop, she was "completely exhausted and weak."[54] Despite her exhaustion, this author continued going to the city to see the doctor, but not every woman decided to do the same. Another author who also lived in a village wrote: "I do not even have a doctor here, and since I am too weak to walk, I do not have physical strength, I do not go to Warsaw to see a doctor."[55] Disability experiences, then, were shaped not only by gender and employment status, but also by location.

Written Through Suffering offers multiple descriptions of life in the countryside. An anonymous writer discussed the hardships associated with it: "I need other people's support, especially because I live in a village. For example, I need help with cooking dinner and doing the laundry. In the village, we do not have running water or a bathroom. My village is isolated; the closest city is 25 kilometers away. The store, which is located in a bigger village, is 7 kilometers away."[56] Perhaps inadvertently, the anthology serves as a commentary on Polish socialist geography and reveals the unequal distribution of services between the cities and the countryside. One of the authors summarized it this way: "I should admit that for people such as myself it is easier to live in a big city. It is easier to access health care, get necessary supplies, and there are plenty of stores around. Now that my abilities are diminishing, this is what matters."[57] According to *The Situation of Disabled People and the Condition of Rehabilitation in the Polish People's Republic*, the majority of disabled people—roughly 70 percent—lived in cities under socialism in Poland.[58]

However, the author quoted who wrote about needing support with performing daily tasks stated that she ultimately preferred living in the countryside than in the city: "In the winter I live with my eldest sister because it is more convenient. She has central heating, hot running water, so I can take a bath and it is easier for me to take care of myself. But I am bored there during the summer, I prefer to live in the countryside. There are plenty of people in the city, I am ashamed of going outside. In the village I feel free, I feel comfortable."[59] *The Situation of Disabled People and the Condition of Rehabilitation in the Polish People's Republic* also includes brief information on disabled people living in the countryside: "Physical fitness, health, strength, and vitality are more important to people living in the countryside than to the urban population; however, countryside inhabitants do not care about aesthetic and normative appearance."[60] Both the anonymous memoir and this report depict disabled women's ambivalence toward living in the countryside, which turned out to be synonymous not only with constraint, but also with relative freedom from able-bodied aesthetic norms.

One author in *Written Through Suffering* described her activist efforts at trying to improve disabled people's lives in Poland. Her memoir chronicled her engagement with the Polish Association of the Blind; she eventually joined the board. Coming from a poor family led by a single mother (her father died during World War II), her story represents socialist social mobility. This anonymous writer spent her early childhood in institutions for the blind, and later she got involved with the Scouts and then with the Polish Association of the Blind, the biggest disability organization under state socialism in Poland with around forty thousand members.[61] At the same time, she studied at university and graduated with a master's degree in history. Though her memoir does not offer many details about her activism, she wrote: "I was involved in the blind women's movement from its very beginning in 1963. I traveled across the country a lot to meet blind women at the places where they lived. I was especially interested in elderly women who lived in state-run institutions. I prepared two reports discussing their situation, which I submitted to the central authorities."[62] She visited all the schools for the blind in the country, where she organized memoir competitions for blind girls and women so she could get a better sense of what their life was like.[63] "I was interested in how the schools prepared female students for outside life," she wrote.[64] The topics of the memoir competitions she organized included: "What did school have to offer?," "Being around other people," "My regular day," "My household." She also organized a survey distributed among students: "Do you move around on your own?" She added that she also worked as an editor of a magazine for blind women, *A Woman's Voice*, which at the time of writing had around a thousand subscribers.[65] And, while this anonymous writer did not discuss the nuances of her activist work—except for those mentioned above—her memoir reminds us that some disabled populations organized themselves and actively lobbied for their rights in socialist societies.[66] In other words, disability activism in Poland did not emerge after 1989, but existed long before, even if constrained by socialist regulations and thus adopting different forms than those we know today.

For example, Zofia Krzemkowska, a blind Polish activist and member of the Polish Association of the Blind and of various socialist blind networks, published an article in 1974 on the intersection of gender and blindness, "International Women's Year 1975," in *The Review of the European Blind*. She opened by saying: "International Women's Year has bearing also upon the community of the blind. Wherever a sighted woman lacks equal rights and suffering from obstacles to her vocational career as well as separation from political life, the same rights will be absent from a blind woman, too. Yet the problem will be further aggravated due to the specific nature and severity of the disablement concerned."[67] The obvious political tone of these lines runs throughout the piece. Krzemkowska raises the issues of vocational training and employment for blind women and poses a question that still resonates today: "Are they given equal pay for equal work?"[68] She did not limit her focus to the public sphere but recognized that the personal is political, openly tackling the discrimination that blind women experienced at home and, specifically, the unfair distribution of domestic duties (which, as I will examine further, was also part of the daily life of the anonymous authors of *Written Through Suffering*). Additionally, she touched upon blind women's access to love, marriage, and having kids (topics that were of utmost importance to the authors of *Written Through Suffering*). This short article constitutes just one example of blind women's activism under socialism in Eastern Europe, but it proves that disabled women fought for their rights and explored multiple avenues to make their voices heard.

For some disabled women, having children was a way of "rehabilitating" their disabilities and assuming the normative role of a woman. For most authors in this collection, motherhood brought the most happiness, but even this was fraught with heartache and pain. Nearly all the disabled women authors had at least one child, but with motherhood came considerable apprehension, even before their children were born. Prospective mothers with congenital disabilities worried that their children would inherit their conditions. This desire for the absence of disability must have been at least partially reinforced by material and social conditions. One author described lying awake all night in the hospital, praying to God, asking and demanding that her child be "normal": "I insisted [to God] that the child is normal."[69] Another woman wrote: "I have always dreamed of having a home and big family. . . . Against the doctor's advice I decided to have a child. What is a family without a child?"[70] She thanked God that she gave birth to a "healthy son that did not inherit my blindness. There was a risk, but I am happy I took it."[71] Passages like these make clear that these disabled women, even those without children, unequivocally identified womanhood with motherhood. They perceived motherhood as a woman's destiny and believed that a family without children was not a true family. At the same time, they approached the reproduction of disability as harm done both to the child and the family.

Disabled women's understanding of family might point to Polish socialism's investment in traditional conceptualizations of family and feminine roles. Studies by scholars working on the topic of state socialism have confirmed that motherhood was a defining and normative experience for women in socialist Poland.[72] Their feelings were so strong that some disabled women decided to have children against medical and familial advice. In his history of polio in socialist Poland, Marcin Stasiak writes that disabled women who survived the disease were actively discouraged by the medical establishment from having children.[73] The decision to have them was therefore an act of will: For an able-bodied woman under state socialism, bearing children was an expected life trajectory, while for a disabled woman it was an act of defiance. However, it is striking that these disabled women did not want to have disabled children and embraced narrow understandings of "normality." While this may reflect the internalization of the eugenic and ableist values upheld during the period of state socialism, it may simply be the expression of a hope that by not having to struggle so much to survive, nondisabled children would have a "better life." In other words, it was a response to the material conditions under which disabled people lived. Many of these authors appear to identify disability with suffering and cannot divorce the experience of being disabled from unhappiness and hardship.

The intersection of gender and disability and the social exclusion at the center of the collection does not leave room for descriptions of disability pride.[74] Neither do the memoirs depict any group identification that could translate into a movement or organized solidarity, even though the authors, as individuals, appear to identify as disabled women. Most of them do not know other disabled people (except for the blind author active in the Polish Association for the Blind) and display no interest in meeting any. Apart from those who found employment in sheltered workshops, disabled women rarely had a chance to forge relations with other disabled women; most remained isolated from the sites in which these relationships and communities have been known to form. The collection confirms what I discussed in the introduction: Disability under state socialism in Poland was confined to the domestic sphere, and institutionalization was not a dominant experience of people with disabilities at that time in Poland. The authors did not live in institutions and only visited hospitals on a temporary basis. Additionally, some had difficulty accessing rehabilitative institutions even when they wanted to: "I had to beg the doctor in order to get to a sanatorium."[75] The same author added that "I have enormous troubles to get a prescription that allows me to go to a rehabilitative center. . . . I was humiliated a lot [by doctors] to get this."[76] When she finally did get it, she was sent to a sanatorium that worked with people with different kinds of disabilities.[77] But most, it seems, could not afford to spend more time in these institutions: Parents needed help with household tasks and childrearing and, later in life they needed to take care of their own husbands and children. The gendered expectations placed upon them were not modified because of their disability.

Disability did not prohibit the authors of *Written Through Suffering* from performing household duties and care work; in other words, it did not redefine domesticity in this context.[78] Domesticity resisted the subversive potential of disability, and disability became integrated into preexisting patterns of homemaking. Disabled women often combined taking care of children, husbands, and elderly parents with work outside the home. This work could take longer and be more difficult than it would for a nondisabled person, and even produce physical pain; nevertheless, these women usually performed these duties with little help and little choice. The dominant models of both womanhood and domesticity did not change because of disability. On the contrary, homemaking and taking care of parents and families shaped these authors' experiences of disability, which reflect the 1980s research on disability that states: "Most disabled people had to perform all the household duties: they simply had no choice."[79]

The authors of these memoirs identified as both women and disabled persons. One woman openly embraced her identity as a "sick" person, believing that it provided her with "a deeper understanding of life. . . . I would not be able to learn how to be healthy now. What would I be like if I were not sick?"[80] This important but solitary analysis posits disability as a condition that is learned and can be generative of new understandings of life. Without fully explaining her rationale, the author also stated that health could be performed, though she believed she would not be able to learn healthiness at that point of her life. Additionally, she defined disability as a form of otherness and drew an analogy between disability and race. Her thinking of disability, articulated in her memoir, written in 1991, resonates with the British social model of disability formulated around twenty years earlier, which she probably had no opportunity to encounter. She wrote:

> I dream of writing books. I would like to make it clear to each and every reader that to be different, to be other, does not mean being inferior or superior—simply other. One's skin color or the way one moves or speaks, etc., can be different.

> I would like to provoke goodness in the reader, so that he/she would be willing to eliminate the barriers which limit others' freedom: architectural and urban barriers, legal regulations and personal biases that usually stem from lack of knowledge.[81]

It is remarkable that this author located a disabled person's lack of freedom and opportunities in the physical environment and the societal approach toward disability. She did not mention illness or the ailing body; instead, she discussed architecture, design, law, and societal prejudice, and, in line with what anglophone activists proclaimed, put the burden of eliminating these barriers not on the disabled individual but on the shoulders of "the reader"—in other words, society. She explained that it is the fact that she was born in a small provincial town that made her aware of her otherness and revealed the potential source of her insights: "I spend all my life in the countryside. This is a peculiar population that subjects its entire existence to the demands of field work and farm work, and all forms of otherness are either fought against or discriminated against. This approach shaped my life."[82] In other words, her beliefs about disability as produced at least in part by societal discrimination stemmed from her embodied knowledge. Therefore, it is evident that what anglophone scholars and activists understand as the social model of disability was also experienced and known to people with disabilities from different global locales, even though they did not necessarily refer to it as such.

Moreover, the author connected this social understanding of disability with religious understanding and added that "if God decided that illness would not take away my intelligence and capacities, I cannot lose these gifts."[83] Disability not only produced suffering, but also "a deeper understanding" of the world. This interpretation of sickness and disability cannot be detached from Catholicism, in which suffering is viewed as an uplifting, redemptive experience, determined by God.

Many of the memoir authors refer to God as the main authority figure and a potential force behind any improvement in their lives. As previously mentioned, the cover of *Writing Through Suffering* features a photograph of Pope John Paul II, who is the only person connected with the Catholic Church discussed in the memoirs. Mostly the authors focus on God, often invoking him in their final paragraphs—for example: "I am deeply religious. Faith in God provides me with strength, patience and hope."[84] These comments about God and religion, largely absent in disability memoirs published in Poland during the 1970s and 1980s, reflect both the deep roots of Polish Catholicism and changes in publishing laws during the transition.[85] In some cases, mentioning God appears to help the authors accept their situation. One stated that through God, suffering was "beautiful and makes sense."[86] The author of the memoir "To że urodziłam się chora dało mi głębsze spojrzenie na życie" ("The fact that I was born ill gave me a deeper understanding of life") interpreted the injustices she suffered as a challenge from God, with happiness depending on how people approached problems, whether "as a wall that stops us, or a test given to us by God that we need to pass as well as possible."[87] One author stated that God was the reason that newly disabled people did not commit suicide: "Religious faith is very important in disabled people's lives: it protects people who had accidents from taking their own lives; it protects those who are mentally broken and mentally weak."[88] In a similar vein, another stated that "a deep belief in God helped me survive all my troubles."[89] The title of her memoir reiterates this sentiment: "Głęboka wiara w Boga pozwoliła mi przetrwać" ("A deep belief in God helped me survive").[90] One title references Saint Mary: "Wszystko osiągnęłam dzięki pomocy Matki Bożej" ("I have achieved everything thanks to Saint Mary's help"). It is important to underline, though, that it is not clear whether the titles were given by the authors themselves or by the editor. Nevertheless, these direct appeals and references to God appear to show—perhaps unintentionally—the tension between the Church as an institution that was not a viable outlet or comfort for these women's grievances and suffering, and the authors' need for faith and spirituality.

The topic of pain recurs in complex ways throughout the memoirs, with many authors discussing the impossibility of its alleviation. One author stated that her medications had little effect: "My legs and back hurt more and more. There are nights I am unable to fall asleep."[91] She expected to "start using a wheelchair soon. I cannot afford to have surgery."[92] This short fragment highlights the ways in which social conditions and lack of access to medical services exacerbate pain. A woman with a motor disability that was not apparent to most people she met concluded her memoir by stating that she felt "like every other normal human being no one ever looks at my legs. Even though the pain sometimes makes me cry, I do not show it around other people."[93] This pain, a constant element in her life, could neither be alleviated nor explained to other people. Arseli Dokumaci, a Canada-based disability studies scholar, claims that "pain comprises many kinds of experiences and many different responses," and it seems that a memoir that discusses pain might be a form of response to it.[94]

Additionally, for the authors in *Written Through Suffering*, pain functioned as a sensation of both individualization and isolation. Pain, whether the result of disability or sickness, is clearly exacerbated by societal indifference. An author who suffered from chronic fatigue stated that no one understood how she could "experience exhaustion as a result of getting dressed or washing."[95] However, pain is also a product of scarce resources and a lack of surgical options. One author described how her suffering from poorly manufactured and incorrectly fitted prosthetics in postwar Poland was due to the retirement of prewar medical experts retiring who were not replaced: "The state of Polish orthopedics did not make my life easy. What was most difficult was getting a good prosthesis. The pre-war medical experts were retiring at that time and there were no successors who would be able to produce an equally good prosthesis. The poorly made new prosthesis hurt my stumps and bent my spine."[96] People whose disability had its origin in polio also discussed the poor quality of available prostheses.[97] Moreover, the waiting time to attain a prosthesis was long and "required much determination."[98] In other words, historical circumstances—a lack of doctors and high-quality materials for the production of prosthetics during the early 1950s—were responsible for her pain. Pain emerges as a complex experience produced by societal, historical, and material circumstances; disability itself; and the relationship between a body and the world.

The "suffering" in the collection's title refers not only to the pain that authors had to endure, but also to the extraordinary violence inflicted on disabled bodies, often by the people closest to them. To a certain extent, the collection is composed of images of violence: of parents who beat and abused their daughters to punish them for having a disability, and husbands who raped, tormented, and beat their disabled wives. In one memoir, "Najwięcej krzywdy doznałam od męża" ("The one who abused me the most is my husband"), the author describes the beating she received from a husband addicted to alcohol. She states: "What he liked best was to bully a weak cripple."[99] The author of the memoir "Życie, które mogą wyrazić tylko skargi" ("A life whose meaning can be expressed only as a complaint") reminisces that the physical labor she had to perform as an eleven-year-old child was too hard for her because of her already deteriorating health, and when she complained to her mother, "she thought it was an excuse, that I was lazy. I would often get whipped."[100] In their accounts, the brutality experienced by these authors were not followed by help or intervention. The violence often went unnoticed by others and remained largely unpunished. Consequently, disabled women's bodies become texts bearing the stamp of cultural expectations they could not meet: of parents who had expected a nondisabled boy, or a husband who was ashamed of his wife's deafness. These forms of violence are rooted in heteropatriarchal, ableist understandings of fit, attractive, and useful bodies.

What is particularly striking here is the social acceptance of familial violence that testifies to the state's abandonment of disabled women, which started long before 1989 and continued after the political and economic change. The lives of disabled women are violated and disrupted at home, within familial circles. Disability and gender made their lives unworthy of protection. Violence against disabled women was practically state-sanctioned: the memoirs rarely refer to any kind of help, and in the few instances where women brought charges against their husbands, the men were either acquitted or given extremely short sentences.[101] Historian Barbara Klich-Kluczewska writes that nondisabled women victims of domestic violence received similar treatment from the courts: the husbands who beat them got, usually, very short sentences (for example, six months). After the imprisonment, the perpetrators returned home in most cases.[102] Klich-Kluczewska adds that under state socialism "the Polish state institutions left the victims without real support," and that, despite the presence of the topic of domestic violence in expert and public discussions of the 1970s and 1980s, as well as the socialist pledge to women's rights, the problem remained a private one throughout the period of state socialism in Poland.[103] Her analysis emphasizes the social acceptance of domestic abuse.[104] As a result, violence against disabled women can be understood as part of a continuum of violence against women that was pervasive, normalized, and in most cases unpunished.

As stated above, the domestic violence and state abandonment experienced by disabled women during the period of state socialism did not end with the political transformation of 1989. *Written Through Suffering* reveals that the shift to capitalism did not secure citizenship rights for disabled women despite some analyses in the early 1990s that declared the transition a part of "the resurrection of rights in Poland."[105] By "citizenship rights," I do not mean the more explicit rights, such as suffrage and legal protection, but, rather, in a broader sense, the right to access state resources, gain recognition as a subject, and be included in the social, economic, and cultural fabric of the polity.[106] This collection shows that women's citizenship was second class, not grounded either in the domestic sphere or in the labor force. As the political situation of 1989–91 perpetuated and reinforced the social exclusion of disabled women and the privatization of disability experiences, a break from state socialism was not established.

Writing Trauma

These memoirs disrupt official historical periodization. The collection presents the entire scope of the Polish People's Republic, officially starting in 1948 and ending in 1989, as an ongoing crisis. It makes no mention of the landmark periods and events in Polish socialist history: Stalinism between 1948 and 1956;

the "thaw" that followed Stalin's death; the series of student demonstrations demanding democratic rights in 1968 and the coeval antisemitic campaign against and expulsion of Polish Jews; the workers' strike in the north of Poland due to sudden price increases in 1970; the subsequent removal from office of Władysław Gomułka as first secretary of the Polish United Workers' Party; or the establishment of the Workers' Defense Committee in 1976, following the brutal suppression of protests in a number of Polish cities. The authors do not refer to the strikes of 1980, triggered by further price increases and the firing of Anna Walentynowicz and Lech Wałęsa from the Gdańsk Shipyard for their independent trade union activities, nor to the subsequent recognition of Solidarity or the introduction of martial law between 1981 and 1983. They do not mention the pope's visit to Poland in 1987, or the worsening economic situation in 1988, which resulted in 40 percent price increases for food, cigarettes, and alcohol, prompting strikes organized and supported by Solidarity. A reader of this collection will find no information about the first "capitalist" reforms of 1988 that failed to prevent the Polish economy from collapsing, or the start of the Round Table discussions between the government and the Solidarity-led opposition in February 1989, parts of which were broadcast on TV. There is no reference to the 1989 elections, or the first democratic government under Tadeusz Mazowiecki, established in August of that year. While these authors narrate their own lives in a normative, linear, and chronological fashion, none of these events appear in their accounts. Perhaps it is the interconnection of gender and disability that leads them to cast themselves out of history, to discursively depoliticize their lives and focus on the private.

However, of more import is the fact that these events, often presented in historical and sociological analyses of Poland as "unprecedented" catastrophes, did not constitute "unprecedented" crises in these authors' lives.[107] For example, the only allusion in the entire collection to the start of martial law in 1981 appears in the context of one author's discussion of the problems she faced continuing her education: she had graduated from primary school that year, but as "people were busy with other things, they did not concern themselves with one girl's education."[108] While it may not be unusual for a teenage girl to center her own experiences and embed historical catastrophes within the ordinary, none of the other memoirists, some of whom were adults in 1981, noted the serious social, economic, and political consequences of martial law. The logic that recognizes only certain events as "unprecedented" results in negating a crisis that has no clear-cut beginning or end.

Thus, *Written Through Suffering* negates "the positioning of crisis as a singular and exceptional event."[109] Challenging the focus on "exceptional shock and data loss in the memory" within trauma theory, Lauren Berlant has demonstrated that trauma and crisis do not constitute exceptions and, what is more, are not divorced from the ordinary.[110] The crises described by the authors of *Written Through Suffering* are ongoing, and their memoirs testify to the poverty, abandonment, and violence they continue to experience. In many cases, for a woman, disability cannot be separated from the hurt and injury perpetrated by their parents, husbands, and partners. Traumatic events—never identified as "traumatic" by the authors themselves—are often normalized through a banal retelling. Moreover, as one of the authors commented, "for us, the impaired, there has always been a crisis in Poland": "There was a constant lack of wheelchairs and cars for the impaired, and there was no money for modern equipment. Until recently, I had no idea that in other countries people have access to equipment that helps people who have only one arm. This equipment is unavailable here."[111] Another stated that "we have a crisis in Poland now, but I remember an even bigger crisis we had when I was a child."[112] Disabled women living through the fall of state socialism in Poland did not experience a transformation, but rather a continuation of their "crisis ordinariness."[113]

Written Through Suffering constitutes a document of trauma. The collection belongs to the corpus of writing known as "social memoir," a popular genre in interwar and postwar Poland, when memoir competitions were organized among various social groups, including peasants, miners, and the unemployed. These competitions were a way of learning about the nation, newly reestablished in 1918; due to the partitions, Poland had not existed as an independent country since 1772.[114] Memoir competitions also provided a space for people from marginalized groups to share their life stories. Therefore, it is feasible to think of the social memoir as a genre that democratizes writing and enables people representing various social groups to claim a voice and narrative authority. Having analyzed Polish memoirs from the interwar period, Katherine Lebow has defined the genre of social memoir as a "form of grievance and complaint."[115]

But *Written Through Suffering* offers more than a testament to injustice and a chance to air grievances. The collection's title rearticulates a discourse of Polish martyrology that centers on an individual's sacrificial suffering for the nation. While this is closely linked to the religious rhetoric of self-sacrifice, this disability life writing rejects the redemptive potential of pain. As the authors demonstrate, it is the state that has inflicted violence and suffering upon disabled women: Their trauma did not originate in disabled bodyminds, but from "the social structures that unequally distribute life chances and resources toward a livable life."[116] Thus, the highly politicized language of suffering that in Polish culture refers to one's public role as an insurgent or freedom fighter is here appropriated by disabled women to illustrate the political and social character of feminized disabled trauma. This trauma is not exceptional; it is expected. As a result, the memoirs constitute a collective critique of violence, poverty, and state abandonment.

It is difficult to determine to what extent intrafamilial violence is a direct corollary of the violence inflicted by state neglect. Yet domestic violence has been empowered by the public silence surrounding the topic and the state's unwillingness to intervene in "domestic affairs." In *Trauma and Recovery: The Aftermath of Violence—from Domestic Abuse to Political Terror*, American psychiatrist and gender studies scholar Judith Hermann has noted that, due to concealment of the "real conditions" of women's lives in the private "sphere of the personal," to speak about sexual and domestic experiences is "to invite public humiliation, ridicule, and disbelief."[117] It is telling that the one place these authors can openly share their experiences—marked not only by violence, but also loneliness—is an anonymous memoir. Thus, this normalized and common experience of trauma remains "confined to the sphere of private life, without formal recognition or restitution from the community."[118]

Anonymity enables this collective protest: It is both a recognizable convention—many memoirs published under state socialism were published anonymously—and a condition of possibility for this collection. Some authors told no one about their entries, with one author stating that they "would never tell my family I participated in this competition."[119] The protection of anonymity allows authors to remain "untraceable," to keep their social position as mothers, wives, daughters, sisters and workers, while at the same time criticizing the society in which they live and openly discussing the abuses to which they are subjected.[120] Anonymity gives them the power to establish new identities as writers.

Slow Transformation

On June 4, 1989, after forty-five years of socialist rule, the first "free" elections took place in Poland. This liberation was not necessarily expected: Many dissidents active during the 1980s did not believe that the socialist system would end in their lifetime,[121] and the Polish economist Tadeusz Kowalik has claimed that Solidarity's success came as a surprise to both sides.[122] The largest trade union in Eastern Europe, Solidarity had around ten million members at its peak in 1981.[123] As well as organizing mass protests in factories and other workplaces across the country in August 1980, the trade union formulated the "twenty-one postulates," a charter addressed to the ruling Polish United Workers' Party.

These postulates did not include the abolishment of state socialism, but demanded a day of rest on Saturdays, increased wages, improved working conditions, better health care, and the right to strike. Norwegian academic Johan Galtung has described the strikes of August 1980 as a "socialist revolution."[124] In December 1981, the period known as the "carnival of Solidarity" ended with the introduction of martial law, intended to undermine Solidarity's popularity and, according to the government and army, prevent a Soviet intervention similar to those that had taken place in Hungary in 1956 and Czechoslovakia in 1968. To this day, it is unclear whether an intervention would have occurred had the government not taken this step. Many opposition leaders were imprisoned, and those who managed to escape went underground. Some dissidents and Solidarity activists were incarcerated for violating martial law, and many people lost their jobs due to their involvement with the trade union.[125] Although martial law was lifted in 1983, Solidarity did not regain its earlier power or popularity. The army consolidated its own power and, according to some historians, became more influential than the socialist party itself.[126]

The 1980s were a time of heightened economic and political crises. The relative prosperity of the previous decade was shattered by an ever-increasing cost of living, falling wages, and 15 percent inflation during the first half of the 1980s.[127] Following the imposition of martial law in 1981, the US government introduced sanctions against Poland, putting an end to the series of loans the country had secured from the West during the 1970s.[128] Protests continued, despite the imprisonment of many dissidents and Solidarity leaders, and Wałęsa's authority was strengthened when he received the Nobel Peace Prize in 1983. Nevertheless, the lifting of martial law the same year did not bring an end to literary expressions of weariness, frustration, helplessness, and hopelessness, and, rather than the triumphant result of activism, the unexpected end of state socialism appears to have been instigated by economic and political collapse.

None of this can be found in *Written Through Suffering*. Although authors do allude to the post-1989 situation, as I will discuss below, not one describes voting—or not voting—in June 1989. One author does acknowledge the elections in the context of disappointment and disability policy: "Before the elections, everyone promised that they would improve the quality of life of sick and disabled people, but these were—for the most part—empty words. The galloping inflation and constant price increases exacerbate our already difficult situation. Most of us are afraid of the future."[129] Similarly, there is no reference to broadcasts of the Round Table discussions that led to the elections. Neither is there any indication of support for either the communist Polish United Workers' Party or Solidarity, or any expression of opinion about the ongoing upheavals in Eastern Europe. Reflecting the marginalization experienced by these anonymous disabled women, this lack of reference to both national and international events disrupts official accounts of the late 1980s and early 1990s.

Of course, this does not negate the joy and optimism experienced by the Polish people as a whole. In a famous public news broadcast on October 28, 1989, Polish actress Joanna Szczepkowska announced with a smile, "Ladies and gentlemen, on June 4, 1989, communism in Poland ended." Her happiness is obvious. Additionally, her statement marked an ostensibly clear move from the "communist" past to a democratic future, a linear progression from state socialism to capitalism.[130] But the victorious tone in Szczepkowska's voice and many other analyses is absent from *Written Through Suffering*.

For most of these authors, there was no qualitative difference between before and after the transformation; thus, in their writing, the two periods merge. At times it is difficult to distinguish the socialist past from the present not-yet-capitalist moment of transition.[131] While "then" and "now" do appear in a number of memoirs, both are characterized by violence, poverty, and the struggle to keep going. Clearly, this way of reporting—or, rather, disregarding—the 1989 political transformation challenges the mainstream Polish narrative that cleaves national history into "socialist" and "postsocialist" periods. The Polish historian Tomasz Żukowski has described the effect of this division: "There is no recognition of continuation between the two systems and thus the relationship between the present and the past is erased. The question of 'continuation' does not spark any interest, because it does not fit the collective fantasy. What is more, even historians give in to the pressure from public discourse and emphasize the differences between the two systems."[132]

With their embodied experiences making it clear that no discontinuance exists between the socialist and early post-socialist periods, disabled women do not adhere to this collective fantasy. For these authors there is only a perpetual crisis marked by fluctuating states of anxiety: "it is difficult to write letters now when there is no work, no enthusiasm, only impatience and anxiety";[133] Poland "is no country for poor people and I need to pay out of pocket for everything. . . . I try to save up as much as possible";[134] "The only thing I want is to work the way I used to. Is it too much to ask for? In competition with able-bodied women disabled women have no chance to get a job."[135] One author states that the "changes" have "impacted my life very negatively since I have no chance to make additional money."[136] Another worries whether she will be laid off, as she receives a disability pension, and is "afraid to think about" what she would do if that happened.[137] If anything, the rising unemployment and worsening housing situation that accompanied the shift to capitalism heightened the anxiety and precarity of these authors, who do not use such terms as "socialism," "communism," and "capitalism" any more than the names of political leaders and activists. As I have previously argued, their lack of reference to major events and personalities suggests that, for these disabled women, political change simply had no effect on their deep and enduring sense of abandonment by the state.

The speed with which economic reforms were introduced, often referred to as "shock therapy," has been emphasized in recent literature on the transformation. The Polish iteration of shock therapy was a long time in the making: The works of Friedrich van Hayek, Robert Nozick, and Milton Friedman had been read, discussed, and championed by a number of Polish dissidents and scholars during the 1980s. Among these scholars was Leszek Balcerowicz, who was responsible for economic reform during the early 1990s as minister of finance. In an anthology on capitalist transformation in Eastern Europe, Philipp Ther has described the passing of the Washington Consensus in 1989 by the International Monetary Fund, the World Bank, the US Ministry of Finances, and high-ranking members of the US Congress. Its "first prescription" was "an austerity program intended to stabilize the macro-economic situation and fight inflation."[138] Poland was the first country to follow this "new economic doctrine," through the Balcerowicz Plan.[139] According to Ther, the reforms aggravated the existing economic crisis.[140] Increasing unemployment, prices, and privatization, which often involved the closing down of major state companies and factories, impoverished many and led to industrial action during the early 1990s.[141]

The anonymous writers of *Written Through Suffering* described their own precarious economic situations. One wrote of being wished "hope and optimism" by everyone—emotions she could no longer feel: "On June 13, 1990, my regular job ended. The institution I worked for was reorganized and has a new owner. The institution [a school for the blind] stopped providing vocational education because, as is commonly known, there is no work for the blind. And not only for the blind. So, the teachers are not needed anymore either. My work hours have been significantly reduced."[142] Another author described the worry that she would be unable to meet the "constant price increases: the apartment maintenance, electricity, gas, food" in six months' time.[143] Only one of these writers openly criticized capitalism, stating that "an invalid has no chance to thrive" in the new economic situation. "Living as surviving" was all they could do, and even the "educated and rehabilitated" would be passed over for a job if an able-bodied person was available, as where "there is business, there is no room for a human being."[144] In 1990, there had been very little opposition to the Balcerowicz Plan from a Polish society that, if not overly enthusiastic and optimistic, was convinced of the need for radical change.[145]

Reflecting on the transition in a 1994 interview, Deputy Prime Minister Leszek Balcerowicz described his goal as "a swift and permanent implementation of the reforms, which I understood as indispensable should Poland enter the path of constant development."[146] In his biography of Polish capitalism, *Zimna Trzydziestoletnia (A Cold Thirty-Year-Old)*, the journalist Rafał Woś claims that the government had initially intended to implement reforms at a more gradual pace.[147] This "leap into capitalism" has been described by the economist and activist Tadeusz Kowalik as "Thatcher's notion of shock therapy."[148] According to the architects of the transformation, this was an accelerated moment of introducing new capitalist reforms, practices, and discourses. In other words, there was no time left. However, the notion of speeding forward described by Kowalik is entirely absent from *Written Through Suffering*.

For disabled women, the capitalist transformation equated to extended waiting: They waited longer than previously to access ever scarcer and more dispersed medical therapies and facilities, and for government housing. As prices and demand escalated, one *Written Through Suffering* author was afraid she would no longer be able to afford her own apartment.[149] Thus, in some cases, the transformation did have an effect: It led to deteriorating living conditions. To be a disabled woman in Poland in the early 1990s was to experience slowness on a regular basis: a slowness that offered no healing or respite, only an increase in suffering and weariness.[150] American anthropologist Katherine Verdery has described a seizure of time by socialist state governments, presenting "the immobilization of bodies in food lines" as "the most obvious example."[151] As socialist states "compelled people's bodies into particular activities," I argue that the new Polish state deployed similar tactics when it came to disabled women.[152] Waiting for access to resources was part of the temporal politics of the transformation period.

Producing Disability Knowledge

While *Written Through Suffering* provides unique insight into disabled women's experiences of the transition, it is important to attend to how this knowledge has been produced. To this end, I believe it is helpful to think of these women as theorists of the 1989 Polish transformation. Disability knowledge is rarely created or brought together in university libraries or the halls of parliament buildings; far more often it is shaped by embodiment and arises from the conflicts and frictions that characterize a disabled person's interactions with social, architectural, and political spheres. In other words, it is knowledge that stems from and reflects the embodied experiences of "misfitting."[153] Disability knowledge not only describes; it also intervenes within the social sphere. Thus, this world-describing and world-making knowledge is inherently politicized.

American literary disability studies scholar Thomas Couser has noted that life-writing, which appears "to require only that one have a life—or at least, one considered worth narrating—and sufficient narrative skill to tell one's own story," may be the most accessible genre to people with disabilities.[154] However, the accessibility of autobiography can be illusory: Not only are narrative skills required, but the process of writing itself may pose difficulties for some, and can be physically and mentally exhausting.[155] One *Writing Through Suffering* author expressed doubts that she had written what she wanted to "in a clear manner": "Perhaps my sentences are too long and there might be errors. I am sorry, but I have no patience to consult the dictionary. I wrote all of this myself, because despite my disabled hands, I can still do it."[156] Another stated that it had taken her a whole summer to write her memoir, and it was only the "long deadline" that had enabled her to contribute.[157] The author of "Niepokoją mnie zachowania ludzi wobec siebie" (The way people react to each other scares me) described her own fears:

> I have no idea how I found the courage to participate in this competition. Maybe because I am expected to write, because I would never share these things orally. I apologize for the errors, ugly handwriting, but I have written it myself. I hardly see anything, but I have written it all by myself. I would never tell my family I participated in this competition. I write when I am at home alone, I have already been working on this for two months.[158]

The recurring claims of authorship without assistance in these memoirs suggest that the activity of writing enables disabled women to reclaim independence and agency. But writing about being a disabled woman also has the potential for embarrassment, as for the woman who could never tell her family what she was doing.[159] Equally striking is the information provided on how long it has taken to complete these memoirs, which reveal writing as a practice that requires physical strength and patience. Perhaps the apologies for errors and imperfect handwriting—whether to readers, competition organizers, or someone else—are a gendered tendency. By attending to the sections in which authors touch upon the writing process, one can see that writing is neither a gender-neutral nor a disability-neutral activity.

Moreover, analysis of these fragments indicates that disability is not only a topic of the memoirs, but, importantly, a mode of their production. Disability determines the rhythm and pace of writing. The seemingly innocuous and cryptic phrase about writing "When I am at home alone, I have already been working on this for two months" reveals that gender may also be a mode of production.[160] The phrase forces the reader to ask whether it takes the author a long time to write due to her disability and the physical or emotional difficulties she struggles with, because, as a disabled person, she spends most of her time at home surrounded by family members—or is it because, as a woman, she spends most of her time at home taking care of others and thus is rarely alone? While no definitive conclusion can be reached, close reading shows that disability and gender are responsible for the ways in which this writing and knowledge have been produced.

Conclusion

Written Through Suffering disrupts the dominant and victorious narrative of the 1989 transformation, which, in the words of the popular Polish sociologist Piotr Sztompka "constituted a major break in historical continuity, a complete and radical change at all levels of social life, for great masses of people."[161] These memoirs force us to recognize continuities rather than radical ruptures and, in order to more accurately reflect all experiences, attempt alternative ways of conceptualizing the Polish transformation. Similarly, the employment of disability and gender as analytical tools enables one to ask whose perspectives are represented in dominant historical narratives of political change. Reading *Written Through Suffering* also impels us to ask what other voices have been lost from the transformation narrative. As discussed earlier, one example is that of the Roma community. The violence they experienced in socialist Poland did not cease in 1989. Under democracy the Roma have continuously suffered economic neglect and marginalization: Their houses and settlements have been consistently raided and destroyed by state and city authorities, in Warsaw in 1996,[162] and Gdańsk in 2014 and 2019;[163] and they have been the victims of individual and organized attacks in many cities and towns across Poland.[164] While the experiences of the Roma and disabled communities are distinct, it is clear that ableist and racialized devaluations of certain lives have characterized both Polish socialism and capitalism.

Although my analysis centers the silenced experiences of regime change, *Written Through Suffering* also serves as a commentary on the tradition of memoir competitions in socialist Poland. According to cultural studies scholar Magda Szcześniak, these competitions were intended to illustrate social mobility among the working class, thereby demonstrating that socialism provided access to the social ladder.[165] Conversely, *Written Through Suffering* testifies to crisis ordinariness and impasse, remaking what we have been led to believe about socialist mobility.

By focusing on the precarious ordinariness these writers continued to experience, the memoirs contest boundaries between political and domestic spheres and present the family as the site of a state-sanctioned form of violence. In *Written Through Suffering*, family often disrupts and violates disabled lives. Disability does not threaten or redefine domesticity; rather, it becomes confined within a private and perilous domestic realm.

Not only do these authors inscribe pain into politics; they also inscribe themselves into a symbolic order from which they have been excluded. Construction of the autobiographical subject is an act of agency, one that enables these authors to counteract the abandonment I analyze in the chapters that follow. Krystyna Kersten and Tomasz Szarota have argued that the anonymous writers of socialist autobiographies were driven by a desire to "include their <I> into history, to mark their presence, to participate in the public sphere."[166] The same desire animated the twenty-one disabled women whose life-writing is at the heart of this chapter. In the next, my focus shifts to state abandonment and the familialization of disability, which I will address through the experiences of nondisabled mothers and their disabled children.

2 VIOLENT INTIMACY

Although this chapter changes perspective, from the attempts of disabled women to navigate the often hostile and ableist environments under state socialism and through the transformation of 1989, to the lives of nondisabled mothers with disabled children between 1989 and 2022, I remain focused on the abandonment of the disabled population by the Polish state and the privatization of disability. To this end, I bring together a range of literary and factual sources.

Whether in a fictional or nonfictional context, almost all cultural texts produced in Poland after 1989 frame a child's disability as a disruption to familial life or an exceptional crisis that needs to be overcome or cured.[1] Depictions of disability being integrated into the fabric of a family are rare. In this chapter I analyze texts that focus on this disruption, particularly the impact on the mother, who is generally expected to be the primary caregiver.

The central themes of this chapter are the notion of "violent intimacy" and the meanings of care. Violent intimacy, as an intervention into disability and family discourses, is in and of itself a major disruption to the ways in which the Polish family and the maternal relation with a child in particular are imagined. As I discussed in the introduction, violent intimacy is an affective structure that binds a mother and her disabled child; it not only disrupts families, but also commonly accepted ideas about motherly love and the emotional and financial cost of care and dedication.

Violent intimacy binds a mother to her child. It is crucial to keep in mind that there is no violent intimacy without love: it is an intimacy marked by love and commitment, but also—and equally importantly—by a lack of choice. It is simultaneously loving and oppressive for both mother and child. Violent intimacy does not trespass on kinship boundaries: its boundaries are biological ties. It is an enduring intimacy, and its length adds to its violence; it often only ends—as the texts featured in this chapter demonstrate—with the death of one participant.[2] In other words, the bind and the expectation of maternal care are infinite. There are no limits to the tasks a mother is required to take on, and no accepted means of exit for either mother or child. Unlike a stranger receiving payment from the state or private funds, this caregiving relationship is nonnegotiable for both parties.

Violent intimacy, like all care situations, is deeply enmeshed in power relations.[3] Both the caregiver and the care receiver are trapped, a condition that testifies to their shared vulnerability. Theirs is an intimacy that benefits and is enforced by the state. Violent intimacy is a constant, reinforcing dynamic, a dialectical process: It enables the state to relinquish its duty to citizens, just as state withdrawal from the sphere of care creates the intimacy itself. According to American philosopher Nancy Fraser, this kind of affective structure underpins and enables capitalism: "The capitalist economy relies on—one might say, free rides on—activities of provisioning, care-giving and interaction that produce and maintain social bonds, although it accords them no monetized value and treats them as if they were free."[4]

This is not a new idea. Many scholars have noted capitalism's dependence on gendered care work. Raj Patel and Jason W. Moore have claimed that without unpaid care work, "wage work would be simply too expensive."[5] What is perhaps new (as I outlined in the introduction and alluded to in chapter 1), is that both state socialism and capitalism in Poland have relied on unpaid care work for disabled subjects. In other words, I would venture that as a specific form of care work, violent intimacy is independent of either state socialism or capitalism: Both have taken it for granted that mothers will perform this work. While investigating the political economy of violent intimacy is not my principal focus here, following this aspect through state socialism and capitalism in Poland illustrates that the two systems differ little in the politics of care and disability. By fashioning care for a disabled subject as an issue of maternal dedication, both systems have exploited motherly love and concealed the central role of this kind of care labor in the state economy.

I must emphasize that care work and violent intimacy are not one and the same. Clearly, "care work" is a broader term and a form of labor that can be performed by a nonfamily member. It is undervalued and often performed by migrants, but the person performing it has—however limited—a choice.[6] While care work can be exploitative, this is not the same kind of cruelty that characterizes violent intimacy: While violent intimacy is predominantly a form of coercion rooted in love and lack of choice due to social and moral beliefs about the maternal role, the coercion of low-paid care work is rooted in economic necessity and labor market constraints.[7] Coercion defines both, yet their ideological and material roots differ.

The consequences of violent intimacy differ for mother and child. While oppressive for both, violent intimacy removes a mother's freedom, career, and, at times, her personal life: It is not uncommon for a husband or partner to leave such situations. Violent intimacy positions a child as the mother's burden, as a care receiver, rarely a care provider.[8] Needing maternal help to survive, a disabled child simply has no choice. Unlike the father, the mother herself has little choice but to accept violent intimacy: To refuse it would be to defy deeply entrenched ideas about maternal sacrifice and the duties of women.[9] As long as the state does not provide long-term, high-quality care assistance, violent intimacy remains inescapable for both the mother and her disabled child.

When viewed through the lens of adoption, the biological ties underpinning violent intimacy become increasingly clear. The only book that I have located on adoption and disability published in Poland opens by stating that "finding a family for a child with a disability is an extremely difficult task."[10] As had been the case in the United States a few decades ago, "adoption professionals, doctors, and psychologists all frame disability as a major risk of (and to) adoption."[11] Before 2017, when the government placed restrictions on the foreign adoption of Polish children, most adoptions of disabled children in institutional care were made by families from Italy and the United States.[12] These restrictions have increased the numbers of disabled children in Poland who will move from an orphanage to an institution for people with disabilities at the age of eighteen. As adoption studies is a new and underdeveloped field in Poland, an examination of the intersection between violent intimacy and adoption has yet to be undertaken.

By putting forward the notion of violent intimacy, I intend to nuance Polish narratives on family and disability. First and foremost, an exploration of violent intimacy reveals the multifaceted aspects of care, and its inherent nature as a power dynamic. Described in the texts I analyze, without being named as such, violent intimacy disrupts the mainstream narrative of the family that routinely glosses over experiences of disability and the toll of motherly care. The notion of violent intimacy enables me to emphasize the simultaneously oppressive and loving dimension of this form of care, which "is simultaneously a vital aspect of positive intimacy as well as grueling work that can be both difficult and unpaid."[13] By challenging narratives that showcase *natural* maternal sacrifice and the autonomous choice to take on care work, violent intimacy enables us to recognize the deeply ambivalent character of care.

Violent intimacy is neither an aspect of every mother–child relationship nor a synonym for a child's dependency on a caretaker. It identifies a relationship in which the necessity for long-term everyday care work does not end when a child reaches their teenage years or adulthood. Violent intimacy is present when an "autonomous" future for either child or mother is inaccessible due to a lack of state support, adequate policy, and care infrastructures. To put it differently, the foreclosure of a future in which a disabled child can move to a supportive group home and a mother gains time for anything other than providing care is a condition for violent intimacy. Violent intimacy is not a gesture of refusing this normative future vision; it is a lack of choice in the matter.

I trace care and violent intimacy across a diverse corpus of texts published between 1995 and 2022. Thematically organizing this wide range of texts illustrates the enduring mechanisms of enacting care and the entrenchment of violent intimacy within families with a disabled child. The texts include a young adult novel, *Poczwarka* (*The Pupa*, 2001) by Dorota Terakowska, one of the most important Polish authors writing in this genre during the 1990s and early 2000s, in which the idyllic life of a married couple is "destroyed" by a daughter with Down syndrome. I read this alongside another young adult novel, *Wyspa mojej siostry* (*My Sister's Island*, 2011) by Katarzyna Ryrych, a deeply stigmatizing and ableist depiction of an intellectually disabled protagonist that met with critical acclaim. Among the nonfiction texts I examine are *Mieć dziecko z porażeniem mózgowym* (*Having a Child with Cerebral Palsy*, 1995), a forgotten anthology of life writing by mothers of disabled children edited by Zofia Chodkowska; *Emil i my: monolog wielodzietnej matki* (*Emil and Us: A Monologue of a Mother of Three*, 2021), a political approach to disability and care work by Magdalena Moskal; a book by the chronically ill journalist Jacek Hołub with a title that expresses the concerns of many parents with disabled children, *Żeby umarło przede mną* (*Hoping My Child Dies Before I Do*, 2018); and a 2022 article by the writer Agnieszka Szpila, "Gdzie są te dzieci? W dupie!" (*Where Are These Children? They Are Fucked!*) that focuses on carers and their right to self-fulfillment. As *The Pupa* and *My Sister's Island* sold thousands of copies, *Hoping My Child Dies Before I Do* was turned into a theater play, and a few received literary awards and public acclaim, the meanings of disability and care they present have circulated widely in Polish culture and merit analysis: they present a window into complex experiences of caregiving and participate in building knowledge about disability.

In all these texts, care is privatized. Most often, care work is only provided by a family member and only within a family. Not only do the authors of these texts demonstrate that the Polish family is the only site that guarantees care—and thus survival—for a disabled subject, they also emphasize that the post-1989 Polish state does *not care*: It provides no long-term support for disabled subjects who need sustained help with daily living. As the state has abandoned disabled subjects, mothers and, at times, grandmothers must provide the unpaid and socially underappreciated labor of care. State abandonment is not the result of deinstitutionalization, which has not taken place in Poland.[14] Facilities are limited in number, however, and there is cultural resistance toward placing disabled children in particular in institutions. (I will return to the topic of institutionalization below and in the epilogue.)

The cultural imperative to care for a disabled family member survived the 1989 political transformation. In other words, the privatization of disability could be seen as a legacy of Polish socialism. Polish gender studies scholar Dorota Szelewa has described a "familialization of social policy" in Poland that she attributes to post-1989 austerity and shrinking social benefits (as I discussed in chapter 1), ableism, and the patriarchal tradition that positions the mother as primary caregiver.[15] Additionally, this model of care politics has long enjoyed the support of the Catholic Church, one of the most powerful actors in Polish social life.[16] A lack of interest in disability policies and care provision by the state strengthens family kinship and leads not merely to the familialization of care, but, more precisely (as attested by the texts I analyze in this chapter), to the "mothering" (*umatkowienie*) of care and a subsequent precarization of women's lives.[17] Thus, to live as a disabled subject without a mother is to be utterly alone, and, conversely, to live as a disabled child with a mother, or as a mother of a disabled child, is to never be alone. Care operates as a tool of oppression for both mother and child.

These texts privilege the perspective of nondisabled mothers who take on the labor of caring. They discuss the devaluation of care work and the coercion of women into becoming caregivers by a negligent state, disrupting the nineteenth-century ideal of sacrificial motherhood still present in Polish culture. Forcing mothers into care work implies a simultaneous process of compelling disabled children to be care receivers. Yet these narratives rarely include disability voices and pay little attention to the imposed dependency of disabled subjects. My decision to focus on caregiver experiences in this chapter was driven by the fact that texts centering on the perspectives of nondisabled carers are (at the point of writing this at the end of 2022) far more popular in Poland than texts about and by people with disabilities.[18] Moreover, mothers of disabled children are among the most vocal advocates for disability rights in Poland and have produced the majority of mainstream disability knowledge during the 1990s and 2000s, thereby shaping public understanding of disability, a topic I continue to explore in chapter 3. Thus, despite coming into conflict at times, the rights of women and disabled people in Poland are intricately interconnected.

This potential for opposing needs is not always apparent in the texts under discussion, mostly due to a lack of disabled voices, thereby neutralizing their disruptive capacity. While violent intimacy is depicted in all of the texts I analyze in this chapter, apart from *Emil and Us*, this aspect remains unproblematized and is therefore naturalized. The same is true of ableism. Accordingly, there are two ways to understand this chapter: as an exploration of the notion of violent intimacy, and as a more or less unified interpretation of six post-1989 Polish care narratives that discuss disability. Alternatively, this chapter can be approached as an attempt to describe and analyze the effects of an archive of violent intimacy that excludes disabled voices: while these texts focus on both care and disability, only the former is politicized, and ableist beliefs about disability are at times upheld. As a result, the disruptions these texts provoke are mostly limited to the concept of care and the situation of caregivers.

This chapter consists of three sections. In the first section, I delve into the meaning and operations of violent intimacy through an analysis of two works of nonfiction: *Having a Child with Cerebral Palsy* and *Hoping My Child Dies Before I Do*. I show how these texts, while criticizing state noninvolvement in disability issues, do not politicize disability or violent intimacy but reinforce the maternal primary caregiver status. In the second section, I argue that the deaths of the disabled protagonists in two young adult novels, *The Pupa* and *My Sister's Island*, constitute a literary solution to violent intimacy. In the final section, I discuss the widely circulated article "Where Are These Children? They Are Fucked!" in conjunction with the memoir *Emil and Us* to address the binary between remunerated labor and care and to explore the ways in which this complicates my discussion of violent intimacy.

A Disabled Child Is a Mother's Child

In post-1989 Poland, as in the pre-1989 era, a disabled child is a mother's child. The state's disregard of the disabled population has not generated an extension of kinship networks, or what US-based scholar Akemi Nishida has described as "care collectives," wherein "community-based mutual-care structures" are organized by disabled people and their allies.[19] The aforementioned "familialization of care" has merely been strengthened. By declaring their commitment to traditional Christian values, as Dorota Szelewa has noted, the first post-socialist government under Tadeusz Mazowiecki endorsed women's "return" to the roles of mother and wife, after the somewhat unsuccessful emancipation of the state-socialist period.[20] In practice, the "familialization of care" has been facilitated by both the increasing cost of childcare, and the privatization of care as part of the neoliberal "shock therapy" I discussed in chapter 1.[21] The familialization of care gained a new facet during the 2000s, as parents of disabled children attempted to secure a safe and relatively independent future for their children by collecting funds and contacting sponsors to build and run their own community homes.[22]

In *Hoping My Child Dies Before I Do* (2018), the mother of a disabled daughter describes the restrictions imposed on her life. With a husband at work, and an older nondisabled daughter who wants to spend time alone in her own room, she wishes she could go out, but she cannot, "because this is my child."[23] As I stated earlier, the mother of a disabled child is never alone: She is always with the child. Despite the political and cultural changes that have taken place this millennium—Poland joined the European Union in 2004, signed the UN Convention on the Rights of Persons with Disabilities in 2012, witnessed the first major protest by disabled people at the Parliament in 2014, and introduced the program Za Życiem (In Support of Life), to provide benefits and additional resources for families raising a disabled child in 2016[24]—care is overwhelmingly a mother's burden, as illustrated by the texts I analyze in this section.[25]

Having a Child with Cerebral Palsy (1995) is an anthology of eighteen anonymous essays by mothers of disabled children edited by the special education professor Maria Chodkowska, who also edited the *Written Though Suffering* collection I analyzed in chapter 1. Published by an NGO devoted to disability issues, Fundacja "Masz Szansę" ("You've Got a Chance" Foundation), these texts were also produced in response to a memoir competition organized by the Maria Curie-Skłodowska University in Lublin, entitled "Different Childhood—a More Difficult Youth." In her introduction, Chodkowska states that over two hundred memoirs were submitted, but she gives no information on the selection criteria.[26] The competition was open to both people with disabilities and their caregivers, but only texts from the latter were published.

Having a Child with Cerebral Palsy does not neatly fit within the genre of disability memoirs. The essays are preceded by a foreword and a long section entitled "To Be a mother of a Child with Cerebral Palsy," both authored by Chodkowska. The section "To Be a Mother of a Child with Cerebral Palsy" consists of eleven chapters on issues such as how to recognize cerebral palsy, mother's role in children's with cerebral palsy societal inclusion, and potential problems with education. Adding medical and psychological commentaries to quotes from the memoirs in this section, Chodkowska discusses the importance of early diagnosis, dispels myths about cerebral palsy, and names some of the more popular therapies. She states that children with cerebral palsy can be "very intelligent; however, unfortunately, they might also be intellectually impaired, sometimes even quite severely."[27] According to Chodkowska, who emphasizes the active role a mother should take in her child's rehabilitation, cerebral palsy is a difference that can be eliminated via medical therapies and a mother's efforts.[28] In this sense, the text is prescriptive, strengthening the idea that a disabled child is a mother's child, and that rehabilitation is the mother's labor.

Thus, without naming it as such, Chodkowska depicts violent intimacy as a necessary aspect of life with a disabled child: The motherhood she anticipates is a sacrificial one, reminiscent of the nineteenth-century ideal. In their introduction to the 2012 edited collection *Pożegnanie z Matką Polką?* (*Farewell to the Polish Mother?*), Polish sociologists Elżbieta Korolczuk and Renata Hryciak describe Polish motherhood as forming both "the basis of a woman's identity" and "a vehicle for women's participation in the national community."[29] They go on to claim that "being a mother takes much more engagement than being a father" in Poland.[30]

Despite such ideological foundations and Chodkowska's investment in the medical model of disability, *Having a Child with Cerebral Palsy* does constitute important historical material and sits as a bitter testament to the early years in a post-socialist state. Several of the authors articulate their disappointment with a democratic rule that is often synonymous with financial deprivation. Whether middle- or upper-class mothers were not included or simply did not respond to the call is unclear, but the anthology overwhelmingly presents the perspectives of lower-middle-class women. Noting that "many people do not live but only desperately try to survive," one author blames the situation on "the mismanagement of funds and bad policies."[31] Another reminisces about the beginning of democratic rule, when "hope was approaching"; despite a general belief that "we could have a good life," the "great opportunities were not available to all," and the possibility "passed us by," leaving her family with wages too low to provide her disabled daughter Zosia "with a future."[32] This mother notes how little difference the transformation has made for disabled children: "Do these kids have to be on the losing side only because they are sick? There was no money for them during the communist rule, and there is no money for them now. But there is money for other things."[33]

It is highly likely that the protagonists in *Hoping My Child Dies Before I Do*—published twenty-three years later—would agree with these sentiments. This text consists of five lengthy interviews that Jacek Hołub conducted with mothers of disabled children, with his questions and comments removed. Published by the prestigious publishing house Czarne, this book received significantly more public attention than *Having a Child with Cerebral Palsy*,[34] was adapted into a play in 2020,[35] and was read by lay readers, journalists, and scholars of disability studies, including Klaudia Muca, who described the text as emancipatory in her 2024 book, *Opowiedzieć niepełnosprawność* (*To Narrate a Disability*).[36]

Living with chronic Lesniowski—Crohn's disease, Hołub identifies as a disabled person and claims that this enabled him to sympathize with the feelings of his interviewees during an event to promote the book.[37] Referring to his own illness in the afterword serves as a gesture of claiming affinity with his interviewees and their children. From this perspective, the book constitutes both a commentary on his own experiences and a form of allyship, even disability kinship.[38]

The success of *Hoping My Child Dies Before I Do* may have been partly fueled by the widespread popularity of nonfiction in Poland as a whole.[39] However, it is also likely to be a direct result of the protests and occupation of Parliament by disabled people and carers in 2018, which I discuss in greater detail in the following chapter. The book was published just a few months after the forty-day protest—shown daily on Polish TV and analyzed in the press—came to an end. Rather than presenting alternative understandings based on disability activism and theory, the text confirms the generally held view that disability is a predominantly medical and individual matter—a framing that could also have added to the book's popularity.

Hoping My Child Dies Before I Do approaches disability not only as a medical but also a charity issue. A section entitled "Możesz pomóc" (You Can Help) follows Hołub's afterword, on the last page, which asks readers to donate to the mothers and children featured in the book. Prompting readers to think of these duos as one entity—one body—their names are bound together, first the mother's and then the child's, reinforcing the fact that a disabled child is a mother's child: her responsibility, her charge. Consequently, this page emphasizes the violent intimacy that binds mother and child. Individual donations are presented as the only action a reader can take to help: a solution to structural deficiencies and the lack of care policies.

While, in his afterword, Hołub identifies with the mothers and children, thereby legitimizing his position as the author of a book on disability, the absence of his name from the donation list sets him apart. He both belongs and does not belong to the world of his protagonists. Hołub is not an object of charity: It is he who organizes it for others. Thus, the book simultaneously performs disability identification and disidentification, demonstrating the difficult and precarious nature of disability kinship. Additionally—yet probably unintentionally—the book emphasizes the precarity of life for mothers of children with disabilities, and their experiences of poverty and violent intimacy. In this sense, *Hoping My Child Dies Before I Do* serves as a commentary on the intersection between disability and gender.

Published twenty-three years apart, the two texts analyzed in this section reveal that the mechanisms of enacting care have not undergone any meaningful transformation: The labor of providing care has been and continues to be disproportionately placed upon women. Additionally, they testify to the shrinking resources dedicated to the disabled population—for example, *Having a Child with Cerebral Palsy* refers to a reduction of state-provided accessible transportation for disabled people and the increasing cost of public kindergartens and medical services,[40] and the lack of social services for disabled people and need for fundraising feature in *Hoping My Child Dies Before I Do*.[41] The juxtaposition of these two books illustrates state withdrawal from the sphere of care and assistance, and the subsequent forcing of mothers into the roles of caregiver and fundraiser. For one of Hołub's interviewees, "Beata," the physical and emotional labor of caring takes "all of her time," thereby reducing life to providing care. Describing how she feels, another interviewee perfectly encapsulates the binding of mother and disabled child: "I feel like I don't exist. In fact, I truly don't exist. I don't exist as myself. I don't have my own life. I'm only an addition to Justysia. We're inseparable; I take care of her all the time. And I don't think that this is ever going to change."[42]

Tasked with sustaining a disabled life, a mother may also feel compelled to consider humane ways of ending that life. This is a recurrent theme among contributors to *Having a Child with Cerebral Palsy*: "I cannot think about what happens later. How am I going to manage when my son grows big and heavy . . . ? What happens when I die?"; "I keep thinking: what happens next, what happens when I die?"; "I am afraid for my child's future; in our society, invalids face great problems on a daily basis. They are at the margins of society; society doesn't want them."[43] Hołub's interviewees share the same fears: "sometimes when I think about what happens next, I come to the conclusion that I want Paweł to die before I die. I want to die without being afraid for his future"[44]; "I am afraid of what happens when I am seventy or eighty and I won't be strong enough to take care of Justysia. Sometimes I think that when I am old and sick I want to have some meds that I can give to both Justysia and myself. So that we can die together."[45] Joanna Marnik raised this issue in the 2024 interview I examined in the introduction: Given the absence of state support for those with disabilities, she advocated for the right to euthanasia. A mother's wish to die with her child reveals that death is as much a part of violent intimacy as life. Dying is imagined as a familialized event by those who cannot imagine alternative ways in which their children can continue to live with dignity.

These dramatic passages illustrate how disability disrupts normative visions of the future. These mothers believe that when they die, their children's futures end. These books and Marnik's interview show that the future of a disabled subject was not a concern for the Polish state during the mid-1990s, and that this disinterest has continued. One of the consequences has been the partial privatization of many services, including nursing and community homes,[46] in which conditions have often been horrifying, reinforcing the fact that a disabled person in Poland without a family has no safety net.[47] Therefore, from a maternal perspective, a premature death may well appear to be the only desirable and humane outcome for their disabled child.

The cost of survival for a disabled child is their mother's normative life. Certainly, the women interviewed by Hołub and the authors in *Having a Child with Cerebral Palsy* have sacrificed their own futures and personal lives. While this is a choice, it is a choice constrained by familial expectations and religion: In a conservative and Catholic country invested in the Polish Mother, the dominant cultural model of sacrificial motherhood is hard to escape. In 1995, one author, whose husband divorced her after she gave birth to their disabled daughter, stated that she did not have a personal life or a husband, and now never would.[48] At no time imagining she would have "a sick child," another author described having "dreams and plans for the future" like everyone else. She now knew she would "never be able to make my dreams come true."[49] In 2018, one of the women interviewed by Hołub described the same loss of options: "When I think of what I lost, of how my life could be if she were healthy, my heart breaks. When a child is born, they drool, vomit, wet themselves, but then they grow up, become autonomous, and the mother gains her own leisure time. I never had this with Justysia and I never will have."[50] As well as confirming the durability of the sacrificial motherhood model in post-1989 Poland and the affective structure of violent intimacy, these confessions compel us to rethink terms such as "agency," "autonomy," and "subjectivity" in relation to those parents with children whose dependency will never end, especially mothers: Their autonomy, agency and subjectivity are as relational as their children's and just as fraught.

Since the 1970s, activist and academic disability studies and projects have been invested in challenging the common understanding of disability as a loss and a tragedy; however, the passages quoted above do not lend themselves to reading disability as anything but loss. Obviously, these are structural deficiencies that determine the meaning of disability as loss. Disability leads to the loss of a mother's subjectivity and her previous life, while also disrupting the lives of nondisabled siblings. In *Having a Child with Cerebral Palsy*, one author describes her nondisabled son as the person she and her husband "lost the most," as they "forgot about a four-year-old who was doing very well, but still he was a small, sensitive child."[51] A similar sentiment is shared by an interviewee in *Hoping My Child Dies Before I Do*, who states that the needs of her disabled daughter dictate her own life and that of her nondisabled daughter.[52] Many of these multiple losses and disruptions could be avoided or mitigated through state involvement. In other words, disability as loss is conditioned by state withdrawal from the sphere of assistance.

Both disability as loss and the affective structure of violent intimacy binding a nondisabled mother with her child are essentialized in these collections. Contributors note the expectations of their nuclear and extended families that they will perform as life-long caregivers—a naturalization of violent intimacy that stems, at least partly, from the gendering of dependency work. Even texts that denounce state abandonment of the disabled population tend to provide instructions on how—invariably—mothers should perform care or bind mother and child together in titles and calls for financial assistance. As a result, these two collections simultaneously amplify the voices of nondisabled caretakers and normalize violent intimacy.

Death as a Solution

Memoir and interview collections are not the only texts to uncritically describe violent intimacy and seek solutions that ultimately advance the rights of neither disabled people nor women. In this section, I analyze two novels for young adults that conceal symbolic violence toward a disabled subject under the guise of compassion: *The Pupa* (2001) by Dorota Terakowska, and *My Sister's Island* (2011) by Katarzyna Ryrych.[53] In both novels, the death of a child with a disability liberates a female family member from the burden of providing care.

The Pupa takes place in Kraków during the late 1990s, where rich and successful Adam and Ewa—the biblical names are not coincidental—own a large house in the suburbs. Having waited until their thirties to have a child in order to ensure their financial security, the couple are devastated when Ewa gives birth to a daughter with Down syndrome: "Adam dreamed about a child. Gaining knowledge, work, and making money made sense only because of the child he wanted to inherit everything he had. A quickly developing company, accumulated capital, buying stock, a house with a garden—it was all for a child. . . . But not this child."[54]

The novel begins with Myszka's birth. At first, Adam and Ewa decide to send their daughter to an institution for disabled children. However, at the hospital, the mother of a girl with Down syndrome shares her experiences with Ewa, and, much to her husband's disappointment, Ewa changes her mind. Although Adam does not leave the family home, the couple stop communicating and live separate lives. Ewa gives up work, stops seeing friends, and devotes herself entirely to taking care of the child: "She and Myszka are surrounded by the fortified walls of the house. She and Myszka are isolated from the world. She and Myszka are sufficient for each other."[55] The possibility of Ewa accessing any state-provided social or educational disability services is never raised, despite it being clear that providing continual care herself is unsustainable. This novel positions the family as the only space for a disabled subject, while also emphasizing that this space is incompatible with disability.

The Pupa depicts violent intimacy between a disabled child and a mother who feels both deep love and disgust for her daughter. It also shows how the relationship between Ewa and Myszka disrupts the love and intimacy Ewa previously shared with her husband. There is no room for Ewa to maintain other close attachments to kith or kin. Adam, who provides for the family by running a successful company, is ashamed of and repelled by his daughter. His decision not to divorce Ewa is driven purely by a fear of social condemnation.

In this novel, disability affords a way for Dorota Terakowska to critique Polish capitalism of the late 1990s, with its emphasis on large houses, expensive watches, and other signs of material success. The deep disappointment experienced by Adam and Ewa when their child is born illustrates that happiness cannot be secured by wealth and success, and that achieving a "perfect" life with a "perfect" child is an illusion. And yet Terakowska undermines the lesson she wishes to impart with the ending of the novel. Myszka suddenly dies at the age of nine. Since she had wanted to die, her death is not presented as a tragedy. However, shortly before her death, Adam and Ewa had started to accept Myszka's disability and no longer felt shame about it. As an apparent reward for this laudable transformation, they reunite and have a new, nondisabled child. A disabled child disrupts a heterosexual marriage; a nondisabled child stitches it back together.

With the death of Myszka, Adam and Ewa are able to reclaim their lives. In other words, *The Pupa* tells the story of a family that is inhabited by a disabled person but should not be.[56] Terakowska's book sends the message that there is simply no room for intellectual disability in contemporary Poland, and that a disabled child will destroy a marriage: Family is exclusively understood as a heterosexual marriage between healthy bodies.[57] Ultimately, Myszka's disability is a setback, not a permanent disruption. Continuing to live in the same large suburban house with their new child, Adam and Ewa ultimately "have it all," despite only going through the briefest value realignment. In other words, once Myszka had taught her parents that material possessions cannot guarantee happiness, and that there is no perfect genetic makeup, she becomes redundant.

The Pupa offers no alternative, more accommodating version of capitalism. Terakowska uses a religious frame to illuminate the incongruity of disability and capitalism, thereby rendering a discussion of either disability services or accommodations and rights for disabled people unnecessary: Disability is "God's gift." Alongside the inspirational discourses that interweave disability with the changes that Adam and Ewa undergo, the novel contains more blatant religious references. Chapters titled with numbered days of the week allude to the book of Genesis; Ewa reading the Bible to Myszka becomes a significant element of the plot; Adam reads Pope John Paul II's encyclical on disability; and, of course, there are the Garden-of-Eden-evoking names of Adam and Ewa. The most important function of these religious references is to enable the death of a disabled child to be posited as a happy ending for both her and her parents. Put simply, religious discourse masks ableism or, rather, is ableist itself. Therefore, rather than presenting Myszka's sudden death as a tragedy, or as the result of her parents' cruel wishes or systemic neglect, Terakowska has Myszka discuss her future with the biblical Adam and Eve, as well as the serpent. By having Myszka tell the serpent she will join them all in the garden that represents heaven, Terakowska attempts to present death as a choice. Yet it is clear that Myszka lives in a world in which there is no choice, as her reasoning reveals: "There, I am locked up at home, because mom is afraid to take me to the park, supermarket, and even to the street. . . . There, children do not want to play with me and look at me as if they were afraid of me or disgusted by me. . . . Here I can dance. Yes, I will stay with you."[58] By introducing Myszka's internal monologue, Terakowska absolves the reader from feeling guilt when the novel is resolved with the restoration of "normal" family life.

The regimes of heteronormativity and compulsory able-bodiedness are reinforced by the Catholicism that shapes Myszka's internal monologue, drawing a veil over the fact that her desire to die is driven by a mother who does not understand her and is exhausted by providing care; by a father who rejects her; and by the disgust of a hostile world. Although Myszka's monologue is cogent and rational, her actual speech is largely formed of disconnected and therefore nonsensical syllables. Polish literary scholar Przemysław Czapliński has noted that Myszka represents "an embodiment of otherness,"[59] particularly through her inability to normatively communicate.[60] Within the logic of this novel, Myszka's incomprehensibility indicates her incompatibility with the world: The impossibility of Myszka integrating with family and society implies a nonhuman status. Czapliński also claims that *The Pupa* suggests "a trace of genius" in Myszka, yet gives no examples.[61] If he is referring to the internal monologue, is the humanity of an intellectually disabled person to be equated with genius? Overall, Czapliński's reception of *The Pupa* demonstrates that a disabled subject cannot be culturally normalized and humanized: She is either a genius or the ultimate other.

Terakowska shows death as a happy ending for Adam and Ewa, and also for Myszka, who meets other disabled children in heaven, where, now nondisabled, she is finally able to express herself. Thus, able-bodiedness is located in heaven, and death is a liberation from disability. Positioning death as synonymous with a disability-free future, *The Pupa* rejects the chance of any reparative reading of disability. There is no place for disability on Earth or in heaven: "God's gifts danced and felt joy that they had spent a brief moment on earth and experienced true feelings: love, hatred, acceptance, rejection, isolation or loneliness. . . . The butterflies hidden in the pupa of their bodies fluttered invisible to other people's wings."[62]

With Myszka dancing in heaven alongside other disabled children who, like her, wanted to die; Ewa is released from her duty; and the failure of Adam and Ewa to fully accept a disabled child, the failure of the state to introduce services to support people with disabilities and their families, and the death of a child are triumphally justified. It is religious discourse that facilitates this triumph, by positioning disabled subjects as "God's gifts" rather than citizens or even fully human beings. Religious discourse forecloses any discussion of disability rights, the politics of care, or, equally importantly, the political dimension of Myszka's desire to die. It posits disability as a deficit and a tragedy, divorced from the domain of politics.

Katarzyna Ryrych, author of *My Sister's Island*, published ten years after *The Pupa*, in 2011, also appears to believe that heaven is the place most suited to young disabled girls. In her widely acclaimed novel, which reached its fourth edition in 2019 and received the Astrid Lindgren Literary Award (given to contemporary Polish novels for young adults and children), Pippi, a protagonist with an unnamed disability, dies suddenly and seemingly without reason in her early twenties.[63] Pippi and her younger nondisabled sisters had been raised by their father following the death of their mother. Their father did not remarry:

As she did not want to raise Pippi, the woman he wanted to be with ended their relationship. Thus, once again, a happy heterosexual coupling is precluded by a child's disability. Being incompatible with the social world, disability prevents Pippi and those around her from entering social and romantic relations.

This is the only text I analyze in this chapter that does not feature a maternal figure. Yet violent intimacy is still present: in the absence of a mother, it is the younger, nondisabled sister who is bound with Pippi. It is she who truly mourns when Pippi is first sent to an institution and later dies. The father, who appears to have a good relationship with Pippi, remains a secondary protagonist, as men are excluded from the affective structure of violent intimacy: It is always a nondisabled woman who is party to it. While this book normalizes the fact that care is women's work, the logic of the novel does not allow for a nondisabled sister to be a lifelong caretaker or companion for Pippi; such a life would be "wasted." Thus, the disabled sister must die: As in *The Pupa*, death ends the violent intimacy engendered by the presence of disability.

The disappearance of the disabled subject enables able-bodied family members to have a future. There is no hope for Pippi of an independent or semi-independent life, such as in a small community home, but the institution to which her father takes her in her late teens has compassionate staff and good resources. Thus, this novel both reflects and skews the lived experience of institutionalized people in Poland. Disabled children are not often placed in institutions, which largely accommodate elderly citizens and disabled adults. Often these are people with intellectual disabilities, whose parents have either died or are no longer able to provide daily care. Debate about the possibility of deinstitutionalization has increased since ratification of the UN Convention on the Rights of Persons with Disabilities in 2012, yet has produced no "tangible" results.[64] *Disability Disruptions* covers the period 1989–2022, but it is worth mentioning that in 2023 a document entitled "Personal Assistance Standard for a Person with Disability" was released, the result of a three-year project coordinated by Państwowy Fundusz Rehabilitacji Osób Niepełnosprawnych (State Fund for the Rehabilitation of Disabled People), the Ministry of Family, and two NGOs: Polskie Stowarzyszenie na Rzecz Osób z Niepełnosprawnością Intelektualną (Polish Association for People with Intellectual Disabilities) and Fundacja im. Królowej Polski św. Jadwigi (Saint Polish Queen Jadwiga Foundation).[65] Also in 2023, President Andrzej Duda submitted a bill on personal assistance for people with disabilities. In response to increasing criticism of institutionalization, these initiatives attempt to offer solutions in the form of state-funded personal assistance. No law on personal assistance had been passed by the time this book went to press.

In *My Sister's Island*, institutions are the only recourse for the families of disabled people. As there are no care assistants or community homes, care is either provided at home by a blood relative or in an institution by a female employee. The labor of care not only oppresses the nondisabled sister; it also puts her in danger—Pippi is shown to be physically violent. As care cannot be imagined in any other way, the only solution is to move Pippi into an institution.

With Pippi at the institution, her father reunites with his former girlfriend, and her sister grows up. The family, as the able-bodied sister narrates, not only cease to visit Pippi, but they never speak about her, making it appear "as if she has disappeared or was never here in the first place."[66] When the sister learns to drive, she starts to visit Pippi and realizes, despite earlier descriptions of Pippi making friends at the institution, that she is like "a lonely island."[67] The book conveys the idea that it is disability, not societal treatment or a lack of adequate social policies, that has separated Pippi from her family and the world, thus turning her into "a lonely island." The sister decides to study medicine at university: "I decided to look for an answer to the question I kept asking: 'WHY?' I think that many people have tried to do it before, and similarly to them I hope that I will be the first one to discover the cause and I will make the lonely islands disappear."[68]

The sister aspires to find and eliminate whatever has caused the genetic mutation responsible for Pippi's condition. The neoeugenic idea of eliminating disability and disabled people permeates this novel: Not only must Pippi disappear from her family, but all children with this unnamed disability must also disappear from humanity, and medical eugenics is depicted as a response to and the end of violent intimacy. Rather than addressing Pippi's loneliness and asking what accommodations could be provided by the family and society, the sister muses on how to create a world without disability. For Ryrych, this is a noble desire. While searching for a medical solution, the sister imagines Pippi in heaven: "Where are you, Pippi, in your blue dress? I believe that you sail the warm seas; the bed becomes a ship and all the pirates escape to their islands and hide their gold."[69] Heaven is imagined here as a sea-playground. Although Pippi died in what appears to be her twenties, she is presented as an eternal child: not an adult, not a citizen with rights, as reflected in the fact that she is never afforded more than her nickname. Pippi is an object of care, which an institution is the only suitable place to provide.

The Pupa and *My Sister's Island* tell stories of temporary familial disruption caused by disabled people. What these two novels truly disrupt is the normative and widespread expectation of maternal and paternal love: Here, parents are happy when their children die. Obviously, this is possible due to the disabilities of the two protagonists and is probably why this cultural transgression has been overlooked in all academic analyses of these novels. Polish disability studies scholar Alicja Wang has praised *The Pupa* for presenting a nuanced representation of an intellectually disabled protagonist,[70] and she has paid similar compliments to *My Sister's Island*.[71] Przemysław Czapliński, in his analysis of Terakowska's novel, notes that Myszka has to die for normality to win, but also emphasizes that "a person such as this . . . does not share with us a common language" and exemplifies an "ultimate and impenetrable otherness," thus reinforcing the strongly-held belief that people who do not communicate in a normative manner cannot be considered human.[72] The inability to extend humanity to Myszka precludes a much-needed critique of normality.

Thousands of copies of these two novels were sold, and they received praise from readers and journalists alike.[73] *The Pupa* even made a bestseller list in 2003.[74] Thus, violence toward disabled subjects is acceptable when it masquerades as benevolence, charity, and religious creed. Rather than complicate public understandings of disability, these books confirm the belief that disabled lives are worth less than nondisabled lives, and only the death of a disabled subject can end violent intimacy.

Care as Oppression and Allyship

In the final section of this chapter, I analyze Magdalena Moskal's memoir, *Emil i my: monolog wielodzietnej matki* (*Emil and Us: A Monologue of a Mother of Three*), published in 2021, and Agnieszka Szpila's article "Gdzie sa te dzieci? W dupie" (Where Are These Children? They Are Fucked!), released the following year. Bringing these texts together will nuance my discussion of violent intimacy: While Szpila calls for an end to it through the provision of state benefits, Moskal's memoir of a nondisabled mother's relationship with her disabled child testifies to a shared struggle and advocacy and, to a certain extent, challenges my argument.

Juxtaposing these texts also underscores the fact that care operates as a tool of both exploitation and allyship. By concluding this chapter with two fairly recent narratives, I illustrate the multiplicity of contemporary Polish disability and care accounts and discuss how, in different and often contradictory ways, they redefine and at times disrupt the meanings of care, mothering, and work. The "social fund of knowledge about disability" created by these texts may not be consistent, yet it is critical for any refiguring of care politics in Poland.[75]

Partly a memoir, partly an essay on motherhood, family, disability, and the ethics of care, *Emil and Us* contains many references to scholarly texts. Although it did not spark the degree of controversy generated by Szpila's narrative, it was widely addressed in both print and social media.[76] It tells the story of making disability part of a family: from the initial trauma, fear, and uncertainty of a familiar familial rhythm experienced by a mother, father and two children, to inclusion and coming to terms with disability. I read *Emil and Us* as a challenge to the idea of disability as crisis, a memoir written as an account of familial inclusion to serve as a model of societal inclusion.[77]

Magdalena Moskal states her purpose in writing this book at the outset: "I wanted to fight for my subjectivity and Emil's subjectivity as a child with disability, to fight for our subjectivity in the face of the health care system, the education system, and so on."[78] Strikingly, Moskal distinguishes between her subjectivity and that of her child in the first part of the sentence, then merges the two, indicating the erasure of a mother's sense of self in the "fight" for the rights of her disabled child. Accessing health care and educational services in Poland is identified with combat, which necessitates that a mother relinquish her subjectivity to support her child. And yet, as noted above, these passages speak not of violent intimacy but of shared struggle and advocacy.

Moskal further emphasizes interconnection of mother and child by the persistent use of "we" and the first-person plural. When her son is not invited to yet another child's birthday party, Moskal hopes that "maybe one day we will receive an invitation."[79] When people stare at her son, she states that "each time it becomes easier for us."[80] When her son attends a kindergarten for children with disabilities, she notes that "the environment of children with disabilities became natural and comfortable for us."[81] The first-person plural denotes an intimate binding of mother and son as well as, perhaps, social exclusion and the reduction of a woman to solely her role as the mother of a disabled child. Moskal notes that any social acceptance of her family, at school or elsewhere, is always "conditional."[82] Yet these fragments do not present a reinforcement of violent intimacy; rather, they depict the way a mother, child, and the rest of the family navigate and negotiate the stigma associated with disability. Moskal declares that she is "not troubled by his illness and otherness; I am troubled by people's reactions to it."[83]

Violent intimacy gets replaced here by intimacy that allows for an alignment in the struggle for rights. Moskal employs this language and references the disability rights movement in her book; in other words, her memoir owes a debt to both disability theory and disability narratives. She quotes both anglophone and Polish disability scholars, inserts fragments of other disability memoirs, and, a few times, provides Emil's musings on his own life and disability. She states that she rejects "the objectification of people with disabilities in important public debates"; thus, her strategy of integrating her own words with analyses offered by various scholars as well as other disabled people seems to be a conscious solution that enables her to avoid objectification.[84]

The familial intimacy discussed by Moskal helps to introduce a sense of collective intimacy: One reviewer noted that the titular *Us* stands not for Moskal's family but for society as a whole.[85] Both Moskal and this reviewer recognize that disability is not an exclusively familial matter. Moskal reminds us that, as the "weakest members," the conditions under which disabled people live "reflect" the values of a wider society.[86] Moreover, she believes that fewer Polish women would opt for abortion following the discovery of fetal abnormalities if it were not for the "common belief" that "a disabled life" equates to a "slow dying and never-ending suffering."[87] She attempts to counteract the construction of disability as a tragic burden in Polish public discourse by providing positive examples of people with disabilities and an understanding rooted in disability justice.

The intimacy depicted in *Emil and Us* makes space for an empathetic allyship that extends to others. In stark contrast to violent intimacy, this voluntary intimacy is grounded in interdependence. Once fetal anomalies had been detected, a doctor made it clear to Moskal what to expect: "It will be your son who will be disabled, he will encounter some obstacles. You need to be strong to support him."[88] Emil's experience is never appropriated by his mother. Moskal relates his integration into the family and attempts to envision a way in which disabled people can be integrated into society. With the aim of persuading people to "start looking at disabled people differently," Moscal attempts to build a community of allies to share her "anger" at a system that abandons disabled people.[89]

Emil and Us goes beyond the family and the mother. Although the text principally focuses on her children and husband, Moskal also discusses the various institutions and actors that play critical roles in Emil's life, including the health-care, social services, and education systems, but also nondisabled children and their parents, as well as the family's neighbors. By gesturing toward the larger community, Moskal attempts to show that Emil's future should depend not on his family's financial and cultural capital but on a collective effort. The book itself is an attempt to introduce readers to a sense of disability kinship and allyship.

A year later, in September 2022, a writer and mother of twin teenage daughters, disabilities, Agnieszka Szpila, published "Where Are These Children? They Are Fucked!" on the left-wing website Krytyka Polityczna (Political Critique).[90] Although the tone and scope of her text are very different, like Moskal she addresses the issues of care, violent intimacy, and inclusion. Despite the focus of her title, Szpila only briefly touches on the lives of disabled children in Poland and instead emphasizes the forced care labor of nondisabled mothers.[91] Consequently, the article shows—more directly than the other texts I discuss in this chapter—that there is no distinction between mothering and care labor in the context of disability in Poland. The text clearly testifies to Szpila's profound exasperation with a highly inefficient support system; it is, in fact, a frustrated and exhausted outburst resulting from years of attempting to secure help.

At the center of the article is the monthly state benefit for which parents who provide full-time care for their disabled children can apply.[92] In exchange for this small payment, caregivers are prohibited from engaging in any wage labor. Thus, Szpila, a published novelist, screenwriter, and columnist, must ask others to sign her work contracts. In the opening lines of the article, she describes her intention in writing this text: to show how this "fucked-up Polish government's policy" forces her to engage in a "scam" that "dehumanizes" her by taking away her identity and rights.[93] While emphasizing her own dehumanization, it is notable that Szpila does not dwell upon the dehumanization experienced by many people with disabilities (a topic I will return to in the next chapter).

Szpila's goal is to make care labor an issue of state policy, not motherly commitment. She demands to be granted the right to work while caring for her two disabled daughters, Helena and Milena. With the state benefit as her only stable source of income, Szpila simply wants to make some additional money and escape the constraints of providing constant care. For her, wage work constitutes a respite from violent intimacy: "I want you to understand what work is to me as a carer of people with disabilities: it is the only escape from children who are completely ignored by the state."[94]

This article generated significant media debate about the situation of carers, particularly mothers, and inspired a series of protests during the fall and winter of 2022 in various large cities, including Warsaw, Poznań, and Kraków. Thus, the text disrupted public order and revitalized the topics of disability and care within public discourse at a time when media interest produced by the disability protests at the Polish Parliament in 2018 (which I discuss in the next chapter) had diminished. Following Szpila, demonstrators highlighted the ban on carers receiving the benefit engaging in wage labor. Subsequently, Szpila gave a number of interviews and was awarded a Grand Press award for the article she published in December 2022. I draw on these interviews in my discussion of her analysis of disability and care, as well as her 2015 memoir, *Łebki od szpilki* (*Pinheads*).

For Szpila, the cost of her disabled daughters' survival is her normative life and well-being. In an interview with Justyna Nagłowska, she stated that "everything depends on the mother," and "everything is about the children," going on to add that "we do everything because the state does nothing."[95] Having given up a job to stay home with her daughters, she mocks Virginia Woolf's concept of a room of one's own: not only does she not have one, but she also does not have a desk to write on, as hers was destroyed by one of her autistic daughters: "I write on my bed, behind the bed, in the bathtub at 4 a.m. . . . , under the radiator in the kitchen; I'm under barricades, like those who fought in the Warsaw Uprising [in 1944], the only difference being that I'm hiding from my own children."[96]

At various times in her articles, interviews, and memoir, Szpila compares life with her autistic daughters to living with Vladimir Putin or being in a concentration camp.[97] While these comparisons are problematic, since raising disabled children has little do with genocide or war, I read them as an attempt to convey the intensity of the arduous struggle required. As Akemi Nishida has stated, "Care is functioning and intensified as a mechanism of oppression and exploitation that alters people's bodyminds."[98] Both Szpila and her husband, the father of her third, nondisabled daughter, suffer from PTSD due to the constant anxiety of living with one of the disabled twins, Milena, who is aggressive and often destroys and throws heavy things at family members. It is work in the form of writing that enables Szpila to continue living: "I write in order to get the fuck out of life, out of a state which forces me to oscillate between life and death, in particular when glasses, shoe cabinets, chairs, tables, and plates are thrown over my head. . . . I won't survive without writing. Without the escape into the world of writing, I'll take my daughters' psychotropic drugs. . . . The state does not provide help in anything. It does not provide any hope for the future."[99]

In the absence of state support, Szpila deteriorates under the name of love, commitment, and care. Prohibited from working means "the right to freedom and self-determination is taken away."[100] Enabling an escape from violent intimacy, Szpila equates work with freedom, self-actualization, and satisfaction. Work, it appears, stands in opposition to care: Through care one deteriorates, while through work one thrives. Thus, as care oppresses, work liberates. Of course, while work certainly can be liberating, it is worth remembering that Szpila is describing the creative process of writing rather than manual labor, and that a miner, shop assistant, or factory worker may not experience similar emancipation. Yet it is significant that a text that galvanized public opinion and shaped public knowledge about disability and care—even featuring in an article for the online edition of Polish *Vogue*—calls for the right to work.[101] Rather than advocate for access to care assistants, independent living, disability justice, or higher benefits, Szpila calls for care providers to be allowed to work both inside and outside the home.[102] This text not only acknowledges but appears to be invested in the fact that inclusion in capitalist Poland hinges on participation in the workforce. There is no attempt to redefine the meaning of work, but rather to strengthen the belief that an individual's value lies in their productivity.[103] This belief, as much capitalist as socialist, demonstrates the continuation of the two systems I discussed in the previous chapter. It is perhaps this unwillingness to redefine the terms of societal inclusion for care laborers and to insist on the right to work that is at least partly responsible for the article's positive reception.[104] Not only does it ask very little of people, but it also asks very little of the state: In many ways, the text is a demand for the ability not to be a societal burden.[105]

For Szpila, the inability to participate in the labor force makes her socially nonexistent. Writing about herself in the third person, she claims that "Agnieszka Szpila does not exist legally on any work contract, if she exists at all."[106] Owning no copyrights to her own texts, the only thing Szpila has "a right to are her disabled children" and the chaos they create: "to broken windows, to furniture knocked over by one of the twins during a rage attack . . . to broken plates and glasses."[107] Disability is therefore identified with a destructive force. According to Szpila, the right to her children is far more of a burden. Throughout the article, Szpila relies on binaries: The right to work is desirable, while the right to disability is undesirable. Ultimately, the article reinforces the social understanding of disability as a hindrance and establishes that, as a care laborer, a mother is downgraded by her association with disabled subjects.

Nevertheless, Szpila underlines a crucial paradox: By prohibiting care-providing mothers from engaging in other forms of wage work in a world that deeply values work, the state subjects a large population of women to social marginalization and poverty, and to the status of dependents on public assistance. As Szpila notes, "The only thing we are meant to engage with is *sacrificing life*."[108] Not only is a mother's relationship with her disabled child structured by violent intimacy, but, perhaps equally importantly, this is also the only affective structure of which she is to be a part. It is this that drives Szpila to declare: "I don't want to be a Polish Mother, I want to be a mother."[109] In many ways this declaration majorly disrupts the mainstream Polish narrative, which continues to remain invested in the sacrificial model of motherhood.

When care is compulsory, it becomes a site of tension and ambivalence. In her article, Szpila discusses the love and vulnerability she shares with her daughters and asks for empathy, not pity. However, the text does contain ableist aspects. Reinforcing the understanding of disability as deeply undesirable, Szpila claims to be disabled by the state policy that prevents her from working: "The entire system disables not only my children but also me."[110] In an interview, she states that disability is her daughters' identity, not hers, a distancing that appears to indicate a belief that she has been unjustly disabled.[111]

In her memoir, *Pinheads*, she tells the story of doctors misdiagnosing the twins in early childhood, delaying physical therapy and treatment; thus, she wishes that in hell, after death, the doctors "get diagnosed with autism, cerebral palsy, and Down syndrome."[112] In other words, Szpila politicizes care work and demands that the state get involved in disability issues, but she fails to politicize disability and think about disability justice in her article "Where Are These Children? They Are Fucked!" and in her memoir. Or, maybe more precisely, her thinking about disability is fraught with contradictions. Disability is, on one hand, imagined as punishment for medical malpractice; on the other hand, it is a position of shared vulnerability that enables a new kind of love or feeling, "but not as a heart's gesture from those who have it better to those who have it *worse*; it is a feeling which has nothing to do with the colonization of the disabled and their suffering, but a shared, common feeling."[113]

Szpila's invitations to love and feel compassion for others from "a position of shared vulnerability, unworthiness, and helplessness," and to relate to the world from the perspective of those who are "excluded, denigrated and fucked-up by the system," are attempts to universalize care and disability and invest nondisabled members of society in disability issues.[114] She makes similar efforts in relation to the 2020 ban on abortion based on fetal malformation, which I discuss in more detail in the next chapter. In an interview with Justyna Nagłowska, she highlights the fact that the ban will result in so many more women sharing her fate, as, in a country where access to contraception is restricted, they will have no choice but to give birth to disabled children. Yet again depicting disability as burdensome and undesirable, this approach is obviously stigmatizing. The abortion ban may be highly problematic, but not due to a possible increase in the disabled population of Poland. And, while disability is a universal issue, seeking support for caregivers by invoking a fear of disability is blatantly ableist. These comments have nothing to do with disability justice and suggest a desire to eliminate disability. But this is not the way to end violent intimacy: That can only happen when the state participates in disability matters and listens to the voices of both caregivers and disabled people.

Conclusion

Although, in this chapter, my analysis of violent intimacy between a mother and a child with disabilities is restricted to post-1989 Polish accounts and literary works, the analytic potential of the concept does not share these limitations. As an affective structure that binds the giver and receiver of care and underpins both capitalism and socialism, violent intimacy extends beyond the biological and traditional family. Further research is merited on this phenomenon in all social and political contexts, including those with more expansive kinship arrangements.

As demonstrated by these five texts, published across many years, violent intimacy does not characterize all relationships between nondisabled mothers and their disabled children, yet it is one of the dominant ways in which such relationships are imagined and experienced in post-1989 Poland. A product of the structural injustice and violence arrayed against both disabled and nondisabled bodies, violent intimacy does harm. However, the fiction and nonfiction texts I analyze here are largely unwilling or incapable of positing alternative visions of motherhood and disabled—nondisabled bonding. As a result, they ultimately naturalize violent intimacy by stipulating the mother as primary caretaker of a disabled subject, erase it by fantasizing the death of a disabled protagonist, or seek charitable or legal solutions that enable mothers to engage in remunerated labor.

With the exception of *Emil and Us*, these narratives silence the voices of disabled subjects and think of care and disability exclusively from a nondisabled and non-disability-studies perspective. This neglect of disabled voices can be explained by the simple fact that the interests of caregivers are not always closely aligned with those of disabled people and may actually conflict. To illuminate the disruptive potential of violent intimacy, both perspectives must be taken into account. Thus, reading these narratives while considering disability theory and sensibility illuminates their strategies of silencing violent intimacy or limiting it to the caregiver situation. By positing disabled people as objects, not creators, of knowledge, this archive falls short of a disability archive, yet it offers a window into the perspectives and experiences of caregivers and thereby participates in building knowledge about living as a life-long care provider.

I continue to explore the notion of violent intimacy in the following chapter. My focus turns to the disability protests that took place in Poland during the 2010s and early 2020s, and the statements made by protesters about the intimate and interdependent relationship between mothers and their disabled children. Unlike the narratives in this chapter, these declarations denaturalize violent intimacy and demand state involvement in disability issues. As this chapter witnessed disability plunging families into a crisis, the next sees the predicament of a state faced with disabled people creating knowledge about themselves.

3 DISABILITY CONFESSIONS

One anonymous memoir writer in 1991's *Written Through Suffering* proclaimed that all she wanted to do was "work the way I used to. Is it too much to ask for? In competition with able-bodied women, disabled women have no chance to get a job."[1] The transition to a market economy in Poland had generated a sharp rise in unemployment, prompting numerous strikes and demonstrations against factory closures and redundancies. On June 13, 1991, a group of approximately 250 deaf people gathered in the center of Warsaw; among their demands was a guarantee of workshop employment for people with disabilities.[2]

One photograph of this demonstration features a placard stating "Nie mam pracy. Czy mam kraść?" (I don't have a job. Am I supposed to steal?). The face of the placard holder is in shadow, and the two other placards that are visible are blurred and impossible to fully decipher. What is evident, however, is that people with disabilities were adversely affected by the economic processes of the early 1990s, and, alongside other social and professional groups, that they advocated for job security.

While people with disabilities continued to fight for social and economic rights throughout the 1990s and early 2000s, it was only in the 2010s that these protests gained enough momentum to attract attention from the mainstream media and society in general. In 2014, following lengthy and unsuccessful negotiations over an increase in the carer allowance, caregivers and parents of children with disabilities held a sit-in protest at the Polish Parliament for seventeen days, and a a group of carers for adult people with disabilities established a protest camp outside . Four years later, carers and their children once again occupied Parliament to demand an increase in benefits, this time for forty days. The occupation prompted solidarity demonstrations across the country and increased the visibility of people with disabilities in Poland.

In 2020, following a ruling by the Polish Constitutional Tribunal (CT) that abortions in cases of severe or fatal fetal abnormality were unconstitutional, Poland faced another wave of protests that centered—albeit in different and at times contradictory ways—on disability. While some disabled women supported the ruling, opposing voices were much louder. Albeit in a different context, Polish feminist disability studies scholar Agnieszka Król has noted that "Poland is seeing an increasing involvement of women with disabilities in the articulation of their political demands. . . . Society's definitions of parenthood and women's citizenship are an area of ongoing dispute and resistance," as the 2020 protests and disabled women's participation make evident.[3] And, in the fall of 2022, inspired by Agnieszka Szpila's article (see chapter 2), a series of protests took place to demand that carers of people with disabilities who received the state benefit be allowed to take other paid work. Thus, since 2014, disability and issues relating to care and state benefits have received regular and considerable mass media attention in Poland, and people with disabilities have begun to participate in creating knowledge about disability on a significant scale.

My analysis in this chapter is grounded in the argument that these protests exemplify a refusal: to live in poverty, to be neglected by the state and infantilized by society, and to be treated as second-class citizens. In many ways, it is also a refusal of the violent intimacy I discussed at length in chapter 2. As I will demonstrate, for both people with disabilities and their carers, confession has been the principal tool utilized to articulate their demands and achieve their goals. As these confessions, often posted on social media and republished by print media, are the building blocks of knowledge about disability, the protesters can be regarded as "epistemic activists," whose ways of knowing the social and material world challenge nondisabled perceptions and thus set new terms for understanding the lived experience of disability.[4]

Thus, I present a close reading of protester confessions that have circulated online and in the printed media, and that, taken together, testify to the emergence of what I term a "Polish disability confessional culture." Motivated by a refusal to be ignored and silenced, this culture ultimately disrupts societal beliefs that disability is a private matter, and that disabled people are passive recipients of state benefits. To varying degrees, these confessions can be understood as acts of liberation and modes of self-representation. There is no unified rhetorical script: While all highlight state neglect and societal ignorance, they employ various affective registers and vocabularies. Some utilize the language of human rights and feminist sensibilities, while others rely on a Catholic understanding of suffering or attempt to connect feminist and Catholic terminologies. While some echo the medical idiom of disability, others resonate with vocabulary from the social model of disability: Neither is precisely replicated. This variety in discussion modes suggests that the meaning of disability has not been solidified and is mobilized depending on sociopolitical context and desired goals. Importantly, it also indicates that the dominant ways of theorizing disability, formulated within Western and anglophone disability studies, do not encapsulate contemporary Polish articulations of disability. In sum, this chapter presents both an incomplete archive of recent disability protests in Poland and attempts to show how disabled people located outside global centers make sense of, and politically instrumentalize, their own experiences.

My use of the term "confession" is a considered one. At its most basic, confession is an act of speech, most often associated with Catholicism and the practice of contrition, and with the act of free association in psychoanalysis. My usage of the term echoes the former rather than the latter, not only because Poland is a strongly Catholic country but also because the language used by protesters resonates with Catholic notions of suffering and martyrdom. As Catholic confession takes place within the spheres of the sacred and the private, disclosure to the public transgresses the boundaries of the private—public domain in an almost scandalous manner.[5] Yet it is the suffering they experience, and the social silence that surrounds disability in post-socialist Poland, that protesters present as the true disgrace. These confessions are intended to disrupt the social ignorance of disability by eliciting outrage and empathy.

While the stories of disempowerment contained in these confessions center on the oppression experienced by disabled subjects and their carers, the act of public disclosure can be empowering. Neither a form of self-cure or a "talking cure", as understood by Freud,[6] nor Foucault's technique of self-regulation ("the confession is a ritual of discourse in which the speaking subject is also the subject of the statement; it is also a ritual that unfolds within a power relationship"), confession in this Polish disability context is a tool of resistance.[7] Engendered by the oppressive conditions that these people with disabilities and their carers denounce, the gesture of publicly sharing their intimate stories of suffering has transformed confession into a tool for resisting state abandonment.

As the confessions I analyze here have been produced and shared by disabled and nondisabled subjects, I have characterized them as "crip" in my initial writing of this chapter. However, closer examination has revealed that the majority take a normative approach to disabilities and illnesses. Despite refusing to accept the poverty and second-class citizenship status experienced by disabled people in Poland, the creators of these confessions follow the bureaucratized classification system and do not challenge the medical and legal systems that govern disability issues. If Western crip politics attempts to destabilize the binary disability/ability, is critical of "bureaucratic mechanisms of *inclusion* or *accommodation*," and explores the limitations of disability rights framework, the Polish disability rights movement, to a large extent, does not follow this path.[8] Unlike Western crip politics, it seeks formal recognition and rights.[9] Apart from a number of confessions created in 2020 that center disability and gender, there is little intersectionality, with most of the confessions focusing exclusively on disability. This reappraisal has also led me to question whether "crip" carries the same meaning in Polish and Eastern European contexts as it does in the West, and what kind of experiences and practices could be considered "crip" in Eastern Europe.[10] In other words, is there a limit to the translation of crip? Evidently, these questions go beyond the scope of this project; for now, I will simply identify the narratives I examine here as "disability confessions."

Thus, in this chapter, I analyze the characteristics of Polish disability confessional culture and the ways in which it redraws and disrupts public space. I follow a series of events that not only disrupt the Polish parliament and public spaces, but also lead to the emergence of a politicized disabled subject. At the end of chapter 1, I posited that anonymous disabled women crafting their life autobiographies were perhaps recognizing themselves as public subjects and wanted to participate in the public sphere; here I explore twenty-first-century disability confessional culture as a continuation of the same desire. Additionally, by expanding an archive of violent intimacy, I foreground my analysis in chapter 2. Despite being visible to the public and helping to "expand discursive space,"[11] however, like the forgotten disruption of the Polish narrative of history and maternal scripts, these disruptions did not significantly change and expand social policy.[12]

This chapter follows a chronological trajectory from the 2014 Parliament sit-in, through the 2018 protest and 2020 demonstrations against the CT ruling, to the 2022 demands that the carer employment ban be lifted. This enables me to explore the moment when a disability confessional culture emerged in Poland, and how it has altered over time.

2014

This occupation of Parliament lasted from March 19 to April 4, but a one-day protest that constituted a kind of prelude to the March occupation had happened already on January 23, and, since the demands and the protestors that made them that day overlapped with the March occupation, I decided to include it in the following analysis. According to some news reports, around a dozen carers, largely mothers and their disabled children, took part in the March sit-in.[13] Their primary objectives were to secure an increase in state benefits and professionalize care work: only the former was successful.[14] In what could be read as an attempt to reformulate violent intimacy, the carers demanded both official recognition as professional care assistants and what they deemed fair remuneration for their work.[15] As Polish disability studies scholar Marta Sałkowska has noted, the 2014 protesters did not raise the issue of combining care labor with outside work.[16] This was not the first protest staged by carers in the 2000s, but, as Polish disability studies scholars Paweł Kubicki, Rafał Bakalarczyk, and Marek Mackiewicz-Ziccardi have observed, prior to the "many petitions, statements, attempts at advocacy, education and consolidation of people with disabilities movement by means of the Internet and social media," the 2014 and 2018 protests were "the most momentous" events.[17]

While the pre-2014 protests and advocacy attempts remained invisible to the majority of Polish society, the situation transformed when this small group of protesters refused to leave Parliament.

On March 27, carers of adult people with disabilities, demanding higher state benefits as well as an end to the differential treatment of people who acquired disability in adulthood versus childhood, initiated a protest outside the Parliament building.[18] This event received little media coverage, and it is unclear when it ended.[19] The outside protestors were also largely ignored by politicians, and negotiations were only conducted with those inside the building. It is likely this was due to the mobilizing of the figure of a suffering innocent child, a cultural narrative that the protesters living in the tent city outside could not equal. Nevertheless, the demonstrations inside and outside the Parliament shared an emphasis on disability as inextricable from poverty and suffering.

The 2014 sit-in inaugurated a disability confessional culture within Poland. The confessions created at this time blend intimate stories of hardship with political commentary on disability in Polish society and state abandonment of the disabled population. Some include references to Catholicism and nationalism. Most importantly, the 2014 confessions were primarily shared by carers: I have found very few created by people with disabilities.

Both during the January protest I mention above and March occupation, a major issue raised by protesters inside the Polish Parliament was the amount of state benefit a disabled child received in 2014: 153 zł a month (in 2025, the equivalent of $42). Mothers asked such questions as "Why does my child receive 153 zł when a disabled member of Parliament receives 6.000 zł per month?" (in 2025 6.000 PLN is the equivalent of $1,618, but in 2024—ten years after the protest—the Parliament members received around 13.000 zł per month/$3,600, plus additional benefits) and "How are we supposed to pay for rehabilitation if we get 153 zł?"[20] They also described how their lives had been reduced to begging: "We beg for 1 percent, we beg our friends and acquaintances and strangers. This is really nothing but begging."[21] They believed that professionalizing the care work they performed would solve the problem. Protesters outside the building echoed this narrative by sharing their own stories of poverty and lack of basic resources.

On March 22, when Prime Minister Donald Tusk met with the protesters, one mother asked him to "perform a miracle and cure my child or tie my child's stomach because I can't wait for you to increase the state benefit: I'm not able to offer her any treatment or therapy. If you perform a miracle, I'll wait."[22] As I discussed in chapter 1, the democratic transition period constituted a waiting time for disabled women: In 2014, the mothers of disabled children refused to wait any longer. One of the protest leaders, Iwona Hartwich, stated: "There is no time to seek solutions."[23] Yet the solution offered by the government was a gradual increase in benefits, to take place over years.[24] Tusk declared that "this year we cannot increase the state's deficit because we simply cannot."[25] In other words, the government planned to maintain the politics of waiting to which Poland's disabled population had been subjected for the last twenty-five years. Although the protesters managed to disrupt Parliament and introduce the issues of disability and care to a larger audience, they did not significantly change disability policies.

On March 27, 2014, in Ostrołęka, a midsize town 120 kilometers from Warsaw, carers of children with disabilities held a solidarity demonstration with those occupying the Parliament.[26] They recorded a ten-minute video at the school the children attended in which mothers told their stories of hardship while the children remained silent. One mother stated that she had a solution to the "disability problem in Poland: Maybe they can light furnaces in Oświęcim again?"[27] By referring to the Polish name for Auschwitz, a place that exemplifies the utmost suffering within Polish culture, this mother conveyed the message that the situation in which the disabled population found itself was a moral outrage. This was not the only reference to Nazism. Several of the mothers taking part in the Parliament sit-in alleged similarities between disability politics in Poland and the eugenic measures of Nazi Germany; one claimed that state policies were intended to kill children with disabilities.[28] Similar sentiments appeared on placards held by the protesters outside.[29] These carers claimed that the Polish government had deemed those with disabilities to be expendable.

Given this widely held feeling of abandonment by the state, it is no surprise that during the conversation with the prime minister, one protester stated: "We don't have a president."[30] In another discussion, a mother declared that Parliament was lacking "God, honor and service to the homeland."[31] The motto of the Polish military and an unofficial motto of Poland in general, the phrase "God, Honor, the Fatherland" can be traced back to the eighteenth-century partitions, when Polish territories were divided between Prussia, Russia, and the Austrian-Hungarian empire. This mother therefore claimed that contemporary disability policies are a betrayal of nationalist ideals. To take this further, I read her comment as an assertion that disabled people have not been enfolded into the national polity. These statements are particularly striking as the liberal, center-right party the Civic Platform was governing the country in 2014, and Tusk was regularly accused by the right-wing politicians and journalists of conspiring with Germany to the detriment of Poland.[32]

This was not the only attempt to deploy nationalism in the service of disability. Already during the January protest, a protester emphasized exclusion from the national body: "My child has been subjected to suffering from the moment they were born. Why is even one hour of individual teaching cut? Why does no one want to invest in our children? It is a slow killing, this is euthanasia in white gloves. Are we supposed to file for asylum in Belarus?"[33] While presenting disability in Poland as inextricable from suffering, this mother also showed her audience a photo of her young child undergoing intubation. Besides the physical circumstances, a second meaning of suffering is at play here: one imposed by state disability policies, which, according to this woman, are the policies of slow death. Her rhetorical question about filing for asylum in a neighboring authoritarian country emphasizes the fraught relationship between disability and the nationalist project in Poland.

A few months later, outside the Parliament building, a woman participating in the protest and taking care of a disabled husband expressed a similar feeling of abandonment: "I've been taking care of my husband for four years now; he is partially paralyzed. We have debts, we sell what we can. I see that some women here sell their wedding bands, I haven't had mine for a long time now. Sometimes we have nothing to eat, we get food packages from Caritas, we constantly eat rice and potatoes. That's what our life looks like. We don't have the means to live, we have no medical insurance, we are crushed and humiliated. We feel as if we are not Poles."[34] In this account of suffering and poverty, disability itself is not equated with pain: The woman does not say whether her husband's paralysis is a source of suffering. Instead, she emphasizes the abject poverty in which her family exists. By stating that she does not feel like a Pole, this woman equates Polishness with well-being: What has happened to her family should not have happened because they are Polish. Although words such as "race," "ethnicity" and "citizenship" are not present in this or any of the quoted statements, the confessions I have analyzed are haunted by them. Demands for higher state benefits and better treatment appear to have been partially grounded in the citizenship status of protestors.

Poland has been assumed to be a place where questions about race are absent.[35] However, research by Margaret Ohia-Nowak, Agnieszka Kościańska, Michał Petryk, Łukasz Zaremba, and Magdalena Gawin, among others, shows that Poland not only has a history of colonial pursuits and eugenics, but also has to face its own desire for whiteness.[36] These disability confessions do not directly refer to issues of race—especially those of people of color—but, by invoking feeling as if one was not a Pole or asking for asylum in an authoritarian country east of Polish border, ideas of citizenship and whiteness and its (unclear) status are present. We can read these confessions as suggesting that being a Pole, having a Polish citizenship, and being white have failed to secure the speakers' rights as citizens and carers of people with disability. As Kateřina Kolářová has noted in "Crip Genealogies from the Postsocialist East," the white Western disability studies canon is of little help in "undoing the haunting of the racialized and racist usages of disability" in Eastern Europe.[37] My brief examination of the coarticulation of disability, ethnicity, and citizenship in these 2014 confessions confirms the importance of the intersection of disability and race, and the need to find tools to unravel the two that are grounded in local histories and languages.

2018

On April 19, a day after the inauguration of the protest, Jakub Hartwich, an adult disabled son of Iwona Hartwich, one of the organizers of the previous occupation, said: "We are waiting for a meeting with people who make decisions [in Poland]: the chairman of the ruling party and the president. We are waiting for them, because we want a real change. Sadly, we need to protest to be seen and heard by society. Outside the Parliament no one discusses disability issues, no one advocates for us, we need to come here in order to be seen and heard."[38] I read this confession as a comment on a double abandonment: by society and by politicians. According to Jakub Hartwich, disabled people—despite the 2014 protest—remained invisible to society and continued to be ignored by policy-makers. In other words, the 2014 protest only temporarily disrupted the societal silence surrounding disability.

The 2018 protest, led by the same group of people that had occupied Parliament in 2014, started on April 18 and lasted forty days. Demonstrations in support took place outside the building and in many cities across the country. This protest attracted far more attention from both national and local media than the 2014 protest, with dramatic footage of disabled people sleeping on the floors appearing daily on Polish TV. Protesters were prevented from opening windows or going to a nearby garden, and their access to Parliament bathrooms was restricted. Physiotherapists and other rehabilitation workers were initially allowed to enter the building, but this access was later denied in an attempt to force protesters to leave.

At a press conference held when protesters left the building on May 27, one of the leaders, Iwona Hartwich, announced that "after forty days of struggle for the lives of our children, constant fight, and constant humiliations we suffered from the current government we suspend the protest."[39] She emphasized that the implementation of further restrictions, including to bathrooms and elevators,[40] had made the protest unsustainable.[41] The government did meet one of the protestors' demands: The social allowance for disabled people was increased. However, calls for a monthly rehabilitation allowance of 500 PLN for those whose disabilities had been assessed as "severe" was rejected.[42]

In 2014, demands had centered on the needs of carers; the 2018 protest predominantly focused on the perspectives of disabled people. This was reflected in the confessions that were evident at that time: the media not only underlined the participation of disabled people, but they also interviewed disabled protesters.[43]

Acknowledging the centrality of their children in the protest while positioning themselves as carriers of their message, two nondisabled leaders of the protest, Iwona Hartwich and Anna Glinka, stated, respectively, "We are the voice of our disabled children, since they cannot go out and protest,"[44] and "these are our children protesting, we are only their voices."[45] Obviously, as illustrated by the quote opening this section, these statements contradict the fact that Jakub Hartwich, Iwona Hartwich's son, was interviewed and provided his own confessions. Moreover, as I have discussed elsewhere, it is unclear whether it is disability itself, structural inequities, or other factors that render disabled people voiceless, and in this situation whether these mothers retain their own voice or are simply speaking on behalf of their children.[46] As well as highlighting the material dependence of disabled children on their mothers, these statements testify to the violent intimacy I discussed in detail in chapter 2: A lack of separation exists between mother and disabled child and is enforced and sustained by state withdrawal from the sphere of care and assistance.

The tension that can exist between disabled children and their nondisabled parents was evident at a demonstration held on May 8, in Włocławek, a small town located in central Poland, in support of those occupying the Parliament. After a young disabled woman, Agnieszka, had discussed the architectural, social, and infrastructural obstacles encountered by people with disabilities in the town, her mother added: "I think I know even more than she does about disability issues because it is me who is burdened with helping her in daily tasks."[47] This exchange and the statements by Hartwich and Glinka illustrate how carers can often view themselves as the most appropriate appraisers of disability policies and issues. Bulgarian disability studies scholar Galina Goncharova has noted that mothers of disabled children often engage in "over-responsible mothering," which can deprive their children of "a voice of their own and of any possibility to run their own lives and manage their social chances."[48] Serving as a reminder that tension and competition over disability expertise can underpin violent intimacy, Agnieszka's experiences and opinions were, to a certain extent, belittled by her mother, deemed to be of less value than her own. Because disabled people, while physically present, were not given a platform to share their confessions, this tension was not apparent during the 2014 protest. In 2018, people with disabilities made their experiences and understandings of disability public in the Parliament, the streets and squares of Poland, and the media.

Poland was not the only Eastern European location that witnessed disability protests in 2018.[49] In Bulgaria, mothers of disabled children carried placards announcing that "the system kills us."[50] As Goncharova has noted, use of "the pronoun 'us' suggests the idea of the inseparable biological-and-social bond between the mothers and their children, who are forced to suffer and bear the burden of disability together." Resonating with my notion of violent intimacy, this also shows that systemic failures to provide assistance for families with disabled members cut across Eastern European borders. As in Poland, Bulgarian mothers were also on the front lines, reminding everyone of who is burdened with providing care.[51]

For my analysis, I have decided to focus on confessions made by supporters of the Parliament sit-in—people who did not occupy the Parliament—as these have yet to receive attention: Numerous interviews were conducted with the protesters inside Parliament and circulated on TV, online, and in the press. One of the leaders, a wheelchair user named Jakub Hartwich, became a councillor in his hometown of Toruń shortly after the occupation, and his mother, Iwona Hartwich, was elected to Parliament. As well as the copious national and international press coverage of the protests, Polish academics released articles in English,[52] and Theatre 21 staged a performance entitled "Rewolucja, której nie było" (A revolution that never was) that went on to tour Poland and Europe,[53] and published a book of articles.[54] Thus, the confessions provided by the occupiers have already received substantial coverage and analysis.

At a demonstration outside the Polish Parliament on April 25, an unnamed woman confessed that she and the other protestors were not satisfied with "the scraps that we need to ask for," and that they would not "go to the churches to beg" after Mass, even though this was what the state forced them to do: "We are not beggars, we are normal people, we want systemic solutions."[55] Her words exemplify refusal and resistance toward the positioning of disabled people and their carers as objects of pity and charity. They also strengthen the social meaning of "normality" by setting people with disabilities and their families apart from beggars.

On April 27, an NGO that is no longer in existence, Stowarzyszenie Strefa Wenus z Milo (A Venus de Milo Zone Association), organized a protest in solidarity with the Parliament occupiers in the Old Square, Kraków, one of the largest cities in Poland. Katarzyna Żeglicka, a disabled activist and artist, opened the rally by declaring that "this is the first protest in Kraków in which disabled people will take over and have a voice."[56] Żeglicka was not only emphasizing the emancipatory character of the event; she was also alluding to the slogan "Nothing about us without us." In her second sentence, she inscribed Polish events into the global history of disabled people's struggles by describing how on March 12, 1990, sixty activists with disabilities in the United States had "dropped their crutches, left their wheelchairs and started to crawl the stone-made Capitol steps to fight for dignity and equal treatment."[57] While this passage leads us to consider to what extent the Polish disability rights movement and its strategies are modeled on or inspired by the US example, it is also possible to analyze this remark as an illustration of how global disability histories meet with, and are used to further, local struggles for emancipation. Żeglicka then articulated the goal of the demonstration: "The protest in the Parliament pushed us to manifest our dissatisfaction with the fact that there is no systemic support for us in Poland. There has come the time to make our voice—the voice of people with disabilities—audible. We want to make clear that we do not agree with the violation of our rights by the Polish state."[58]

Having posited disabled people as agents and identified the state as the main violator, not protector, of their rights, Żeglicka reminded her listeners that "some of us are not here, because of the barriers we encounter; those barriers were installed by the Polish state."[59] In a succinct fashion, this short fragment summarizes one of the main tenets of the social model of disability: People are disabled not by their impairment, but by societal barriers. Discussing disability as a political matter rather than an individual issue, Żeglicka strengthened her message by adding that "we are not harmed by fate, but by the system." As she concluded her speech, Żeglicka denounced the infantilization of disabled people, appealing to the public to "remember that people with disabilities are adults. We don't want to be called kids, we are not kids."[60] Thus, her confession was directed not only at state violence, but also at the nondisabled majority, who often fail to recognize disabled people as autonomous, agentive producers of disability knowledge.

The confessions created during the Kraków demonstration did not center exclusively on state violence and the societal paternalization of disabled people. Piotr Zasadzki emphasized disability identity and sociality: "For a long time I haven't recognized myself as a deaf-blind person; I thought of it as a sort of illness. It changed when I joined the Society for Deaf-Blind People; other members taught me how to live with this disability."[61] This passage is particularly striking, as few people in Poland recognize disability as a form of identity. To emphasize that disability is just one—and not the dominant—attribute of an individual, institutional actors, including disability activists and NGOs that address disability issues, advocate for use of the term "person with disability" rather than "disabled person." The latter has been deemed derogatory by many, including, for example, Agnieszka Szpila.[62] Although a disability rights movement is rapidly emerging in Poland, the issue of disability pride is—thus far—rarely raised.[63]

Zasadzki ended his testimony by discussing the effects of the capitalist transformation during the early 1990s: "I dream of a job that would enable me to live an independent life, that would provide me with an income and an apartment. But there is no assisted living in Poland, because in the 1990s we put our trust in the free market, because all the ruling parties gave away our state to the market."[64] What is most noteworthy about this statement is how Zasadzki makes disability a part of the post-socialist transformation. As I discussed in chapter 1, this association has not been made by either journalists or historians. According to Zasadzki, disability emancipation and independent living are related to capitalist policies—or, rather, the capitalist transformation is the very thing that has denied the possibility of independent living.

An open-mic format was adopted at a demonstration that took place outside the Polish Parliament on May 2. An anonymous nondisabled protester also referred to the shift to capitalism:

> I had a friend whose name was Michał, he had cerebral palsy and we used to spend a lot of time together. We talked about video games and sports, we were very much interested in football. . . . And today, thanks to the Polish 1989 transformation I do not have a friend. Michał and his family left Poland, because they did not receive any support from the Polish state. They left for France. I lost a friend because of the Polish state and its negligence of disabled people. . . . The Polish 1989 transformation has its victims including disabled people.[65]

Like Zasadzki, this man inscribed his and his friend's experiences into the history of the Polish transformation. A disabled mother of an autistic son at the same demonstration stated that, in relation to disability, the system had not changed in Poland since 1989.[66] These confessions demonstrate how disabled people and their allies used the 2018 protest to rewrite and enter one of the crucial moments of recent Polish history. While the contributors to *Written Through Suffering* cast themselves out of history and silenced the democratic transition (see chapter 1), the 2018 protesters reversed this process: By emphasizing the impact of the 1989 transformation on their lives they wrote themselves into history. A societal shift occurred over the twenty-seven years that separates the publication of *Written Through Suffering* and the 2018 protest in how the democratic transition could be discussed. It is now possible for disabled people and their allies to recognize themselves as subjects of history and challenge the official narrative of the post-socialist transformation—a narrative that tends to erase disability.

Also, at the demonstration on May 2, an anonymous mother of an adult disabled son, Jaś, emphasized the "mothering" (*umatkowienie*) of disability in Poland:

> All of us, healthy people, have many expenses: we pay for water, gas, toiletries, rent and many other things. Beside all of these things, I need to pay also for other stuff which I will allow myself to list now: I spend 440 PLN [$121] on diaper pants per month. . . . At some point Minister Radziwiłł [Konstanty Radziwiłł, Minister of Health 2015–2018] promised that the drugs for drug-resistant epilepsy would be free: They are not. I pay 220 PLN [$60.5] for these per month. Extremely basic toiletries: 60 PLN [$16.5] per month. I have to pay for Jaś's baths even though I would prefer not to rely on someone to do this. This is not cheap and it is difficult to find someone. It costs 300 PLN [$82.5] per month. Additionally, if I would like to go out every other day, no, not in order to watch movies or go to

> a theater, but in order to do some stuff for myself and my son, I would have to pay 13 PLN [$3.6] per hour. . . . Several years ago when my son stopped eating for two months because of a drug change he almost died from hunger. . . . These two months cost me more than a dozen thousands of zlotys. But Jaś is alive.[67]

I present this confession virtually unabridged because it relates to a number of important issues—first, the cost of care. Care requires both money and labor, and, as I discussed at length in chapter 2, the individual responsible for providing both of these in post-socialist Poland is almost always the mother (as in the many cases I analyzed in the previous chapter, Jaś's father is no longer around). This mother's confession illustrates how disability is intimately interwoven with financial deprivation. Other than mentioning the minister of health in the context of an unfulfilled promise, she makes no reference to the state and its institutions. Moreover, this confession shows how the life of a nondisabled person can be determined by someone else's disability. With very little information about her disabled son, this confession testifies to a mother's suffering and sacrifice. Disability confessions can collectively constitute a form of resistance and refusal of the politics of austerity, ableism, and the exclusion of disabled people. However, rather than resistance, this confession is a narrative of survival and debilitation.

Equally importantly, by depicting this woman's entire life as dedicated to providing care, this confession provides a graphic and detailed illustration of violent intimacy. Her life and future are bound to her son's life and future, and there is no room for anything but the organization of her son's survival. This particular form of time manipulation leaves little time for protest. Though not directly referenced, the state is not absent from this confession: By providing only basic support and expecting individuals to organize their own lives, whatever the physical, mental and financial costs, the state benefits from this woman's determination that she and her son will survive.

As well as enabling a revision of history, the Parliament occupation of 2018 also engendered the envisioning of a new future. At a Warsaw demonstration on May 5, former Paralympic medal—winning swimmer and disability activist Karolina Hamer loudly proclaimed that "we will build a normal state that is based on tolerance, openness and modernity."[68] Influenced by the liberal values associated with Western democracies, Hamer's vision includes no "normal" state where disabled people are not afforded first-class citizenship. While her use of "we" is unspecific, given the context of the protest it seems safe to assume she is referring to disabled people and their allies, thus casting disabled people as agents and active creators of a newly imagined state.

The May 5 demonstration produced another important intervention in the public approach to disability. At some point, the marching protesters started to chant: "We want health, not Hail Mary." While it is not clear what they meant by the first part of this statement, whether cure or simply better healthcare services, it is clear what they did not want: prayers and pity. While the contributors to *Written Through Suffering* referenced God and Pope John Paul II as possible sources of improvement in their lives, these protesters rejected religion: In their view, rituals and prayers had nothing meaningful to offer disabled people.

It was perhaps partly the lack of support the occupation and the solidarity demonstrations received from the Catholic Church that provoked this renunciation of prayer. Catholic priest Stanisław Jurczuk had publicly announced that these "arrogant" demonstrators should have chosen a form of protest that did not amount to "tormenting disabled people."[69] Describing the protest as "politically motivated,"[70] Archbishop Henryk Hoser had advised the mothers of disabled protesters to revise their demands and proclaimed that "the Church is not a party to this conflict."[71] Priest Tadeusz Isakowski-Zaleski, president of the Saint Albert Foundation for people with intellectual disabilities, had supported the Parliament occupation in 2014, when the center-right party Civic Platform led the country.[72] In 2018, however, he called on the protestors to end their demonstration.[73] It has been suggested that the 2018 protests received little support from the Catholic hierarchy due to close relations between the Church and the Law and Justice party, which came to power in 2015. It is also likely that the rejection of the Church's model of a passive, suffering disabled person by the demonstrators, who presented themselves as agents capable of formulating political demands, is of equal import. Polish disability studies and media studies scholar Magdalena Zdrodowska notes that the protests "encourage a view of these [disabled] citizens outside the model of a submissive and eternally grateful object of care and assistance," which have been dominant in postsocialist Poland and additionally enforced by the Catholic Church in Poland.[74] It bears pointing out that Polish Catholic representations of disability are extremely uniform. Disabled people, whose "miserable" circumstances can be a source of solace for the nonafflicted, are depicted as helpless and thus in need of support, and Pope John Paul II emphasized that disabled people should be provided with care in his teachings.[75] One Catholic textbook for schools promotes charity initiatives for the disabled population.[76] Another presents disability as a condition that should be cured.[77] As theology scholar Anna Maliszewska has noted, some Catholic theologians do not appear to distinguish between disability and evil or sin.[78] My analysis of the young adult novel *The Pupa* (see chapter 2) also illuminates some of the ways in which Catholicism and Pope

John Paul II inform understandings of disability in post-socialist Poland. Given this context, the declaration "We want health, not Hail Mary" is a rejection of the Catholic Church's attitude to disability. And given the overwhelming influence of Catholicism in Poland, it is quite notable that the Church is not discussed in any of the disability confessions I have found.

2020

On October 22, 2020, the CT ruled that abortions in cases of severe or fatal fetal abnormality were unconstitutional. Announced during the COVID-19 pandemic, this decision initiated a wave of demonstrations across the country through the fall and winter of 2020 to 2021. Despite widespread disbelief, the change in legislation that followed this ruling was not entirely surprising: Many attempts to restrict access to abortion have been made since 1989. These efforts intensified when Law and Justice came to power in 2015. The possibility of prohibiting abortion in cases of both fetal abnormality and rape was debated in Parliament in the fall of 2016, prompting mass demonstrations across the country on October 3. A black umbrella became the symbol of the Czarny (Black) Protest. In response to more attempts to restrict the law in 2017–18, alternative proposals to legalize abortion up to twelve weeks were debated by Parliament but rejected. In the fall of 2020, it was not Parliament, but the CT that deemed unconstitutional the premise that a fetus suspected of "severe disabilities" could be legally aborted.

Abortion has been legal in Poland since 1956. Further liberalization in 1960 gave women the sole right to decide whether to continue or terminate a pregnancy.[79] Polish gender studies scholar Agata Chełstowska has stated that, abortion was "accessible and affordable" under state socialism, as the law was interpreted "in a way that allowed the woman to decide if her social conditions allowed her to have a child."[80] This (almost) unrestricted access to abortion lasted for around twenty years, until shifts in public and political discourses on the issue took place during the 1980s—largely, Malgorzata Fidelis has claimed, in response to pressure from the Church and leaders of the Solidarity trade union.[81] Agnieszka Graff has noted that use of the neutral term "fetus" in published material began to be replaced with "unborn child" at this time.[82] Additionally, Kazimiera Szczuka has described how the Polish Catholic social movement started to refer to abortion as the "killing of unborn babies" and hold communism responsible for the existence of legal abortion.[83] Despite protests in the streets and a petition with over a million signatures, Parliament enacted restrictions on access to abortion in 1993. Under the new law, abortion was possible in only three situations: that the pregnancy constitutes a threat to life or a serious threat to the woman's health; the fetus is irreversibly damaged; or the pregnancy is the result of an illegal act.

As Szczuka has stated, the ban on abortion and introduction of Catholic lessons to school illustrate how effectively the Church "took over" Poland after 1989.[84] From the perspective of reproductive rights, this political transformation had actually been initiated far earlier, with the Church organizing and fighting, in different ways, against the abortion law of 1956 already in the 1960s, and campaigning openly—alongside the "Solidarność" Independent Self-Governing Trade Union—for a ban on abortion from the early 1980s.[85] Due to this "ideological offensive," as Chełstowska has noted, the number of legal abortions dropped considerably between 1988 and the implementation of the new law in 1993.[86] But Poland was not the only country in which a political and economic transition was accompanied by a restriction of women's reproductive rights: As Katherine Verdery has noted, similar trends took place in Hungary, Croatia and other parts of Central and Eastern Europe.[87]

The CT ruling of 2020 can be understood as a continuation of these politics: an escalation of the manipulation to which women's bodies are subjected and a further reduction of their reproductive rights. Disability had now been situated at the heart of this ideological conflict. Following the ruling, a new subject, term, and slogan entered public discourse: the disabled fetus.[88] The CT, the Law and Justice government, and other supporters of the new law hailed the protection now afforded the unborn disabled. However, there was no provision for increasing support for families raising children with disabilities: "Protection" of disabled fetuses did not translate into protection for disabled children.

While there were certainly women with disabilities who supported the CT ruling, as almost all the demonstrations that took place were against the restriction on abortion, their confessions have not circulated as widely as those created by women with disabilities who opposed the legal change.[89] As I will discuss, these women employ diverse rhetorical strategies to claim rights and citizenship: They utilize medical terminology to describe disability, Catholic imagery of a suffering Christ, and a vocabulary of social justice. As well as supporting the right to abortion, these women denounce the social marginalization and oppression of people with disabilities and advocate for a life of dignity. These confessions are especially important given that, as noted by Agnieszka Król, "discourses around abortion tend to disregard the voices of women with disabilities, yet both proponents of the pro-choice position and their opponents address disability. The experience of women with disabilities lines up across contemporary debates."[90]

Ola Mosioł

On November 3, 2020, in response to the CT ruling, OKO.press published four statements by women with disabilities. They had originally been collected by Katarzyna Bierzanowska, a well-known disabled activist, and published on her popular Facebook page, Pełnoprawna, where she discusses disability rights and issues. The opening of Ola Mosioł's statement is particularly powerful: "I'm upset. No. I'm pissed. Pissed and terrified. Can anyone tell me what is this glorified *protection of life*? Why does only the interior of my uterus get to be protected, and not me? Why is it protected only for nine months? Because, after giving birth, no one is interested in the baby I just had."[91]

By pointing out that a disabled life only receives protection prior to birth, Mosioł challenges hypocrisy in Polish attitudes to disability. Using her own identity and experience of living in a disabled body, presumably in a hostile environment, Mosioł continues by stating that, as a woman with a significant disability, she is "fully aware of what it means to give birth to a fetus with irreversible defects."[92] The phrase "irreversible defects" underlines the gravity of the situation and, equally importantly, individualizes and pathologizes impairment. Mosioł goes on to address the pro-life worldview that a woman's role is to bear and rear children, adding that the official diagnosis she received from the medical establishment had "a wonderful addendum: *unable to live an independent life*."[93] Here, she highlights the contradiction that characterizes the lives of disabled women: as women they are expected to have children, but as people with disabilities they are assumed to require constant support and thus be unable to provide for others. In her confession, Mosioł does not distance herself from the medical assessment of her bodily condition; rather, she underlines how her life is made challenging by both social contradictions and the material reality of living in a disabled body.

In the next part of her confession, Mosioł discusses suffering: "Throughout my life I have seen many suffering people, including children. And thus I don't want to give birth to a life that will end soon after in pain. And what if I don't want my child to live in pain for many years?"[94] Crucially, rather than address the possibility of passing down "defects" to a baby, Mosioł speaks of passing down pain: In other words, her refusal to give birth is a refusal to bequeath pain. Through this positioning of pain as a legacy of disability, Mosioł's confession can be read as a criticism of the cultural imperative to silence impairment and pain.[95] It could be argued that the CT ruling enabled women with disabilities to publicly discuss the pain they endure and propel the issue into public discourse.

Ola Mosioł was not alone in her centering of impairment and pain. In 2019, American scholar Courtney W. Bailey published "On the Impossible: Disability Studies, Queer Theory, and the Surviving Queer," in which, drawing upon her own experiences, she discusses the limitations of disability studies synonymous with the social model of disability. She distances herself from the dominant strand of contemporary disability studies and said: "Given my experiences with chronic pain and depression, I feel ambivalent toward the primary counter-narrative offered by disability studies/activism and based on the social model."[96] She continues by saying that disability studies and disability activism rely on the social model of disability advocate for the rejection of cure, medical treatment, and rehabilitation and opt for "'choosing' disability, choosing disability represents a triumph of the authentic self over ideology and oppression, proof of enlightenment and moral authority, and the path to self-actualization. Those who un-choose disability make things worse for themselves, succumbing to dominant ideology, siding with the inauthentic and unnatural, and disabling themselves even further."[97] According to Bailey, the problem with "choosing disability" is that it entails the silencing of pain, suffering, and the need for medications, which are a part of her life, and the lives of many other disabled people, including some of the women with disabilities who protested the abortion ban in 2020 in Poland. "Choosing disability" does not leave room for narratives that include the undesired material effects of living with disability.

Propelled by what seems like the same impulse to voice suffering instead of silencing it, Mosioł contests a definition of disabled life: "Yes, misfortune is a life that does not have much to do with life itself. For what else is a child's fate who is being born with severe developmental defects which do not allow him to live a life in dignity?"[98] According to Mosioł, it is not society that prevents a person with disabilities from living their life with dignity, but impairment. Her words locate disability in the body: Thus, a severe impairment or disease is not compatible with her definition of life. Mosioł recommends that if pro-lifers are to continue "defending the right to life," they should spend a "few months in intense therapy, in ICU, or in a hospice. Have a look at children whose lives are nothing else but surviving epilepsy attacks; and they might experience several attacks every day."[99] By reducing disabled life to the survival of embodiment, the disabled body itself is positioned as a site of trauma and confinement. Unlike many of the protesters in 2018, Mosioł refutes the social model of disability and its emphasis on the injustices that stem from social infrastructures. While addressing the hypocrisy of pro-lifers, Mosioł's confession forms an accusation of the body, not society.

Before we conclude that what she says is an expression of internalized ableism, we need to sit with the discomfort her words might provoke and reflect upon her confession. It reminds us that disabled people around the world do not necessarily subscribe to Westernized models of thinking about disability and modes of articulating demands. They might follow different sensibilities and deem them fit to fight for their rights in their local contexts. This confession can be approached in a twofold manner: as a reflection of Mosioł's understanding of her own situation and her embodiment, or as propelled by an intention to shock society given the gravity of the consequences of banning abortion based on disability status. As feminist disability studies scholar Magda Szarota writes, "Women with disabilities are a large minority characterized by great diversity."[100] Thus, paying attention to Mosioł's words is one way of recognizing the diverse ways disabled women employ to express their anger and frustration and present themselves as agentive and, equally important, to acknowledge that Western disability discourses are only one among many.

Patrycja Polczyk

On October 28, 2020, a weekly feature, "Wysokie Obcasy" (High Heels), in one of the most popular Polish dailies, *Gazeta Wyborcza* (Electoral Newspaper), included a letter previously published on Bierzanowska's Facebook page. Entitled "I'm Not a Mother, I Don't Want to Be One," the letter was written by Patrycja Polczyk, a writer and activist with spinal muscular atrophy (SMA).[101] As SMA does not impair the mind but "takes away other things," Polczyk declares her unwillingness to burden her body with "something that might be broken."[102] Like Mosioł, Polczyk does not adopt the social model of disability discourse. In her account, a potential fetus is "broken," and the genetic disease she lives with is responsible for unnamed losses: Polczyk does not want a child to live as she has been forced to live. She does not differentiate between disability and disease, and her confession medicalizes and pathologizes the former, echoing the medical model of disability. From the perspective of disability studies, the distinction between disability and illness matters, and much effort has been put into the demedicalization of disability.[103] However, it seems that some disabled women might not be equally committed to maintaining the distinction. In other words, the official classification of the condition may have no personal or political significance for some disabled women. What counts are the daily experience of pain, inaccessibility, and material inequities that make life difficult.

However, Polczyk does state that her reluctance to have a potentially disabled child is also due to the lack of a social support system for disabled people:

> I read some comments, opinion columns, articles about the CT's decision. There was a woman saying that no matter disability and fetus's condition, the child needs to be born, and if the mother does not want to raise the child, she can give it away to an institution. . . . What kind of institutions does this woman have in mind? Where are those institutions? The parents of disabled children know that if they do not organize things and fight for resources, no one will support them.[104]

This is a denunciation of both the state, for abandoning people with disabilities and their carers, and of those nondisabled people who are unaware of this abandonment. It is also an illustration of how disability confessions can participate in building social knowledge on disability and addressing misconceptions.

In chapter 2, I discussed mothers' desire for their disabled children to die before they do. Polczyk refers to this, confirming the impossibility that disabled people can live without a mother: "Each and every one of [these mothers] hopes that her child dies before she does. . . . Personally, I would like to die before my mom does. I do not have siblings, I do not have financial means to hire a 24–7 personal assistant, and I do not want to live in an institution. . . . The conclusion is simple."[105] This individual desire to die is socially and politically engineered: State withdrawal from the sphere of assistance can compel a person with disabilities to want to die, and care-providing parents to want their children to die. As her disabled future is beyond the interests of the state, Polczyk believes she has no future without her mother. Thus, to a certain extent, opposition to the ban on abortion in cases of severe or fatal fetal abnormality expanded into a protest against the Polish state's neglect of people with disabilities.

Without relinquishing the desire to live a disabled life in dignity and have a viable future, the confessions of both Polczyk and Mosioł center "broken" bodyminds. Polczyk oscillates between striving for disability rights and medically pathologizing the disabled body. To defend the right to abortion, she enfreaks the disabled fetus. Calling on the reader to imagine they are carrying a fetus that is "just a piece of flesh without a brain, eyes and is unable to breathe on its own," she asks, Would they want to give birth to this "cluster of cells and observe it dying immediately after birth?"[106] Elsewhere she states that "a requirement to give birth to a cluster of broken cells should not exist in any sort of reality."[107] As her emphasis is a *broken* body rather than an inhabitable world, the language of rights and the social model of disability are largely absent. The CT ruling and resulting demonstrations enabled many women with disabilities to articulate and politically instrumentalize their negative experiences of impairment.

Polczyk concludes her confession by demanding the right to choose for all women:

> I do not want to be a mother. . . . There are more women who think the way I do. Women with disabilities, nondisabled women. Poor and rich women. Women who wanted to be pregnant and those who did not plan it. Every woman has a right to make decisions about herself. She needs to have this right! Her body, life, and health cannot be subjected to the forces of patriarchy: of priests and fascists. A woman is not anyone's property. . . . Together we will fight the regime. We will support all women and we will not be told that we cannot do it. There has come the time to fight. It will not be nice.[108]

In this passage Polczyk connects her two identities: a woman, and a person with a disability. Setting aside the issues of pain and the lack of social support for disabled people, she focuses on attempting to reclaim women's rights, noting that only an alliance of women, both disabled and nondisabled, can force a change in the law. This is a feminist-disability call for liberation made in a spirit of solidarity and affinity.

Bogumiła Siedlecka

While Mosioł and Polczyk rely on medical and social justice terminology in their confessions, these were not the only approaches used to narrate disability experiences and express anger about the CT ruling. On October 20, 2020, Bogumiła Siedlecka, a disabled activist who runs popular social media accounts under the name Anioł na Resorach (Angel on Wheels), posted a ten-minute video on Instagram. The video was viewed over three hundred thousand times, and nearly a further ten thousand times when posted on YouTube. Siedlecka opened by addressing her audience and identifying her position: "I want you to know what a person with severe disability thinks and feels about the current situation. The CT's decision concerns all of us, not only women. It concerns future fathers, whole families and our state."[109]

Rather than focus on a woman's autonomy and the right to choose, as Mosioł and Polczyk do, Siedlecka positions the ban on abortions in cases of severe or fatal fetal abnormality as a universal issue, extending beyond women's rights to affect future fathers and families. Siedlecka then addresses suffering: "I have an impression that the most important decisions are taken by people who know nothing about suffering and how it is to carry the cross of child suffering. Of course, I also do not know much about it, but I have seen the suffering of parents at the hospitals and in other places; I have seen my own parents and they were very brave. They carried the cross of my disability."[110]

Here, Siedlecka identifies disability with the Catholic cross and equates providing care with carrying it. The Crucifixion is the ultimate representation of innocent suffering and the popular Polish phrase *nieść krzyż cierpienia* (to carry the cross of suffering) is often used to describe a life with disability. To a certain extent, Siedlecka's confession does not significantly depart from the others I analyze here: It presents disability as inseparable from suffering and pain. However, in addition to Catholic imagery, Siedlecka deploys a very different affective register: Rather than utilizing the medical model of disability, she references the Catholic symbol of innocent and redemptive suffering. What is more, she highlights the importance of embodiment in reproductive rights and assumes that those who want to ban abortion do not live with disability.

What is particularly significant about this confession is that the visual rhetoric of the cross, used by various Polish religious and conservative groups to portray the suffering of aborted fetuses, is employed here to represent the irrevocable torment undergone by disabled children.[111] It is also highly significant that it is parents who are described as carrying the cross. Siedlecka's confession illustrates both the pervasiveness of Catholic rhetoric in public discourses on reproductive rights in Poland, and the way Catholic imagery, particularly of the Crucifixion, can be politically mobilized to advocate conflicting causes.[112] In her cultural history of the cross in Poland, historian Magdalena Waligórska has claimed that "no other symbol is as multilayered and contradictory."[113]

Siedlecka makes it clear that she is not advocating for abortion on demand: "It is not a contraceptive, absolutely not. I support a woman's right to decide about herself in very dramatic situations. . . . Each woman should be able to make a decision if she wants and if she is able to carry the cross of disabled child."[114] In contrast to demands by feminist groups in Poland, Siedlecka believes that abortion should only be an option in undefined "dramatic situations." As she supports the right of women to decide whether they are able to bear and rear children with disabilities, perhaps she also believes that they are capable of determining when a situation is sufficiently "dramatic" to justify abortion.

In an interview a few weeks after she posted her video, Siedlecka again addressed the right to choose whether to continue a pregnancy when the fetus is impaired: "I can be afraid of such a pregnancy, too. I also want to be able to make a decision. I do not know if I will ever be pregnant or if I will not—this is a choice, too. But if I am and it turns out that I carry a genetically impaired fetus, I want to know that I can make my own decision."[115] Feminist undertones are far more evident here. Siedlecka goes on to state that some people who watched her video had expected that, being religious and disabled, she would support the CT ruling. However, Siedlecka does not believe that practicing Catholics should be able to dictate how others live, and she thinks that the law "should not be passed with only one group in mind."[116]

In both the video and the interview, Siedlecka attempts to negotiate and reconcile positions that often conflict: while she employs the symbolism of the cross, she believes that religion cannot and should not be translated into law, and she speaks about the freedom to choose, if only in limited and loosely defined situations. As her followers on Instagram and YouTube appear to be a rather diverse group, this may be intentional. But it could also reflect the fact that discourses on reproductive rights in Poland have long encompassed both feminist notions of freedom and autonomy, and the restrictions imposed by the vast influence of the Catholic Church.

2022

In September 2022, as I discussed in detail in chapter 2, the popular feminist fiction writer Agnieszka Szpila published an article entitled "Where Are These Children? They Are Fucked!," in which she described her experience of mothering two autistic teenage daughters. Her principal focus is the work ban placed on carers receiving the monthly state benefit in exchange for providing 24–7 care, which covers any kind of paid work, including the writing of her article. Not only did Szpila give countless interviews and receive a prestigious journalistic award in response to her article, the public discourse it engendered resulted in a new series of protests in Warsaw and other large cities, such as Poznań and Katowice, through the fall and winter of 2022. Although she did not organize the protests and was not their only spokesperson, Szpila became a public face of the movement they represented.

Organized by Katarzyna and Karolina Kosecka, the mother and sister of two autistic men, the first protest took place on September 17, five days after the publication of Szpila's article. As this demonstrates, the confessions of carers for people with disabilities perform a significant political and cultural role in contemporary Poland: Not only do they produce and disseminate disability knowledge, but they can also shape public understanding of issues relating to disability and care and galvanize a movement.[117] However, accounts by people with disabilities themselves do not as yet exert similar power within Polish society.

Although calls for people with disabilities to have access to care assistants and the right to an independent life had been added to their list of demands by the spring of 2023, the 2022 protests centered on the rights and voices of carers. Photos were posted on social media of carers and their allies holding posters with such slogans as "2.119" (the amount in PLN of the monthly benefit for carers), "Let us live," and "We want the whole of life," the latter referencing the words of Polish feminist writer Zofia Nałkowska as she concluded her speech at the first Polish Women's Congress in 1907. Protesting carers in Katowice were filmed describing their lives, which had always been difficult and were now a "disaster," and asking why young mothers were made to "count every penny."[118] These statements testify to an ongoing humanitarian crisis among carers and, equally important, to a shift in their approach to the state. The 2022 protests illustrate a realization on the part of carers that the state does not want to—and will not—get involved in disability issues. Unlike the protesting carers of 2014, who viewed the professionalization of their work as a solution, the carers of 2022 have accepted that they are on their own: The only way to improve their lives and those of the people under their care is to perform labor outside the home. This acceptance stems, probably, from memories of the protests in 2014 and 2018, and the awareness that since little changed then, little will change now, and therefore the only way to improve their children's lives is to get permission to work legally outside the home while retaining state benefits.

The 2022 protest was also the first time that highly educated women were visible among those taking action against disability policies in Poland. As stated, Agnieszka Szpila is a writer, and Karolina Kosecka, one of the principal organizers of the protests, studied theater and movement in London. As part of her confession at the demonstration in Poznań on November 19, an anonymous woman described her academic background:

> Apart from being a mother and wife of a person with disability, I graduated from university and before I gave birth, I was engaged in doctoral studies. Carers and people with disabilities in Poland are forgotten, . . . , they live on the brink of poverty. . . . We want the state to let us make additional money, we do not ask for charity, we want to be ourselves for a little while. Let us be ourselves, let us do something different. In my case this means being an academic, in someone else's case it means being a writer, a singer, or something else.[119]

It may be that the change in demands relates to a shift in the educational and class backgrounds of protestors. It certainly appears that the spokespersons of the movement represent a different social group than those of 2014 and 2018, and the remarks by this former academic resonate with Szpila's discussion of work as a mode of self-fulfillment, as I discussed in chapter 2. In this view, care labor stands in opposition to being oneself, and, according to this woman, being oneself is synonymous with self-realization through a professional career. This passage demonstrates the power of the capitalist (and, similarly, the earlier socialist) ideology of work as the main mode of individual self-expression; yet, understood in these narrow terms, it also emphasizes how a child's disability restricts the productivity of a nondisabled mother. Or perhaps these women have decided—like the mothers of children with disabilities who protested against austerity measures in Bulgaria in 2018—that embracing a work and productivity logic was the strategy most likely to gain support from the nondisabled public.[120]

The 2022 protests illuminated another aspect of the caregiver experience that rewrites the 2018 confession on invisibility by Jakub Hartwich. As she and her mother met with many other carers to organize the protest, Karolina Kosecka underwent an "extraordinary" feeling of "suddenly" being noticed: Until then, she had "never felt seen in my life."[121] Having added that the exhaustion and debilitation among caregivers noted in Szpila's article "touched upon something we talk about every day,"[122] Kosecka revealed her own disablement, having received a triple diagnosis of depression, anorexia, and neurosis at the age of fourteen.[123] This is reminiscent of my discussion in regard to Joanna Marnik's interview on the relationality of disability and the evoking of new disabilities in family situations with disabled family members (see the introduction), as it appears that her condition was at least partially prompted by living with two brothers requiring constant care. Her words also illustrate the impossibility of drawing a clear line between nondisabled carers and disabled care recipients.

As well as emphasizing the voices of female care providers and their experiences of debilitation and lack of self-fulfillment, the 2022 protest—and Karolina Kosecka's confession in particular—reformulated the notion of violent intimacy. In an interviewed confession, Karolina Kosecka relates how she accompanies her autistic brother Konrad to all his activities, including "sensory integration, hippo therapy, dog therapy, social skills trainings," and behavioral therapy, during which none of the therapists were "bothered" by her presence.[124] Describing how she and her brother interact and her hopes of working with him and other people with intellectual and cognitive disabilities in the future, she adds that "we are perfectly in tune with each other. The problem is that the education system has no room for people bonded in this kind of relationship."[125] Her education in London was "a three-year adventure" that enabled Kosecka to construct herself as "separate from my brother; we were almost inseparable before. I needed this in order to return to him; I had to know that this was my choice, and not my only reality."[126] These statements testify to both the existence of violent intimacy and the attempt to renegotiate this situation. Without dismissing the significance of her relationship with—and desire to be close to—her brother, Kosecka has refused violent intimacy. A larger issue is the extent to which Polish culture and society can accommodate such closeness or create conditions for this kind of "perfectly in tune" relationship to thrive that are not based in violent intimacy.

Conclusion

In sum, the protests that took place in Poland during the 2010s and early 2020s can be described as a series of temporal disruptions: the repeated staking of claims to the public sphere and citizenship rights that have yet to be conceded. The main tool employed by the diverse groups of protesters was confession. These confessions, born out of suppression and oppression, constitute acts of refusal: of the post-socialist politics of austerity; of the second-class citizenship status afforded to people with disabilities and their carers; and of the invisibility of disabled people within Polish society that allows injustices to be uncontested and institutionalized. The confessions emphasize pain, rage, frustration, and hopelessness and attempt to convey an embodied experience of disability and debilitation. While the confessors have not ignored the effects of living with disabilities, they are more concerned with the social marginalization and poverty that disabled people have been subjected to throughout the entire post-socialist period and (as discussed in chapter 1 and by some of the protesters) long before 1989. While personal and specific, these confessions constitute a collective public testimony to the maltreatment of the disabled population and their carers. This Polish disability confessional culture has not only disrupted the decorum of what can be publicly debated about bodies, suffering, and state violence, but has also set new terms for disabled self-representation and introduced new ways of discussing disability in Poland.

The narratives I analyze in this chapter that provide diverse and detailed firsthand accounts of taking care of a disabled child expand what I have designated the archive of violent intimacy (see chapter 2). Unlike published texts by fiction writers and journalists, these confessions call for the state to introduce a more robust set of disability policies, including an increase in state benefits, and thereby dismantle violent intimacy. But the cultural role of these confessions is not limited to the immediate political demands they make: of equal importance is how they shape knowledge about the daily minutiae of living with disability and providing care. In other words, this form of raw storytelling by carers and care recipients is a crucial component in expanding what we know about disability. It is also highly significant *how* society acquires this knowledge; the nondisabled majority were forced to listen to the disabled people and carers occupying Parliament, on the streets of Poland, and in online spaces.

While Polish disability confessional culture is marked by intense anger and frustration, the understandings of disability and idioms that participants employ are diverse and often contradictory. Such inconsistency reveals a fractured complexity: a Polish disability rights arena characterized by competing meanings of disability.[127] This fracturing of the disability rights movement is a major topic in my next and final chapter, in which I investigate the autistic and neurodivergent narratives produced in the 2010s and early 2020s and their uneasy and fraught relationships with disability. By examining autistic narratives authored by both autistic and nonautistic subjects, including parents, journalists, and experts, this chapter will continue my reflection on the ways in which disability and autistic epistemologies are created, and the role of family, and familial caregivers in particular, within the Polish cultural imaginary.

4 AUTISTIC DISAVOWALS

Since the mid-2010s, Poland has witnessed a proliferation of increasingly popular autism narratives. Accounts by caregivers, doctors, therapists, lawyers, advocates and, to a far lesser degree, autistic people themselves and their advocates have appeared in widely circulated newspapers, fashion magazines, medical journals, self-help books, and nonfiction texts by both mainstream and small independent publishers. There has also been a rush to translate—particularly from English—manuals, memoirs, and self-help books that discuss the autism spectrum, such as Steve Silberman's *Neurotribes*, Jenara Nerenberg's *Divergent Mind*, Naoki Higashida's *The Reason I Jump*, Donna Williams's *Nobody Nowhere*, and Simon Baron-Cohen's *The Pattern Seekers*.[1] These Polish autism narratives do not conform to a particular standard: While many are trauma-centered and focus on stories of normalization, struggles for a cure, and prevention, others focus on identity, emancipation, and the sense of self-understanding that can result from diagnosis. In this chapter I focus on the memoirs of two autistic women and one nonbinary subject, a nonfiction book by Jacek Hołub, and the position statements of a number of NGOs. Given the multitude of literary, journalistic, and academic examples to draw upon, this may appear to be a small sample to work with, yet it is representative of the major trends within autism narratives in contemporary Poland.

A tension exists between this and the previous chapters: Many autism narratives ignore or distance themselves from the category of disability. As I will explore, these texts actively disavow disability. In fact, as some speak of neurodivergence rather than autism, they strive for a double disavowal. Following the meditation on trans and mad studies by Cameron Awkward-Rich in his book *The Terrible We*, I not only trace but also think with these disavowals.[2] This enables me to identify how social actors understand disability, and why they would choose neurodivergence over autism as an identity category. The Polish autism narratives I analyze in this chapter do not disrupt or alter social understandings of disability in any meaningful way. Rather, in their unwillingness to engage with disability, they situate themselves alongside disability; unwilling to belong, they have no interest in disrupting the genre of disability narratives. Just as this chapter traces the performance of standing or sitting apart from disability, it stands apart from the previous three chapters while remaining focused on one of the principal themes of this book: the family. The distinct approach of this chapter demonstrates that, rather than fostering coherence and consensus, chronicles of disability and autism are often rife with contradictions, polyphonies, and divergence.

Therefore, it is the issue of disavowal that sits at the center of this chapter. Awkward-Rich has described disavowal as "premised on recognition; precisely by attempting to disavow an attachment, the attachment is foregrounded, sticks around."[3] My analysis of Polish autism narratives and statements by various institutional actors confirms this: By distancing themselves from disability, many of these narratives are haunted by the category. However, my interest lies not in establishing this connection or questioning the wisdom of adopting this strategy in autism narratives, especially memoiristic texts. Rather, I aim to address how and why these disavowals are performed, and what they provide. This is not the only form of disavowal investigated in this chapter: I also explore the ways in which families disavow autism, and how, in return, autistic self-advocates disavow families. In other words, I trace multiple and complex disavowals, which, taken together, show autism to be a contested condition, with meanings and knowledge that are no longer solely determined by caregivers and medical professionals, but shaped by autistic subjects themselves.

First, I address how the authors of the contemporary Polish autism narratives I analyze—though originating from various literary genres and told by diverse social actors with dissimilar aims—distance themselves from the category of disability. In other words, rather than seeking a coalition with disability, these authors question the very definition of disability and its relationship with autism.

Second, I demonstrate that these autism narratives—whether emancipatory from or hostile to the very condition, diagnosis, and experience of autism—form an assemblage of conflicting stories about family. In *War on Autism*, Canadian disability studies scholar Anne McGuire claims that autism is understood in contemporary Anglophone narratives as a form of "cultural crisis."[4] While my analysis supports her thesis, I will show that these narratives also reveal other crises, particularly those relating to family and society in contemporary Poland. In chapter 2, I documented how families approach disability as a disruption of the normative life trajectory; in a sense, by exploring how families rather than disability are responsible for these crises, this chapter forms a response. Thus, my emphasis rests on how autism narratives reveal the ways in which family becomes the primary site of the violence and crisis experienced by an autistic subject. To return to my discussion in the introduction, it is family that disrupts disabled and autistic lives.

In this chapter I engage with a wide range of texts, but my main corpus consists of three memoirs: Dorota Kotas's *Cukry* (*Sugars*, 2021), Ewa Furgał's *Dziewczyna w spektrum* (*Girl on the Spectrum*, 2022), and Karolina Dec's *Aspergerka, czyli życie na obcej planecie* (*The Asperger Woman, or Life on a Distant Planet*, 2020). As a backdrop for these, I also analyze a nonfiction work on autistic children and children with ADHD, *Niegrzeczne: historie dzieci z ADHD, autyzmem i zespołem Aspergera* (*Rude: Stories of Children with ADHD, Autism, and Asperger's Syndrome*, 2020) by Jacek Hołub, whose other book, *Hoping My Child Dies Before I Do*, featured in chapter 2. I also reference articles from various newspapers and magazines, including online periodicals, as well as the websites of leading autism advocacy NGOs and autistic self-help books. As stated, the texts I have selected—despite unavoidable omissions—represent some of the most popular but also novel strands of autism discourse in Poland.[5]

The authors of the three memoirs I explore do not long for a world without autism, nor do they depict the condition as a threat to the individual, family, and society, or as a terrorist or kidnapper of an innocent child. In the next section, I will address texts that approach autism as all of the above. Rather than a reproduction of recognizable tropes, this set of familiar stories serves as a background against which counternarratives complicate, nuance, and disavow hostile understandings of autism. Some of these counternarratives, especially those by Dorota Kotas and Ewa Furgał, have been discussed in the mainstream media and received praise from beyond the circles of autistic advocacy. Their contribution to autism discourses in Poland lies not only in their commitment to autism as an identitarian category and a form of difference rather than deviance or disability, but also their focus on gender and the ways in which experiences of autism and gender intersect. Consequently, standing in opposition to the autistic child in need of cure at the center of the global autism spectrum narrative, a cultural figure has emerged within this particular discourse over recent years: the autistic woman, a self-advocate who chooses autism as both a personal and political identity. This autistic woman is, retrospectively, an undetected autistic child finding diagnostic respite in later life and seeking out other autistic women. Significantly, this woman is not disabled but neurodivergent and well versed in autism and neurodiversity discourses. This leads me to the final observation I will make in this introduction: Some of the most visible advocates shaping popular autism discourses in Poland are women and nonbinary subjects.

Fear and a Longing for Normalcy

The customary, prototypical autism narrative tends to go as follows: Autism is, as yet, an incurable condition that threatens the individual, family, and society and is deeply undesirable to virtually everyone, including parents, educators, doctors, therapists, governments, and, as discussed by McGuire in *War on Autism*, the NGOs that raise funds for autism research and autistic families.[6] While waiting for a scientific method of eradication, this narrative calls for the condition to be remediated through intensive therapies. Joanna Grochowska, vice-director of Synapsis, one of the leading Polish NGOs addressing autism, has stated that "our experiences show that 10%–15% of early diagnosed children can achieve a condition equal to being cured, and among the remaining children it is possible to minimize the consequences of this disability."[7] This claim is prominently displayed on the website of Badabada, a private initiative providing questionnaires and checklists to diagnose children with autism as early as possible. Next to Grochowska's statement is a claim by Agata Bujnik, director of Badabada's diagnostic team, that early diagnosis helps "get the child closer to the normative developmental trajectory."[8] The mainstream Polish narrative on autism is indistinguishable here from the anglophone approach analyzed by McGuire in *War on Autism*: The aim of Polish NGOs specializing in autism, like their Anglophone counterparts, is clearly eradication. In this context, referring to autism as a disability only strengthens this cultural imperative.

The relationship between autism and disability is fraught with tension. Polish NGOs working on autism appear unsure whether to make the connection. In 2022 and 2023, the Prodeste Foundation opened its philosophy statement by claiming that "autism is a divergent form of human development or a divergent way of establishing a relationship with the environment."[9] They also claimed to follow "the social concept of disability, understood as the result of a relationship between an individual and an inaccessible environment."[10] Disability studies activists and scholars know that the definition of the social model of disability the Prodeste Foundation alluded to here is inaccurate. The British social model of disability emphasizes that physically impaired people are disabled by society,[11] and thus it has a clear political character that was absent from the foundation's formulation.[12] The Prodeste website added that "disability is caused, predominantly, by social and economic barriers and not by an individual."[13]

Prodeste provided answers to several questions, including "What is autism?," "What are the symptoms of autism?," "Is it possible to cure autism?," and "Is autism a disability?" Their response to the latter question was that "autism in itself is not a disability. However, autistic people are, sometimes, disabled. Around 35% of the autistic population is diagnosed with intellectual disability." Prodeste then went on to list conditions that can occur with autism, such as Down syndrome, while making it clear that these *other* conditions are disabilities. Thus, according to this NGO, only the co-occurrence of autism and another condition could render a person with autism disabled, and disability cannot be understood as a "divergent form of human development." The foundation concluded its response to the disability issue with a sentence intended to reassure the reader: "Many people with autism live in a way which has nothing to do with disability."[14] Thus, the autistic way of life is not a disabled way of life, and while in this statement the Prodeste Foundation does not entirely separate autism and disability, they do hold any connection between the two at arm's length. Similarly, the aforementioned Synapsis Foundation statement describes autism as "a part of one's identity": "It is not an illness. It is a divergent way of thinking and relating to the world. Sometimes it can lead to disability because it can cause serious problems in life and limit one's independent coping with everyday challenges."[15]

In the framing that has been employed by these foundations, which are representative of other Polish NGOs, disability equates to undefined serious problems and a lack of independence; as part of one's identity, autism has nothing to do with disability. These attempts to disconnect autism from disability testify to a cultural fear of being categorized as disabled. This strategy may also have commercial benefits: Parents, the main recipients of the services provided, are unlikely to want the lives of their children associated with disability.

Whether intentionally or not, the narratives deployed by these foundations present us with an economy of disability and autism in which a sense of scale and hierarchy are at play: Disability can result from too much autism, an excess that presents when the condition is paired with "something else," such as Down syndrome or a lack of self-reliance, and it is this nonnormative autism that cannot easily be "repaired." Believing that the only way to de-otherize autism is to otherize disability, the attempts by these foundations to destigmatize the former inevitably stigmatize the latter. However, as it is predominantly referred to in the context of problems and difficulties, disability disrupts the narrative of divergent development.

While decoupling disability and autism, these NGOs do medicalize people on the autism spectrum. The Synapsis Foundation offers a wide range of therapeutic services, including behavioral therapy, plus training for autism experts and caregivers. In 2022 and 2023, their website informed visitors of their goals. The first of their eight goals was to "strengthen, promote and support the development of familial and societal bonds,"[16] the second "to support the subjectivity and dignity of autistic subjects and families,"[17] and the third was "strengthening, promoting and supporting kinship and communal bonds."[18] It is rather striking that the focus of all these priorities is embedding and strengthening the relationships of autistic subjects within their families and wider communities. Once again demonstrating how autism, like disability, operates within the familial context in Poland, the subjectivity of an autistic person is only addressed within the family unit. While not necessarily advocating for autistic people, the Synapsis Foundation undeniably advocates for families raising autistic children.

At the same time, as has become increasingly clear while reading the discussion of the leading Polish NGOs working on autism and offering support to families raising children with autism, such as the Podeste Foundation and the Synapsis Foundation, the information on their websites regarding autism has changed over the past few years while I was working on this book. These modifications speak, at least partially, to the evolving discourses on autism in Polish society.

In *Rude: Stories of Children with ADHD, Autism, and Asperger's Syndrome*, Jacek Hołub performs a similar allyship with caregivers and presents an equally ambiguous relationship with disability. Although he makes few explicit connections between disability and autism, the language of prevention, cure, and normalization on which he relies echoes the medicalized jargon used in relation to disability. The book was first published in 2020, two years after Hołub's first work of nonfiction, *Hoping My Child Dies Before I Do*, and follows the same format, presenting narratives by mothers, teachers, doctors, fathers, and one teenager with autism: No adults with autism are included. Having conducted his interviews, Hołub removed his questions and comments and restructured the words of his interviewees. There are no interviews with self-advocates, disability rights activists, or people who do not view autism as a curse, and, reflecting an approach to autism as a condition that primarily affects families, most of the interviews were conducted with mothers. Moreover, due to the method employed and selection of interviewees, Hołub offers no critical commentary and does not expose his readers to alternative understandings of autism.

The book received mixed reviews.[19] While some critics emphasized the importance of the topic itself, the insufficiency of state support for families raising children with autism, and the unjust treatment of autistic people in Polish society, no one addressed how the text stigmatizes and others people with autism. Criticism was aimed at the form of the text: that it was made of a few, quickly conducted interviews and did not exhaust the topic, and the fact that the protagonist of the closing interview is a psychologist, thus reinforcing the medical model of disability.[20] I have been unable to locate any review that notes the many instances of violence mentioned in caregiver statements, or the absence of a representative from the disability rights movement, and a sole reviewer has lamented the fact that only one person with autism was given a platform.[21] No one has challenged the way the book strengthens the beliefs that only children have autism and that a family should not include disability. Uncritically, Hołub reminds us that, as Jennifer Fink has stated, "our very definition of the family excludes disability lineage. Our sense of what a family is—who constitutes it, what kinds of bodyminds it can hold, and, crucially, the history of whose it has held—is defined by this exclusion."[22]

At the very beginning of the book, before passing the voice to his interviewees, Hołub declares autism to be a threatening individual condition. In his preface, Hołub presents some figures and states that, while there is "no precise data on the number of children with autism," experts estimate that 1 in 100 people have autism, and numbers are rapidly increasing. From this, he concludes that 384,000 people in Poland have this "problem."[23] Hołub's chosen framework is quite telling of his approach to autism: Located in individuals, autism is increasing, which is a problem, though for whom remains unspecified. The majority of maternal accounts exhibit the same narrative structure: The mothers begin with descriptions of a small child displaying "weird" behaviors or with distressing accounts of their knowledge that the fetus was abnormal, as, for example, "he was wriggling and kicking all the time."[24] This narrative structure corresponds with Hołub's prelude: Autism is located in particular individuals, and this deviance will manifest during pregnancy or infancy.

These origin stories remove autism from the realms of the political and the cultural and relegate it to the biological. They establish a maternal authority based in feelings—these stories inevitably intertwine knowledge and emotion and ultimately place nondisabled mothers at the center of autism narratives. More importantly, they reveal the ways in which maternal origin stories retrospectively produce autism. In other words, autism precedes the child, existing in a fetus that has "something wrong with it." Thus, these narratives revitalize the desire to detect autism at the fetal stage; while the possibility of termination remains unarticulated, it clearly underpins these stories. Unlike the majority of narratives that feature a fetus and a woman's body, these are not stories of fetal violation, but rather a violation of the maternal body. Their significance lies in how they evoke the anxieties and fantasies relating to reproduction, ability, and disability that fuse the intimate with the public.

In *Rude*, stories of pregnancy, birth, and early infancy are generally followed by dramatic descriptions of children's behavior for which parents have no explanation until the moment of diagnosis. As well as making attempts to understand the child and provide them with a safe future, the parents also experience the violent desire that these autistic children would not exist. One anonymous mother states that "maybe this sounds cruel, but everything would be different if Tamara were erased from our life and we had only a son—an emotionally healthy child. Our [marital] relationship would have been stronger and more stable."[25] This mother does not hope for the autism to disappear, as is often the case in such narratives; unable or unwilling to separate her daughter from autism, she imagines a life in which her daughter has been erased. The violence contained in this statement passes without comment.

Rude tells stories of shame, fear, threat, and a desire for normalcy. Afraid of the physical violence their children may commit, these mothers also fear that they will never fit in or be accepted by society. These are stories of shameful difference, of the ways in which these children's departure from the norm affects their parents and nonautistic siblings. Although Hołub individualizes autism in his preface, these accounts demonstrate its relational character. These are also stories of an overwhelming desire for normalcy: Mothers describe feelings of pride when children manage to imitate "normal" behaviors "when he can sit peacefully and manage his own emotions," and "when she does not escape from other people. . . . She sat with us at the table and behaved normally—she even talked with us."[26] Mimicry of normalcy is what parents wish for, and this, too, passes without comment.[27] Advocating for parents and their desires, *Rude* normalizes the belief that autism is a threatening, unwanted part of family life, and that the only possible parental response to a diagnosis is despair and trauma.

Clearly, Hołub is not alone in his emphasis on the caregiver perspective of the "burden" of autism. Since 2016, *Gazeta Wyborcza* (Electoral Newspaper), the most popular liberal newspaper in Poland, has published at least one "big" article a year on autism in its prestigious topical magazine, *Duży Format* (A Large Format). These texts almost unanimously center on the struggles of parenthood.[28] Although the visibility of an expanding disability rights movement and autistic self-advocates is increasing, parents remain the key "producers of the cultural response" to autism.[29] Perhaps autistic subjects are seen as "rhetorically suspect," incapable of telling their own stories and creating their own knowledge of autism.[30] In recent years, however, autistic women have started to publicly share their experiences.

Feminist Autistic Disavowals

As stated, narrators of autism in contemporary Poland strive to disidentify themselves from the category of disability, and any connections that do occur are usually in the context of medicalization and erasure. This is not where the disruptions end: The recent emergence of narratives and memoirs by autistic women has opened a new series of disability disavowals and pathologization. However, these autistic women present an oppositional knowledge to that exemplified by Hołub and the Synapsis Foundation: Rather than families being disrupted by autistic people's support needs, it is families that endanger autistic women, and autistic subjects themselves who require assistance. Driven by anger at the families and society that have subjected them to violence and stolen their voices, these texts represent a backlash against mainstream narratives and, upholding the disability rights slogan "nothing about us without us," position autistic subjects as the principal producers of autism knowledge. But the significance of these texts goes beyond the confines of the autism literature genre: While they do redefine autism, they also reveal that Polish families, especially those with an autistic child, are in crisis. Disavowing the family, they depict mothers and grandmothers in particular as preservers of unintelligible and stifling social norms that inflict violence on autistic women.

As these women are what are usually referred to as "high-functioning" self-advocates, the autistic disavowals I analyze below are driven by and characteristic of a specific group of people on the autism spectrum. However, as Ewa Furgał has discussed, the notion of "high-functioning" is complicated. Noting her suicidal thoughts, unwillingness to observe bodily hygiene, and body dysphoria, Furgał concludes that the binary division between high- and low-functioning is misleading: "Yes, I am high-functioning and my diagnosis is very often questioned. . . . Yet this 'impressively high-functioning' person harms herself while cutting her fingernails, scratches all her wounds, avoids going to the doctor, regularly forgets to take medication, and still falls asleep with her teddy bear."[31] The autistic community is diverse and includes people with little in common. The writings I analyze here are evidently authored by subjects who are verbal and possess the necessary skills to craft and publish their life narratives. These subjects also all work for a living, although some have struggled to maintain employment. Thus, the dilemma remains as to who should speak on behalf of nonverbal autistics and those unable to share their stories and experiences in a fashion that is societally acceptable and understandable. Can "low-functioning" people on the autism spectrum provide their own narratives, and would these narratives contest mainstream knowledge about autism?

However, in this section, I focus on what I would describe as an eruption of feminist autistic writing. Although not all these authors openly proclaim allegiance to feminism, the texts and statements they have published in various media are driven by feminist sensibilities and impulses. With a focus on destigmatizing the neurodivergent mind, challenging its presumed maleness, and revealing the bodily oppressions to which autistic women are subjected, feminism mostly plays out here as an aesthetic. As the primary institution in which gender roles and behaviors are enforced, family is understood as a site of anti-autistic and anti-feminist violence. Dorota Kotas has described making her decision to "give up" her family "very consciously and for my own sake."[32] In this instance, forsaking her family was an act of both life preservation and feminism.

The writings of Furgał and Kotas are both feminist and queer. As Furgał has noted, women on the autism spectrum are more likely to belong to the LGBTQ+ minority than their neurotypical peers.[33] Although she still identifies with the political category of female, Furgał has come out as nonbinary and accuses her family of enforcing not only gender rules but also the sexual norms that privilege heterosexuality. Kotas has described her mother ascribing her lesbianism to her father, using a male version of her name: "Dorek" rather than Dorota.[34] This writing embraces queerness, feminism, and autism as valid experiences, political positions, and identities, but seeks no coalition or alliance with the disability rights movement or disability itself. While not a disavowal per se, Awkward-Rich has adopted a capacious definition of the term and describes such avoidances as attempts to "disavow an attachment."[35] These authors literally skip over and do without the connection. It is important to note that the term "coalition" does not designate an undifferentiated merger between disability and autism, but, rather, as American disability studies scholar Alison Kafer has discussed, the opportunity to think about "difference, relation, and politics."[36] In this context, a coalition would involve exploring the porosity and stability of identities, the distance between these two categories. Such a coalition would not rely upon the politics of separatism but on those of affinity and curiosity.

Despite being published over twenty years ago in a vastly different cultural and historical context, the words of queer scholar José Esteban Muñoz, in his

1999 *Disidentifications*, still resonate: "Although various processes of identification are fraught, those subjects who are hailed by more than one minority identity component have an especially arduous time of it.... Minority identifications are often neglectful or antagonistic to other minoritarian positionalities. This is as true of different theoretical paradigms as it is of everyday ideologies."[37] An unwillingness to engage with other identity categories may well result from navigating a hostile social world as subjects who are already marginalized in more than one respect. Rather than questioning and disrupting identities, the three authors in question strive for recognition of the neurodivergent identity.[38]

The possibility of a coalition with "low-functioning" autistics is also rarely addressed. Few texts examine the relationship between the neurodivergent movement and people who live with both autism and intellectual disability, and those with the more "severe" cases of autism are usually silenced in this literature. The texts I focus on in this chapter imagine the neurodivergent subject in entirely narrow terms. Perhaps, as with disability, voicing such an affinity would interfere with the authors' quest to establish a neurodivergent identity and legitimize it on a broader scale. Nevertheless, even if it allows for more precise definitions of specific experiences, this mode of conceptualizing autism and neurodivergence undoubtedly leads to a fracturing of the movement and weakens its position vis-à-vis the Polish state.

Thus, attempts to consolidate the autistic identity start with negation. In *Sugars*, Dorota Kotas declares that she is "not ill with autism, because this is not an illness. I have a divergent mind. This means that my mind operates slightly differently."[39] Ewa Furgał defines autism as a "difference, not a disorder, deficit or ailment" and approaches the autism spectrum as "a social condition, not a medical one—as a part of human identity."[40] In a Polish *Vogue* interview, "Autism Spectrum Is Not an Illness," photographer Joanna Musiał states, "Yes, I differ from other people, because I experience the world differently and more intensely.... I will never change my divergent sensibility."[41] In these and other accounts, illness serves as a reference to be disputed. Autism is an identity, a diverging manner of relating to the world, a form of difference. And, although autism is recognized as an identity, identity-first language rarely appears in these texts: The preferred phrases are "women with autism," or "women on the autism spectrum." Perhaps "autistic person" too closely echoes the frequently used phrase "disabled person." In Poland, in general, a people-first language is viewed as more empowering. Ewa Furgał is an exception here: At times she appears to use "disability" or "disabled" as synonyms of "autism" and "autistic," and she interchangeably deploys identity-first and people-first language, without commenting on her linguistic and ideological choices. Overall, these self-advocates orient their definitions of autism toward dispelling an association with illness and establishing it as a form of difference. However, it is very apparent that these definitions remain unstable and in statu nascendi. As new, destigmatizing definitions are sought and formulated, autism is in the process of retelling itself.

Diagnosis and the Retelling of Identities

This retelling of autism requires a retelling of one's identity and life. Most of these authors, and the women who tend to feature in media articles on the subject, received their diagnosis as adults. Diagnosis is a story in and of itself: the initial prompting to search for answers, the form of the diagnostic process, and the effect of receiving—or not receiving—this confirmation. For Dorota Kotas it was a story of surprise and "great relief."[42] Ewa Furgał shares not only her own story of becoming known to herself and others as an autistic subject, but also the history of autism as an official medical condition. Containing a multitude of tales, diagnosis also triggers new stories: of a childhood, an adolescence, and an adult life now viewed from the perspective of a recognized autistic subject. It can even inaugurate a story: "Until the moment of receiving a diagnosis," Furgał felt she "did not have a coherent story about myself."[43] Diagnosis filled the cracks and gaps: "There were different things that happened in my life that I understood as a reason for my social maladjustment. However, I could not make a whole picture out of them. . . . Only the Asperger's syndrome diagnosis allowed me to connect the dots. Diagnosis enabled me to make my story whole and find peace."[44]

In most narratives of autism, diagnosis often operates by disrupting a family's life and trajectory: an explanation for the child's behavior, unwanted and unexpected, shatters the parents and rewrites their lives in undesirable ways. Thus, attempts at cure are also attempts to return to normality. In these three texts by adult autistic women, diagnosis offers continuity and coherence rather than disruption. As both a point of departure and a condition of possibility, it enables these stories to be written. In what follows I describe and analyze how Kotas, Furgał, and Dec discuss diagnosis in relation to truth, temporality, class, and medical power.

Although the autism diagnosis is vulnerable to historical and medical developments—as proven, for example, by the emergence and then disappearance of Asperger's syndrome as a separate condition in DSM—many autistic subjects perceive it as the long-awaited truth of their identity. In the recent eruption of writing by feminist autistic self-advocates, diagnosis functions as an individualizing feature. In the introduction to *Sugars*, by discussing the moment she received her autism diagnosis and what it meant to her, Kotas makes this the lens through which one reads the chapters that follow. As "a person with a diagnosis," Kotas believes that writing about her "singular experience is the best thing I can do. It is my truth and my perspective."[45]

Kotas goes on to explain that, rather than presenting the information about autism and its symptoms that can be found in "expert literature," all she has "to offer" is herself.[46] This is her writing strategy: embedding autism within the personal and intimate and turning the authorial "I" into a narrative. In his article "Body Solitaire: The Singular Subject of Disability Autobiography," David T. Mitchell discusses how an emphasis on the self can result in the rejection of "disability as communal identity" and "reif[y] the longstanding association of disability with social isolation."[47] This association becomes even more pronounced in the context of autism. Anticipating such criticism, Kotas states that, while she knows she might find herself under attack for focusing on herself too much, for centering her own experience—in other words, for being *too* autistic—she had to write this book because "I lack stories about people like myself."[48] Kotas goes on to condemn a mainstream readership that may not deem her experiences worthy of writing and reading: "A singular perspective—this for me constitutes the meaning of writing. . . . If I were a man, no one would hold this against me. I could even write six volumes about my life, one entirely devoted to shitting in the forest. People would be in awe of my honesty."[49] While this alludes to the work of Norwegian writer Karl Ove Knausgård, which is immensely popular in Poland, "shitting in the forest" may also refer to M. Remi Yergeau's discussion of the autistic shitting trope.[50] If this is the case, Kotas is actively and creatively working against the public notion that autism involves a lack of consciousness in regard to rhetoricity and modes of engagement.

This critique of men's writing and defense of the focus on her own experiences reminds us of the vulnerability of both women's and autistic people's stories. Due to its mutability, diagnosis as a story is particularly vulnerable and can engender disbelief. Kotas recalls people responding to her diagnosis by incredulously asking whether she had only been autistic for a month.[51] This testifies to the peculiar temporality of autism: For how long has one been autistic, and what counts as its beginning? The structure of Kotas's book, starting with the diagnosis she received at the point of publishing *Sugars* in 2021 and returning to her childhood in the first chapter, suggests that there is no story of her life without autism.

Similarly to Kotas, Ewa Furgał opens her book on a diagnosis and reflection on the temporality of autism: "I was not a girl on the spectrum until I was thirty-six years old. I mean, I was, but unofficially. Officially, in the beginning, I was an exceptionally intelligent child, then a nervous child, and then just a girl with depression."[52] These two short sentences, depicting how people's perception of her changed and the names and labels she was given evolved, succinctly describe the leitmotiv of the entire text: the long-standing lack of medical interest in nonnormative girls and women, their consequent exclusion from a diagnosis of autism, and the resulting misdiagnoses and mistreatment. Having met a man with Asperger's, Furgał self-diagnosed a few years before her own official recognition as a woman with this syndrome: "I got angry then that I was overlooked, cheated by the system, that once again male experience was seen as representative of the entire society."[53]

Since the 1970s, disability activists and allies in the anglophone world have perceived disability as a result of social oppression and exclusion and thus concentrated on the demedicalization and depathologization of disability.[54] What Furgał is advocating here follows and diverges from this struggle: She believes that society, and the medical world in particular, has set obstacles in place that prevent women and girls—and nonbinary subjects such as Furgał—from receiving the correct diagnosis. However, by emphasizing the importance of medical diagnosis, she appears to (albeit grudgingly) endorse the medical expertise rejected by many anglophone disabled activists. This paradoxical approach to medical knowledge perfectly illustrates the tangled relationship between disability and autism.

From Furgał's viewpoint, it is primarily a widespread disbelief in women's self-diagnosis that strengthens the importance of medical diagnosis. In other words, it is the societal failure to acknowledge women and girls as agents capable of naming and determining the character of their own experiences that enforces medical power: "Women do not believe in themselves; they doubt their own feelings and opinions. It is hard to believe in yourself when your self-diagnosis is questioned by others."[55] Any woman wishing to access support and be understood by others is required by society to secure medical confirmation. Therefore, rather than affirming the medical model of autism, advocating for the right to medical diagnosis is a complex negotiation of medical and social powers.

In the prologue, Furgał describes her hope that *Girl on the Spectrum* will help "girls on the autism spectrum; I want them to feel less alienated in the world."[56] It is a gift to the people she thinks of as her community: misdiagnosed women who are treated by society as "madwomen." Started in 2017 as a blog project that attracted a significant number of readers, *Girl on the Spectrum* is a narrative about a collective experience of omission, exclusion, and lack of belonging, despite the individualism of the title. Furgał describes the history of diagnosis and the ways in which girls and women were excluded from this for much of the twentieth century.[57] While telling her own story, she repeatedly returns to shared experiences of women misdiagnosed or cheated by the system: "They are classified as hypochondriacs, odd ones, loners, hysterics, madwomen, angry women, oversensitive."[58] By discussing how women who "tell stories of their experiences, particularly women with disabilities, are oftentimes infantilized and accused of lying, exaggeration or hysteria" by a society that "does not treat women seriously," Furgał has created a collective memoir.[59]

Even this capacious term does not fully encapsulate *Girl on the Spectrum*. Drawing on her own experiences, Furgał also critically engages with a range of scientific publications on autism and offers advice for women and nonbinary subjects on the autism spectrum: This collective memoir is also a self-help book and critical literature review. And while autism and gender are privileged, they are considered in relation to sexuality and class. For example, elaborating on how the interweaving of her queerness and neurodivergence can problematize her romantic life, Furgał states that "sometimes I still don't know how I should behave as someone's partner. The fact that homosexual couples do not have cultural patterns to follow does not make things easier."[60] This comment reveals the divergence and uneven development of queer trajectories: While present in the anglophone world, such "cultural patterns" are still scarce in the Eastern European context. Furgał also describes how the autistic traits displayed by her mother were mistaken by her husband's parents for the results of her rural, working-class background: these included "her inability to compromise, her sharing of intimate life details, and her sometimes inappropriate dress sense." Her in-laws decided that this insolently honest "*girl from the countryside*" simply did not know how to behave.[61] Covering so many issues, this polyphonic text testifies to the commitment of various social actors and institutions to shape public understanding of autism and, in order to capture the multifaceted ways in which it impacts the lives of women and girls, the need to take an intersectional approach. In Furgał's text, autism is both an individual condition and a deeply familial and public concern.

It bears repeating that this is a collective memoir of autistic women rather than autistic people. Furgał delves into the history of autism from a female perspective and emphasizes the most popular Western theories by Kenner and Baron-Cohen, which take the societal perception of women and gender into account. They underline the need for histories of autistic women to provide "our own heroines, personality patterns, and so as not to feel ashamed of our identities." Having enjoyed "discovering that many female writers, poets and artists I adore are on the autism spectrum," Furgał acknowledges in particular Emily Dickinson and Patricia Highsmith.[62] This gesture speaks to the need to create a genealogy of autistic women artists and, returning to their comment in the preface, allows other autistic women to "feel less alienated in the world." In other words, it is an attempt to establish crip kinship, an idea I return to later in this chapter.

Furgał posits a history of autistic women as separate from the more established and well-researched history of autistic men. However, their book is not only about documenting autistic women's history; more importantly, it is about becoming a part of this history. *Girl on the Spectrum* locates itself within a history of autistic women and their writing tradition. By wishing to be a fragment of a larger history, this memoir, inspired by a decades-long experience and understanding of autism as a solitary and isolating experience, recognizes the importance of community and collective experiences.

The need of community is also brought up in Karolina Dec's book *The Asperger Woman*. Dec expresses a desire for a community of "we, the women with Asperger's" and wonders what it would have been like if her two neurotypical sisters had also had Asperger's.[63] The only self-published book in my corpus of autistic women's writing, *The Asperger Woman* attracted the attention of people on the autism spectrum and experts but has not enjoyed the same wider success as the others. Dec's status as an outsider to both medical diagnosis and the publishing world make this text, which focuses on a self-diagnosed autistic woman, worthy of discussion.

Particularly significant, and noted by a number of readers, is the fact that Dec rarely uses the word "autism": Her commitment is to the Asperger's rather than the autistic community. One reader has accused her of a lack of knowledge about autism research and the removal of Asperger's from the DSM-5 in 2013. This, combined with Dec's lack of medical diagnosis, has somewhat undermined her authority and legitimacy as an autistic person and writer.[64]

Securing an autism diagnosis can be costly. In her role as a public speaker and autistic self-advocate, Furgał addresses the fact that those over the age of eighteen must pay to undergo the diagnostic process in Poland. Due to the gender bias in childhood diagnosis, as discussed above, this has particularly affected women. However, Dec raises another aspect of diagnosis inaccessibility: class. Having unsuccessfully undergone the process twice as an adult, Dec claims that a "girl from the intelligentsia" with similar issues would be diagnosed with autism. Not only does Dec come from a family of blue-collar workers, but her father abused alcohol: As a girl "from a pathological family," Dec alleges, she was always more likely to be diagnosed with "ACA syndrome or a personality disorder."[65]

Claiming that fair treatment and an Asperger's diagnosis are only available "to *the better ones*," Dec describes people "like me" occupying "a strictly defined place in society."[66] This is the only text I have found that openly discusses the possibility that securing a diagnosis in contemporary Poland may depend on one's social and economic background. Dec suggests that only some people are believed deserving of a diagnosis of autism or Asperger's: Those deemed unworthy will receive a "worse" diagnosis, such as a personality disorder. By introducing a hierarchy of diagnoses, Dec shows that diagnosis may operate as a stratification tool, dividing autistic populations into "better" and "worse."

As I discuss elsewhere in this book, disability is interwoven with poverty in contemporary Poland, with many families who live with autism experiencing financial deprivation and abandonment by the state. Yet the public image of a person with Asperger's syndrome is often that of a creative, independent woman, perhaps an artist, activist, or doctor. Having featured many articles about native and foreign neurodivergent women since 2021, the online version of Polish *Vogue* is particularly invested in spreading this classist representation of neurodivergence. Like many other media outlets, *Vogue* has little interest in providing space for autistic people who are unlikely to hail the benefits they have gained from their condition. In what could be interpreted as a response to such representations, Dec presents a manifesto for those she terms the "doubly harmed": those excluded from medical diagnosis and born into families deprived of financial and cultural capital. "Not only are we deprived of good opportunities," she writes, "and only sometimes are we admitted into low-paying jobs, but we are also denied real diagnosis because we are hard cases. Apparently, if someone had an extremely difficult childhood and life conditions . . . , then s/he cannot receive a decent diagnosis, even if the majority of our traits testify to autism spectrum or Asperger's syndrome."[67] In *Sugars*, Dorota Kotas describes some people believing that she had received a diagnosis because she knew how to respond to the doctor's questions, thus framing diagnosis as a matter of expertise in test taking.[68] Dec is making a different claim here: that medical diagnosis is not a question of knowledge but family background and, therefore, determined from birth. Thus, medical diagnosis is a form of gatekeeping.

In the fragment above, Dec displays a great desire for a "real" and "decent" diagnosis. Only at the end of *The Asperger Woman* does she reveal that both her attempts to secure official diagnosis were unsuccessful. This is likely to be a strategic decision: Disclosing the fact earlier may have led to readers questioning her legitimacy. In fact, demonstrating that ultimately she was unable to convince at least some readers of her autistic status, Dec was criticized for not revealing her lack of diagnosis earlier. This lack of trust in self-diagnosis also underlines the Polish autistic community's investment in medical diagnosis. One reviewer, while welcoming the tips shared by Dec, advises caution due to her lack of medical recognition. This investment in medical acknowledgment not only makes it difficult for self-diagnosed autistic people to establish legitimacy, but it also generates another layer of divisions within autistic communities.

Disavowing Family, Looking for Crip Kinship

While family is at the center of most autism narratives, the meanings attributed to this institution are competing and conflicting. The families in *Rude* are under threat: In a state of crisis due to the disruption of autism and abandoned by the state, they seek cure and rehabilitation for their autistic children, rapidly depleting their financial and emotional resources. A family disavowing autism is the standard story, a global narrative of which *Rude* and the other examples I have provided are local reiterations. Here I examine a different story, one in which family is the destroyer of a neurodivergent subject, an ally not of the autistic child but neurotypical society. This oppressive institution enforces gender and sexual norms that violate boundaries, ignore needs, and make love and pride conditional on a child ceasing to be autistic. These neurodivergent Polish women posit family as the ardent advocate of a normality that, as discussed earlier, is closely identified with Catholic doctrine. These narratives, ultimately, disavow family.

However, another aspect of these stories of family is concerned with a lineage of autism and crip kinship. Kotas, Furgał, and Dec all approach autism as a family legacy: They search for autistic symptoms in the personalities and behaviors of their parents and, in many ways, find themselves reflected there. The family that rejected and was often ashamed of these women simultaneously represents the origin of their autism. Nevertheless, while families cannot be written out of these stories, the crip kinship I refer to in this section is yet to be attained. Alexander Kondakov, a researcher based in Ireland, has defined crip kinship as a relationship outside institutionalized interactions that emphasizes the interdependence of people.[69] By expanding beyond blood or legally recognized ties and subverting traditional family structures, the idea of crip kinship echoes queer kinship.[70] It emphasizes mutual support and care. In these three texts, crip kinship is not necessarily imagined outside family ties and to a certain extent overlaps with these, but it is also imagined across time and space. Crip kinship connects readers and authors and a community of autistic women. In these narratives, a family-based crip kinship is envisioned and gestured toward, but not yet realized.

In Kotas's *Sugars*, home is a site of abuse, misunderstanding and exclusion rather than a place of nourishment. "Home was the most difficult for me," she writes. "It was the worst time ever. When I lived with my parents, I thought I was too weak to survive."[71] In many ways, *Sugars* constitutes a chronicle of abuse: "I was constantly laughed at. . . . [I was told that] I looked as if I wanted to murder someone. With a face like this I will never find friends because people will be afraid to approach me; looking at me is a huge displeasure . . . and on top of everything I make myself ugly."[72] Kotas had a particularly difficult relationship with her mother, who "has never apologized for anything she has done to me and she has never praised me for anything."[73] Kotas describes her mother beating her, withholding food for two days when Kotas refused to eat meat, and killing her pet. Perhaps jealous of the love and care Kotas bestowed on her animal companions, her mother gave one of her cats away and appears to have poisoned another.

Sugars has over 220 reviews on the popular Polish reader review website Lubimy Czytać (We Like to Read).[74] While most are positive, even enthusiastic, some readers felt there were too many distressing details about Kotas's childhood. One noted: "It might be surprising that the author is not interested at all in other people's opinions and drags out memories and experiences from her home and difficult childhood." Another was unconvinced by parts of the book that were "almost like airing dirty laundry in public."[75] According to these readers, writing about intimate and difficult experiences constitutes a breach of decorum and shows a disregard for the opinions of others. I would argue that to a certain extent these and other similar reactions testify to a cultural anxiety about the way Kotas describes familial relations and, in particular, maternal abuse: This writing transgresses Polish cultural and social norms, according to which family is the most valued form of sociality.

In *Sugars*, Kotas herself states that she "cannot find a clear boundary between what can be said and what is too private to be said."[76] She relates that Ewa Furgał once pointed out to her how saying too much in an autistic context is often labeled as "oversharing."[77] But can one overshare details in autobiographical writing? Why is it the parts about family and the abuse Kotas suffered that are labeled "too much"? And can autobiographical writing ever be motivated by anything but an impulse to overshare? In other words, does oversharing constitute an autistic or an autobiographical mode of writing? Or perhaps "oversharing" applies to all autobiographical writing; perhaps there is no other way of crafting an autobiographical text. Perhaps every autobiographical text is at least a little autistic.

Classified as nonfiction by the publisher and as autobiography by Kotas, *Sugars* promises readers authenticity. And yet the fulfillment of this promise and the autobiographical pact causes unease in some readers.[78] *Rude* did not encounter such criticism: Those who describe a child's autism destroying family life are not accused of inappropriately thrusting private matters into the public realm. This discrepancy epitomizes the normalization of narratives that accuse autism or disability in general of destroying families. Disavowing autism is normalized; disavowing family provokes discomfort.

Spatially framing her queer and autistic experiences, Kotas also criticizes Garwolin, the small town in which she was born and raised, and its small-town mentality, characterized as a commitment to Catholicism, normality, and an undefined "real" Polishness that has shaped her family. Since the early 2000s, queer theorists have deconstructed the urban and rural binary and revealed that the complex assemblage of relations in a small town cannot be reduced to a monolithic society.[79] However, Kotas resists this reclaiming of rural spaces, and *Sugars* fits neatly within the narrative of a queer person who moves from a hostile, backward, intolerant and deeply Catholic small town to the freedom, safety, and anonymity that a nonnormative subject can find in the capital, Warsaw. A place where "hetero-familial cultures" thrive,[80] Kotas claims that the most popular form of entertainment in Garwolin is the annual pilgrimage to the Jasna Góra Monastery in Częstochowa.[81] A Catholic priest who visited the family at this time attributed Kotas's condition to the "dangerous influences of Eastern religions" and advised that they pay a stipend for a dedicated Mass.[82] For Kotas, Catholicism is inextricably linked with oppression, regression, and the violence she experienced as a child. Her grandmother, who lived in the family home for some time, took on the role of religious educator and gifted Kotas a wooden figure of the crucified Jesus for her eighteenth birthday,[83] and, believing that Kotas and her queer friends had been possessed by Satan, sent text messages urging her to "return to God and save your soul."[84] For Kotas, leaving her family was explicitly interlinked with leaving Catholicism and Garwolin: As the small town was an unlivable location and the family an unbearable set of attachments, both had to be abandoned.

Having been raised in an inherently violent family, Kotas has never wanted children of her own for fear of causing them damage, "even unintentionally."[85] Family destroys and oppresses. It is also, though, a source of autism: "Mother told me that I'm just like my father. To a great extent that was true. We were the same. We didn't look people in the eye and we were interested solely in animals. We didn't know what others who spoke to us thought or what we should do with that. [We are both] unsociable, inflexible, oversensitive, not very kind, and untamable."[86] This acknowledgment of her father's legacy gestures toward crip kinship. While Kotas's mother is almost omnipresent in *Sugars*, her father appears only intermittently, sending her strange text messages and occasionally visiting her in Warsaw to carry out repairs on her home. He rarely defended her from maternal violence and was often absent, seeking companionship from animals. While the bond with her mother and the rest of family is entirely severed, that between Kotas and her father survives, and, although it remains unspoken, this appears to be an autistic kinship, a less oppressive legacy that enables this relationship to continue.

Crip kinship in *Sugars* is not restricted to the family. Having received a prominent literary award for her debut novel a few years earlier,[87] Kotas asks her readers, "Is this book better than the first one?? Please, tell me. You can mark here: yes/no. I will check the answer when I sign your copy."[88] First and foremost, as autistic subjects are often characterized as lacking a sense of humor, this comment is amusing. Second, as Kotas—who believes reading to be "the best kind of social meeting"—establishes her own mode of engagement with readers, some of whom are likely to be neuroatypical, it demonstrates a clear interest in how the text is received.[89] For Kotas, writing constitutes a way to forge connections (crip kinship) with others.

While in *Girl on the Spectrum* there are far fewer details about her upbringing, Furgał—not unlike Kotas and Dec—also depicts home as a place of misunderstanding and coercion. A smart child who learned to read at an early age, she recalls that "my unique skills did not matter; I was not the way I was supposed to be and thus I had to be repaired."[90] Because autistic children, even if not officially identified as such, are seen as *broken*, the primary function of the family as depicted in these texts is to cure them and enforce their compliance to social norms. As I have indicated above, the family is acting on behalf of society and, oftentimes, the Catholic Church; it very rarely acts on behalf of a child. According to her family, what particularly needed to be repaired in Furgał's case was her physical appearance, which did not meet gender norms. In *Girl on the Spectrum*, home is a place of bodily oppression.

Early in the text, Furgał comes out as a nonbinary person who was socialized as a woman. Later, she discusses always feeling like a boy, "but a different boy than the other ones. I wanted to have the shortest possible hair, play with trains and wear boys' clothes. I didn't want to be a boy; I felt I already was one, but everyone treated me as if I were a girl, which was a great source of frustration and anxiety. My gender expression was contested by my family."[91] Furgał attempted to resist the endeavors by her mother and, most importantly, her grandmother to make her "look girlish" and wear dresses.[92] Her father and grandfather, who are both depicted as autistic subjects, did not participate in these struggles: It is the women of the family who are most invested in the upholding of social norms and patriarchy. Furgał lived with her grandparents for a period of time, during which her grandmother acted as primary caregiver. Furgał describes her as "the most important and the most intense figure of my childhood. She explained the world to me, showed me important places, created the tastes and smells which are still a part of my life."[93] But, apart from this mentoring and guiding role, her grandmother was also the person who treated her bowel issues with regular enemas; oversaw—literally—her hygiene practices, including showers; fought to feminize her appearance; and protested when she played football. Her grandmother, in other words, violated her boundaries and subjected her to violence in the guise of daily tasks and care.

As is clear, grandmothers have an important role in the texts by Furgał and Kotas. Their families are not nuclear but extended, with the grandmother often assuming the position of authority. In many ways, this familial structure emphasizes the hierarchy and privileged status of elders but also speaks to the daily realities of the many Polish families who cannot afford to live apart or who need the older generation to help raise their children. The combination of economic, social, and cultural factors that facilitate these multigenerational homes has the knock-on effect of enforcing and strengthening patriarchal and religious norms.

Demonstrating the ways in which gender, queer, and autism experiences are inseparable and coconstitutive, it is difficult if not impossible to determine which of the practices insisted upon by her grandmother were intended to eradicate autistic traits and which were meant to inhibit Furgał's gender expression. Describing gender nonconformity in autistic populations and sensory and bodily reactions and experiences that may be motivated by autism or gender identity, Furgał does not demarcate these identities and experiences but emphasizes their intersection and codynamic nature. This intersection of marginal positions makes her an "oddity" that her family cannot accept: "Only as an adult did I start to understand that as a child I received care and nourishment, but I didn't receive unconditional acceptance. I wasn't the way I was supposed to be, and this was clear from my very early years."[94] The goal of a family with an autistic child is to reproduce normality and sameness: When the child fails to comply, acceptance is withdrawn.

Like Kotas, Furgał indicates that she is reproducing an autistic sameness and gestures toward crip kinship. She identifies autistic traits in both of her parents and her grandfather. It seems that autism binds this family, yet this autistic closeness fails to make family members more intimate with or understanding of one another. Furgał noticed autistic traits in her mother far later than in her father: This familial trait is revealed slowly and gradually. Thus, it is possible to read *Girl on the Spectrum* as a story about an autistic family that does not recognize itself as such and thus attempts to make Furgał "normal." Consequently, though part of the family lineage, the unaddressed autism mistaken for oddity, the working-class background, individual characteristics, and timidity do not serve as uniting bonds or a foundation for familial identity. A larger question that stems from Furgał's memoir is how to make autism and disability not only an acknowledged part of a familial genealogy and history, but also an important element of its identity—that is, how to embrace crip kinship. Autism and disability are often hereditary, and, from this perspective, and in stark opposition to the standard caregiver account exemplified by Hołub's *Rude*, they are not a disruption of the family but rather a continuation and legacy. The mainstream narrative of autism as disruption and "the child kidnapper" conceals the deeply intimate and familial character of autism. It is likely that combatting the impulse of normalization would require the integration of autism and disability within the family and family narratives.[95]

Autism legacy is present in Dec's memoir, too, and, similar to the two other texts, traces family abuse. The author sets the tone of her family descriptions in her opening sentence: "I was born in a blue-collar family ridden with addictions and ugliness which smelled like the cheap cigarettes smoked by my unemployed father."[96] By the end of the third paragraph she has identified her father as odd, deeply unhappy, and addicted to alcohol: "Who was he? Maybe a village fool laughed at by the local community, maybe a genius . . . who has never been offered—just like me—an opportunity to develop normally, whose strengths have never been recognized and who has never been given real support."[97]

The origin of Dec's autism as well as of the despair, fear, and suffering she experienced as a child, her father was "aggressive when he drank alcohol; he was aggressive when he didn't drink alcohol."[98] Her mother was unable or unwilling to prevent his violent abuse. Although her two older, neurotypical sisters also suffered, Dec states that, "for a girl on the spectrum," this was "a double hell of unpredictability, additional sensory overload and ever-lasting fear." By describing her family as "a psychological concentration camp," Dec conveys unimaginable suffering, as well as the mechanisms underlying these two structures: a division between those in power and their subordinates, and an aim to deprive the latter of their identity and subject them to annihilation.[99] Equally importantly, this comparison expresses the normalization of ever-present and extreme violence and thus reminds us that, in the context of disability and autism, family is a site of legitimate violence.

Dec does not relate the process of recognizing herself as a person with Asperger's syndrome; her self-diagnosis is presented at the very beginning of the text and never questioned. Noting that no one in the family "cared about my needs, dreams, and desires. I was silent, invisible and transparent. I was absent," she writes.[100] "I didn't have my own place to sleep, I couldn't live in peace, I wasn't offered a feeling of safety and I didn't receive respect. My frustrated mother never showed me one bit of sympathy or kindness."[101] This is a story of loneliness and abandonment. Not only was Dec the youngest sister, she was the "odd one": "For my mother, I was a stain on her motherhood—so far unpolluted. I was a stain that could not be erased by any possible methods. The meetings with the school counselors did not help; additional activities at school did not help, and the punishments at home did not help."[102] Dec describes her selective mutism, isolation, and, despite it being "a place of horror," an unwillingness to leave home.[103] Her separateness, her unnamed autism, is an unbridgeable disruption within the family. Her parents are aware that she differs from her older sisters, yet are unwilling to help or seek support.

Like Kotas, Dec has no wish to continue her autistic lineage: "There will be no additional Aspie's planet and no additional exclusion and pain."[104] Viewing both family and wider society as irredeemable, Dec appears unable to imagine a nurturing form of crip kinship. In her text there is an obvious correlation between a family that reflects society, and the power dynamics within a family that reproduce societal power dynamics on a small scale. Like family, society will not tolerate deviance from the norm and is eager to punish and expel those who are different. Thus, for Dec, there is no place for autistic subjects to escape violence. School continued her imprisonment: "At the age of seven, I got convicted for the first time. There was no lawyer, no court and no appeal."[105] Operating according to survival of the fittest, society is not an arena in which neurodivergent people can thrive: Rather, it is a world of strict social hierarchies that cannot be transgressed by those who differ on a neurocognitive or class level. As such, it is a world without protection.

Conclusion

In this chapter I have traced complex autistic disavowals of disability in Polish accounts of autism and family. One issue that arises from this discussion is whether, reciprocally, autism is disavowed by the disability rights movement in Poland. It is difficult to provide a clear-cut answer. The mothers' movement that demanded the right to work in 2022, described in chapter three, included mothers of people on the autism spectrum and made no distinction between disability and autism. The protesters in 2018 also made no distinction. At the same time, in a 2021 article, journalist and mother of an autistic son Dorota Próchniewicz described parents of children with other kinds of disabilities and stated that autism was not a "real" disability.[106] Within the Polish Parliament, disability and autism are addressed by separate interest groups. It is highly likely that whether or not disability rights activists think of autism as a disability depends on the goal they are trying to achieve.

Narratives that seek alternative ways of conceptualizing autism and reject the portrayal of autism as a "destroyer of families" are certainly gaining traction in Poland. Ewa Furgał is a prominent public speaker, and the NGO she has established, A Girl on the Spectrum Foundation, organizes popular seminars and publishes self-help brochures and manuals for neurodivergent subjects, caregivers, and autism experts.[107] In 2023, her self-help book for neurodivergent women, *Authentic on the Spectrum*, was launched by W.A.B., a major Polish publishing house. Similarly, Dorota Kotas is not only a prolific writer but also a renowned self-advocate who collaborates with various cultural institutions on projects relating to autism.[108] In 2024, popular writer Katarzyna Michalczak published a nonfiction book—in which the word "disability" does not appear—describing how she has approached her ADHD diagnosis as a form of neurodiversity. The term "neurodiversity" itself has become part of journalistic jargon: For example, in 2022, *Gazeta Wyborcza*, after years of printing articles on how autism destroys families, published an interview in which psychiatrist Cezary Żechowski discusses the importance of destigmatizing ADHD and autism and framing these conditions as neurodiversity.[109]

But these stories have faced a backlash. In 2022, the popular website niepełnosprawni.pl (disabled.pl) published an article, "Autism Is a Problem," by the previously mentioned Dorota Próchniewicz, in which she criticizes narratives that understand autism as a divergent manner of development and being in the world.[110] While acknowledging the complexity of autism, and that the term "neurodivergent" may aptly describe many people, Próchniewicz speaks as the mother of a "low functioning" son whose experiences are very different:

> I cannot calmly read articles which emphasize the uniqueness of autism and discuss the unfulfilled potential of people on the autism spectrum . . . which center on the trauma that autistic people experience because they live in a world created by neurotypical people. I can no longer read articles that do not provide any details about how the world should be changed or designed differently to satisfy autistics. In this world, not only are some autistic people's problems silenced, but also the problems of neurotypical people who live with autistics are

> ignored. I'm thinking of the family members here, but not only. This is a narrow and limited perspective.[111]

First and most importantly, this text expresses frustration with the fact that caregivers are no longer the sole producers of autism and disability knowledge, and that their narratives have been rejected, nuanced or complicated by neurodivergent subjects. Even the title of Próchniewicz's article stubbornly rejects the more-nuanced narratives offered by neurodivergent subjects themselves; moreover, like Hołub's book, it emphasizes a problem located in the individual. Neurodivergent subjects, as shown in this chapter, are no longer simply the objects of caregiver knowledge, but creators. As the texts discussed illustrate, the powers that shape public discourses on autism are now more diffuse and the stakeholders more diverse. However, Próchniewicz's article is also a reminder that, as I have stated, the voices of "low-functioning" autistics are absent from this new narrative, and little effort has been made to include them or even reflect on the difficulty of doing so. In other words, contemporary Polish autistic narratives are often written by those considered not autistic enough, while those who are recognized as "truly" autistic continue to be represented by the caregivers.[112]

EPILOGUE

The End of Care

The events of 1989 have not been the only "crisis ordinariness" to be embedded in the daily life crisis of the Polish disabled population in recent history. Despite persistent references to the "unprecedented" character of the pandemic by Polish political leaders, journalists, and other public figures, the story I relate in this epilogue illustrates that, for many people with disabilities and their families in Poland, COVID-19 created little disturbance. The pandemic did not disrupt disability policies that predated March 4, 2020, the day the minister of health announced the first officially diagnosed case of COVID-19 in Poland.[1] Rather than introducing a radical shift in the lives of Polish disabled people, the pandemic and ensuing lockdowns in 2020 and 2021 only heightened and intensified the various crises that have long been a part of their experiences—namely, social abandonment, the familialization and privatization of disability and care work, and violent intimacy. Thus, the disability knowledge emerging from the material I present here disrupts dominant knowledge and demonstrates that what was viewed as profound upheaval merely constituted a continuation of the "crisis ordinariness" in which many disabled people and their caregivers exist.

On one hand, this epilogue presents a story of a crisis of care—on the other, a story of the mobilization of care. However, this mobilization, in particular the familial, is a sign of crisis, demonstrating the absence of the state structures required to undertake the organization and distribution of care. In her study of the social ethics of Victorian fiction, American scholar Thalia Schaffer has stated that "care is an action, not a feeling."[2] The various articles, reports, and statements by people with disabilities and their caregivers that I analyze in this book reveal that care in Poland during the pandemic was an action that left no room for any other action; it determined the lives of some caregivers but was not always sufficient to sustain, let alone nourish, their dependents. The narrative I craft here returns to a concept I outlined in the introduction: the fetishization of the family as it facilitates the exploitation of families with disabled members. Obviously, as I have discussed, this fetishization and exploitation pre-date 2020, but it intensified during the pandemic. In other words, the story of COVID-19 in Poland in regard to disability is one of violent intimacy, crisis ordinariness, and social abandonment: the pandemic merely served to magnify these issues.

It may come as a surprise that I open this epilogue with a discussion of residential institutions, disability, and care. Although I mentioned the institutions in chapter 2, the rest of the book focused on the familialization of disability. This does not mean that no residential institutions and nursing homes exist in Poland, but mainstream media and books usually omit discussion of this topic.[3] Moreover, the placement of disabled people, especially children, in such facilities is a social taboo and a rarity. Familialization of disability seems to be a much more widespread phenomenon than institutionalization, especially in case of disabled children. Mothers, as long as they are able, choose to take care of their disabled children at home. Residential institutions are often inhabited by the elderly and people whose families are no longer able to care for them. It is worth mentioning that the outbreak of the pandemic sparked an unprecedented discussion in the mainstream Polish media about residential institutions and the conditions prevailing in them. After analyzing institutionalization and COVID-19, I move on to examine violent intimacy and the familial experiences of disability, care, and the pandemic.

Incarceration

What COVID-19 did achieve in Poland was making the social and political issues analyzed here visible to the public. While some of the challenges relating to the raising of disabled children were discussed during the 2014 and 2018 protests, as examined in chapter 3, the COVID-19 pandemic was the first time in post-1989 Poland that both state and private residential institutions for the elderly and disabled people have been extensively discussed. According to the disability policy expert Rafał Bakalarczyk, many residential facilities in Poland at that time were accommodating around a dozen people, but there were also some with over a hundred residents.[4] While, as stated, institutionalization is not common in Poland, particularly—given the cultural imperative on providing care at home—of children with disabilities, the institutions that provide care for the elderly and adult people with disabilities in Poland began to receive unparalleled attention.

At the beginning of April 2020, barely a month into the pandemic, the office of the Polish commissioner for human rights sent an official letter to the prime minister urging that additional safety measures be initiated for those living and working in institutions for the elderly and disabled people.[5] With so many care workers testing positive for COVID-19, inhabitants in some institutions had been left entirely on their own, and the commissioner believed that the steps taken by the Ministry of Health and the "guidelines and instructions" provided by the Ministry of Family, Labor, and Social Policy were inadequate.

At the same time, dramatic reports of significantly higher death rates and a lack of basic safety equipment and personnel in these facilities started to appear in the Polish media.[6] Some of these reports included references to eugenics, echoing the confessions made by disabled people and their caretakers during the protests in 2014 and 2018.[7] By May 2020, the prosecutor's office was investigating an institution on Bobrowiecka Street in Warsaw in which many senior citizens had died of COVID-19, and where, for at least a short period of time, nursing cover had been nonexistent.[8]

The Polish public also learned that due to low rates of pay, most care workers were employed at more than one institution. Consequently, not only were institutions swiftly understaffed, but carers were unavoidably participating in spreading the virus between facilities. While reminding the public of the existence of institution residents, the pandemic brought to light a crisis within care—or, rather, as I would describe it, the end of care. This multifaceted crisis was the result of both the capitalist undervaluing of care work and a long-term paternalist resolve by the state to house people in institutions.

As the situation worsened during the spring of 2020, various officials, such as the mayor of Kalisz, a town in the Western part of Poland, made dramatic public pleas to health workers:

> I appeal to the conscience and sense of responsibility of all of those who work in the care sector: the nurses, those who work in the social work sector, and those who work in the institutions for the elderly and disabled people but are on health leave at home now. Please, stand in solidarity with those who keep working in the institutions and receive no help from you. Please, stand in solidarity with those who are elderly and need your help the most. Right now in the institution

> in Kalisz there are 30 employees. They provide care to over 160 people who live there. They work non-stop, 24/7, they have no break, they are not able to rest.[9]

The situation in Kalisz received considerable media coverage. An article published on April 7, 2020, informed the public that the 170 elderly people living at the institution were being cared for by 21 employees, 6 volunteers, and 6 soldiers. By that time, 27 residents had died of COVID-19, and over 100 had tested positive.[10] As illustrated by the quote above, those who lived and worked in institutions during the pandemic often became entrapped and received little if any help from the state. It is significant that appeals such as this were made to the public and their "sense of responsibility" rather than to state authorities. Later in the pandemic, in October 2020, the nuns running a Catholic care home in the village of Wierzbowice issued an appeal for volunteers: Having all succumbed to the virus, the resident disabled children had been left without carers.[11] The incidents in Kalisz and Wierzbowice were far from isolated; the Polish press presented many such accounts during the spring of 2020. An article published on OKO.press in April described the situation in 8 institutions across Poland. In the words of one employee: "There is no one to give food, change diapers. We can't hold out much longer."[12]

The Polish government responded to this conspicuous end of care in several ways. In April 2020, the minister of health, Łukasz Szumowski, described the scale of the issue as "not big" and alleged that only 20 of the 830 state institutions in Poland were encountering problems.[13] A few weeks later, Szumowski announced that two legal regulations would soon be implemented: A ban would be imposed on all visitors to residential institutions, and staff at some facilities, particularly hospitals for those infected with COVID-19, would be prohibited from working anywhere else, for which they were promised financial compensation.[14] Following this announcement, workers at some institutions walked out, leaving residents alone until the voivodeship authorities managed to organize replacement staff.[15] The minister of justice, Zbigniew Ziobro, announced that charges would be brought against health workers who refused to return to work.[16] As well as minimizing the problem and then taking prohibitive and punitive measures, the government offered financial support: Marlena Maląg, the minister of family, labor, and social policy, promised additional funds for institutions and individual financial support for people with disabilities whose rehabilitation or therapeutic services had ceased due to the pandemic.[17] This help was equivalent to $115 per month, for three months.[18]

Perceiving the state response as chaotic and inadequate, people with disabilities, their representatives, and NGO disability policy experts presented their own recommendations on how to protect people in residential care facilities at the beginning of April 2020.[19] These included constant monitoring of residents and others who accessed social services, the construction of local databases of people requiring help and the institutions providing support, and the provision of uninterrupted services to people with disabilities and the elderly.[20] Meanwhile, reports of people with disabilities suffering both in residential care and the community continued to appear. In November 2020, health workers who had been called to take an elderly patient with COVID-19 to hospital in Płock, a small town close to Warsaw, left his eight-year-old, intellectually disabled wife alone in their home. Her family only found out about the situation two days later.[21] In late 2020, reports appeared of a sixty-five-year old woman who had fled from hospital, despite being infected, because her ninety-year-old mother was completely alone in their apartment.[22] The pandemic revealed the vulnerability and precarity of both disabled people and their caregivers.

The decision in 2020 to ban visitors from residential facilities for the elderly had profound repercussions. In 2021, despite the majority of residents having received a vaccination, some institutions still remained inaccessible and were reluctant to allow residents to go for a walk or visit a nearby shop.[23] An anonymous, fully vaccinated elderly citizen in one state institution claimed that, despite the manager's claim that there was no ban on leaving, the moment someone left "the gate is closed and s/he is observed as if they were a criminal. What was the point in wasting so many vaccines if we are under conservatorship anyway?"[24] The same article noted other strict restrictions in some institutions: Inhabitants were required to inform a health worker two days in advance of their intent to leave the premises and clearly state the purpose of their journey; two days advance notice was also required for visitors; visits could not last for more than thirty minutes; and no visits could take place over the weekends. Significantly, many of the elderly citizens quoted by the media recognized the penal character of their home institutions and the fact that they were being treated like criminals.

During March 2021, people with disabilities, their allies, and disability experts demanded in an open letter to the prime minister that elderly residents, who had now been "completely deprived of the possibility of participating in social life and cut away from the world" for a year, be permitted to go outside if they wished to do so.[25] At no time during the pandemic did any state authority refer to the need to deinstitutionalize once the situation had stabilized, as the Polish disability studies scholars Zbigniew Głąb and Magdalena Kocejko discuss in an article published in 2022:

> A strategy of strengthening the institution was adopted, which, although effective in some aspects, led to a situation of unprecedented isolation of residents lasting over a year (which was not experienced by any other group in Poland,

> apart from people in the penal system). It should be noted that the situation did not change following the vaccinations of the residents of care homes, who remained in isolation for several months or even half a year after vaccination.[26]

It is clear that during the COVID-19 pandemic, and possibly afterward, residential institutions in Poland became what US-based scholar Liat Ben-Moshe has termed "carceral locales."[27] The logic adopted—segregation and coercion—did not differ from that employed by penal institutions, and government initiatives during the pandemic both isolated those who inhabited residential facilities and intensified institutionalization.[28] Activists voiced their concerns and demanded that the government initiate deinstitutionalization, but the authorities did not listen, and, as I write this in October 2024, there has been no state-led attempt to begin the process.[29] As I stated at the beginning of this epilogue, the narrative I present here relates to care and absent state structures. However, this particular story is of a state implementing a semicarceral social structure and an absence of care: It is the story of how the Polish authorities responded to a global pandemic by violating human rights and normalizing the mass incarceration of disabled people and the elderly.

Strengthening Violent Intimacy

While those living in residential facilities were held captive, disabled people and their caregivers living at home found themselves yet more abandoned by the state. In this section, I show how this further withdrawal from the sphere of care and assistance during the COVID-19 pandemic intensified violent intimacy, a notion I have developed throughout this book, particularly in chapter 2.

On March 12, 2020, the Polish government closed all schools. Initially, this measure was intended to last two weeks but was later extended. Having studied the educational situation of disabled children during the pandemic in Poland, Magdalena Kocejko has noted that despite a government regulation of March 20, 2020, to not prohibit schools from organizing therapeutic sessions or other activities for children with disabilities, these were largely unavailable.[30] In an article published on May 1, 2020, a mother with a disabled child described her life under pandemic regulations:

> In fact, very little has changed. I don't have a social life anyway. I don't have it now, I didn't have it before. The only difference is how much time we spend sitting. We sit all day long, from morning until evening, trying to go through the school material. I'm a teacher, a therapist, and a rehabilitation provider. I don't have time to be a mother for this child or for the younger daughter and older son.

> Yesterday I was asked by a psychologist about my dreams. . . . In fact, I don't have dreams anymore or, maybe, I have just one: I only want to sleep. To close my eyes and fall asleep.[31]

As the statement "very little has changed" suggests, COVID-19 constituted a continuation of the crisis already shaping the lives of families with disabled children. As in the many accounts I discussed in chapter 2, no reference is made here to the father of this family, who is probably either busy working or entirely absent, and, in the absence of state support, the mother has no choice but to take on educative and rehabilitative roles. As proclaimed in the title of the article in which this quote appeared, for a part of the Polish population the pandemic's "new reality" was not new at all: "Trapped in Four Walls? For Many of Us, This Is Our Daily Reality." In an article published in June 2020, Katarzyna Rybicka, the mother of a son with autism, described lockdown as "just another battle we have to fight."[32] COVID-19 simply brought to public attention the fact that violent intimacy is a form of crisis ordinariness in itself.

Magdalena Kocejko has claimed that "children with disabilities were invisible" to the Polish government during the pandemic.[33] Her analysis has been confirmed by parents and other experts, including Anna Duniewicz, founder of the We Want Our Whole Lives! activist initiative and mother of a disabled child:

> Parents are overwhelmed with online education and too many tasks and exercises they have to do. Some of these tasks are not tailored for their children. . . . The Ministry's recommendations have nothing to do with the reality of living with a disabled child. Suddenly, a parent became a teacher and therapist. . . .
>
> The worst of all is that they stopped rehabilitation services and treatment of people with disabilities. The medical visits are cancelled, the surgeries are cancelled and we are not given new dates. The therapy sessions are canceled.[34]

In a different article, an anonymous parent of a disabled child denounced the "significant shrinking of services that help support our children. The less support, the more work we have to do."[35] In order to work, Agnieszka Szpila, the writer and mother of autistic daughters whose article "Where Are These Children? They Are Fucked!" I discussed in chapters 2 and 3, hired people to take her daughters outside for four hours at a time—obviously not an option for many people in similar situations.[36] These statements document the state's failure to provide care and respite not only to people with disabilities, but also their caregivers. It is interesting to consider to what extent the 2022 protests led by

Szpila and other mothers of children with disabilities that I discussed in chapter 3 were triggered by the intensification of violent intimacy during the pandemic.

In their article, Głąb and Kocejko analyze the statements on COVID-19 issued by the Polish government: "One of the last communiqués from the analyzed series, issued in the conditions of starting up and promoting the national vaccination campaign, mentions 'normality' as a central theme ('we will return to normality'; . . . 'that it would be normal again'), which becomes a synonym for the efficient functioning of the institution. The 'normal' state here is therefore institutionalization, embedded in the traditional approach to disability."[37] For disabled people and their families, a "return to normality" would involve a lack of governmental interest in not just initiating deinstitutionalization, but dismantling violent intimacy, ending social abandonment, and developing services that could replace or supplement maternal care. In that sense, the 2022 protests can be interpreted as a cry against any return to normality.

As the state vaccination program in which people with disabilities and their caregivers were not prioritized got underway, the issue of "What will happen to my child when I die?" featured in many articles. In early January 2021, a letter from Barbara Gburzyńska, the mother of a disabled child, appeared in the newspaper *Gazeta Wyborcza* [Electoral Newspaper]:

> I have a question, does the fate of disabled people in our country interest anyone? In the press, on television, on the internet and in other media there is so much talk about the order of vaccinations.
>
> Has anyone considered what will happen to disabled people if we, their caregivers, fall ill or die? After all, our dependents will be condemned to a slow death.[38]

This letter, and in particular the last two lines, remind us of the bond or codependency between the caregiver and disabled subject.

In March 2021, the same paper featured a letter from a "distraught" father expressing a similar sentiment: "Our children have been excluded from life from birth, in one way or another, and now the government has additionally excluded them from social life and is ruling out the option of vaccinating them first, despite the fact that it is obvious that they are more vulnerable to severe infection and death."[39] Despite numerous petitions signed, letters sent to the Health Ministry, and many articles published on the subject, plus the fact that disability experts and activists had campaigned for rapid access to vaccination for people with disabilities and their caregivers since the autumn of 2020, the government was slow to react.[40] By the time people with disabilities were finally prioritized in May 2021, there was a vaccine shortage.[41] Referring to the ruling by the Constitutional Tribunal in October 2020 that prohibited abortion in cases of fetal defect, Agnieszka Dudzińska, a sociologist and mother of a child with disability pointed out the hypocrisy of the government's pro-life stance: "If the government was serious, when they said they cared about life, when they said that disabled life is sacred, then why did they abandon them? People who used to hold a placard saying 'pro-life' lost the placard."[42]

Reactions to the decision not to prioritize the vaccination of disabled people and caregivers echo the 2014 confessions relating to euthanasia that I discussed in chapter 3. In an article published in January 2021, a disabled person described the government's decision as "euthanasia in white gloves."[43] In an article published a few months later, a disabled person claimed that the government wanted those with disabilities to die, and that "the more of us die, the better."[44] By making disabled people wait for vaccination, the state displayed a total disregard for their heightened vulnerability. In other words, the pandemic merely continued the humanitarian crisis for people with disabilities and strengthened the preexisting hierarchies in which disabled lives have less value than the lives of others.

News articles on vaccination and disability not only referred to the increased threat to people with disabilities, but also the deepening sense of isolation and loneliness experienced by caregivers and disabled subjects.[45] Afraid to use public transport, one mother of an intellectually disabled son, who had been in isolation for over a year and relied on other family members to bring groceries, declared that if her son had to go to hospital, "he would die from fear."[46] Pointing out that a lack of vaccination was causing delays in both education and rehabilitation services, Katarzyna Roszewska, a disability expert and mother of a child with autism, asked: "What about the years we spent rehabilitating our children? They are also being wasted away when our children are in isolation."[47] Without access to vaccination, people with disabilities were even more reliant on caregivers to provide for all their needs and prevent them from catching the virus. Now even less able to escape their confines, the home became a site of intensified violent intimacy.

In 2012, after years of lobbying by disabled activists, Poland had ratified the United Nations Convention on the Rights of People with Disabilities. Since that time, some of those same activists have pronounced that the Convention is "dead" in Poland.[48] A significant portion of society, including some caregivers and people with disabilities, appear to have been unaware of the ratification, but this is slowly changing: Since 2018, the Convention has increasingly been referred to by people with disabilities, activists, and the Polish government, which has claimed to be gradually introducing UN recommendations. Nevertheless, the Convention has mainly been a topic of debate between experts and the government and was rarely referenced by disabled protesters or caregivers during the 2010s.[49] Given that this legislation, no matter how revolutionary, did not materially advance disabled people's rights in Poland during the 2010s, it is hardly surprising that no one turned to it during the COVID-19 pandemic. It is still unclear what could generate effective social change for disabled people and their families in Poland.

There are many more testimonies to the state abandonment of families living with a disabled person in the rich COVID-19 archive of violent intimacy. Particularly galling is the fact that throughout the pandemic, the Polish government repeatedly insisted that they would "not leave anyone behind."[50] Minister of Family, Labor, and Social Policy Marlena Maląg declared the government's priority to be "the protection of Polish families, the elderly, people with disabilities as well as employees and employers."[51] It is striking that families, rather than society or simply citizens, are afforded the highest level of protection in Poland. Moreover, given the evidence presented in this epilogue, the listing of the elderly and people with disabilities among the groups under the highest consideration is tragically comic. As I have shown throughout the book, this prioritization is merely fetishistic rhetoric: The figure of the "Polish family" is among the most important fetishes of both the Law and Justice government that governed Poland during the pandemic, and of post-1989 Polish culture in general. Before, during, and after the pandemic, politicians valorized family and promised various forms of support, including for families with disability, yet routinely have failed and continue to fail to deliver on such promises. Government communiqués released during the pandemic serve as further examples of this. At the same time, the disability confessions I have analyzed show that the fetishization of family is inseparable from its exploitation: Fetishization and exploitation go hand in hand.

In July 2023, the Polish government officially suspended the state of epidemiological emergency they had initiated in May 2022 (March 2020 to May 2022 had been designated a state of epidemic). By the beginning of 2023, most prosecutions of residential institutions in which pensioners had died of COVID-19 had ended: The vast majority of cases were dismissed, and no one was found guilty.[52] In early 2022, the Polish commissioner for human rights informed the public that over one hundred thousand people had died due to COVID-19 in Poland since the beginning of the pandemic.[53] There are no statistics indicating how many of these people had a disability.

* * *

This book mobilizes the term "disability disruptions" to point out moments, sites, and relations that disability has reconfigured or impacted since 1989. The first historical moment analyzed via disability disruption in this book is the 1989 political and economic transformation, and the last is the COVID-19 pandemic. While I look at the Polish iterations of these events, both the 1989 collapse of state socialisms in Eastern Europe and the COVID-19 pandemic transcend the local context and have global consequences. I believe that the significance of the intimate, familial stories, experiences, and confessions recounted in chapters 2, 3, and 4 also have consequences that go beyond Polish and Eastern European disability studies and nuance global disability studies narratives. The brutal shortcomings of care policies and support in Poland are not, unfortunately, isolated, and they resonate with care crises around the world. From this perspective, this book serves as a further evidence that "to be disabled is often to be hyperaware of the existing care systems," and that violent intimacy is not a viable solution to a care crisis.[54] At the same time, the disability disruptions analyzed in this book constitute the beginning of an archive and an invitation to think of other historical moments as well as social sites and familial relations that add to and complicate discussions of disability. Both as an analytical tool and a lived reality, disability disruptions constitute an alternative system of thought about historical, social, and familial change and are not limited to a specific geographical location or time period.

APPENDIX: VIDEOS

Jacek Hołub interview

"Żeby umarło przede mną—rozmowa z Jackiem Hołubem" [Hoping My Child Dies Before I Do], 1:16:33, March 6, 2019, https://www.youtube.com/watch?v=ruT40MTD2WY.

2014 protests

"Stop dyskryminacji niepełnosprawnych" [Stop discrimination against people with disabilities], 4:41, January 23, 2014, https://www.youtube.com/watch?v=cViehtzJb6U.

"Zdesperowani rodzice niepełnosprawnych dzieci okupują Sejm"; [Desperate parents of disabled children occupy the Parliament], 3:29, March 20, 2014, https://www.youtube.com/watch?v=VCWacQn3M9M.

"Sorry, ale jest pan kłamcą! Tusk spotkał się z protestującymi" [Sorry, but you're a liar! Tusk met with protesters], 5:23, March 22, 2014, https://www.youtube.com/watch?v=Rf9wXrQA3XM.

"Protest rodziców dzieci niepełnosprawnych" [Protest by parents of disabled children], 3:47, March 26, 2014, https://www.youtube.com/watch?v=q_N6-DIEpz4.

"Protest w Sejmie trwa" [The protest in the Parliament continues], 1:22, March 23, 2014, https://www.youtube.com/watch?v=azLvF40gRSQ.

"Ostrołęka—protest rodziców dzieci niepełnosprawnych" [Ostrołęka—protest by parents of disabled children], 10:32, March 27, 2014, https://www.youtube.com/watch?v=wHvh5wo1SIU.

"Iwona Hartwich do Tuska: Głosowałam na Pana! Protest niepełnosprawnych 2014 r" [Iwona Hartwich to Tusk: I voted for you! Protest by people with disabilities, 2014], 1:04:53, May 26, 2018, https://www.youtube.com/watch?v=ooh4DTEn6yk.
"Opiekunowie osób niepełnosprawnych nadal protestują" [Caregivers for people with disabilities continue to protest], 1:20, April 15, 2014, https://www.youtube.com/watch?v=B_jSeB1ZAp8.
"Zdaniem Seniora TV: Protest opiekunów dorosłych niepełnosprawnych pod sejmem" [According to Senior TV: Protest by caregivers of disabled adults outside the Parliament], 5:20, April 5, 2014, https://www.youtube.com/watch?v=5Me4crXV47c.

2018 protests

"OKO.press przedstawia: Protest osób z niepełnosprawnością w Sejmie 5 maja" [OKO.press presents: Protest by people with disabilities in the Sejm on May 5], 3:32, May 5, 2018, https://www.youtube.com/watch?v=Ox9uk7yT69o&t=10s.
"Łamistrajki! Protest rodziców osób niepełnosprawnych" [Strike breakers! Protest by parents of disabled people], 4:05, April 25, 2018, https://www.youtube.com/watch?v=soZFpYFyGfU.
"Majówka2018 #8: Brak serca Polski—emigracja przyjaciel" [May Day 2018 #8: Poland's broken heart—a friend's emigration], 3:20, May 2, 2018, https://www.youtube.com/watch?v=-1Ps5Nb5osQ&list=PLoHHRVts-QZyaAoXf8xUpclvxY6VjHCtk&index=9.
"Majówka 2018 #12.5: Zmienić system" [May Day 2018 #12.5: Change the system], 7:01, May 3, 2018, https://www.youtube.com/watch?v=fYnwqN2DaXQ&list=PLoHHRVts-QZyaAoXf8xUpclvxY6VjHCtk&index=13.
"Majówka2018 #1: Rachunki za cały dzień stałej opieki" [May Day 2018 #1: Bills for a full day of constant care], 4:56, May 2, 2018, https://www.youtube.com/watch?v=8afVqVksoso&list=PLoHHRVts-QZyaAoXf8xUpclvxY6VjHCtk&index=2.

2020 protests

" . . . by mieć wybór!" [. . . to have a choice!], 12:38, October 29, 2020, https://www.youtube.com/watch?v=mPUpQDLthZg&t=140s.

2022 protests

"Protest niepełnosprawnych w Katowicach 25.11.2022" [Protest by people with disabilities in Katowice on November 25, 2022], 1:52, November 25, 2022, https://www.youtube.com/watch?v=dekmsq4VyoE.
"Żyją za 2119 zł i nie mogą dorobić, bo stracą świadczenie: to los opiekunów osób niepełnosprawnych" [They live on PLN 2,119 and cannot earn extra money because they would lose their benefits: this is the fate of caregivers for people with disabilities], 1:45, November 19, 2022, https://www.youtube.com/watch?v=IY_w_eWOSJc.

NOTES

Introduction

1. Joao Biehl, *Vita: Life in a Zone of Social Abandonment* (University of California Press, 2013), 18.

2. Sławomir Zagórski, "My z Brunem jesteśmy naczyniami połączonymi: Matka OzN prosi o rozszerzoną eutanazję" [Bruno and I are connected vessels: a mother of a disabled child asks for an extended euthanasia], OKO.press, April 16, 2024, https://oko.press/osoba-z-niepelnosprawnoscia-matka-rozmowa?fbclid=IwZXh0bgNhZW0CMTEAAR3ygm6M07qnNX94hSvzU1CPT8sxwHd1H_wr13rzZ2sa31hVozi_m8gpBJ4_aem_ATq308ZEFX71lr3OhRacLSx-ezTmVhPRb_2fskDeSVY_4mcil66q74pMmcUqRown6O3dlzRuPYO13G8ZGzs5vxJx. Translations throughout are my own.

3. Zagórski, "My z Brunem."

4. Zagórski.

5. Zagórski.

6. Biehl, *Vita*, 2.

7. Biehl, 2.

8. Biehl, 2.

9. Zagórski, "My z Brunem."

10. Biehl, *Vita*, 4.

11. Zagórski, "My z Brunem."

12. Biehl, *Vita*, 49.

13. Agnieszka Jędrzejczyk, "Rodzice dzieci z niepełnosprawnościami—niewolnicy polscy" [Parents of children with disabilities—Polish slaves], OKO.press, February

17, 2023, https://oko.press/rodzice-dzieci-z-niepelnosprawnosciami-niewolnicy-polscy-temat-5-7-agnieszki-szpili.

14. Jennifer Douglas, "Toward More Honest Description," *American Archivist* 79, no. 1 (2016): 29.

15. Joan M. Schwartz and Terry Cook, "Archives, Records, and Power: The Making of Modern Memory," *Archival Science* 2 (2002): 3.

16. "Wsparcie dla rodzin to nie łaska, a obowiązek państwa" [Support for families is not a favor, but a duty of the state], *Gazeta Prawna*, June 19, 2023, https://www.gazetaprawna.pl/wiadomosci/kraj/artykuly/8733737,minister-marlena-malag-wsparcie-dla-rodzin-to-nie-laska-a-obowiazek-panstwa.html.

17. Marlena Maląg, "Rodzina to jedno z największych pragnień" [Family is one of the greatest desires], October 4, 2023, https://www.facebook.com/story.php/?story_fbid=752875343312850&id=100057711744489&paipv=0&eav=AfaNMwKGhVibsC1XBkH_R4Jn6mLxFUdoTklpEYkT6BYKq_PkDkFUeLFDhTovzBrWfQo&_rdr.

18. Andrzej Duda, "Karta Rodziny: Duda 2020" [Family charter: Duda 2020], Demagog, accessed January 8, 2026, https://demagog.org.pl/wp-content/uploads/2025/08/Karta-Rodziny-2020.pdf.

19. p.mal, "Andrzej Duda o LGBT" [Andrzej Duda on LGBT], Rzeczpospolita, June 13, 2020, https://www.rp.pl/wydarzenia/art8909311-andrzej-duda-o-lgbt-probuja-wmowic-ze-to-ludzie-to-ideologia.

20. As I write this, during the summer of 2024, the Polish Parliament is debating the introduction of civil partnerships for LGBTQA+ couples. The governing coalition is divided: The conservative wing has declared that it cannot support the use of the same surname, the adoption of the biological child of one partner by the other, or the signing of a marriage certificate in a registry office. These stipulations are intended to "defend" the "traditional" family and heterosexual marriage.

21. Zagórski, "My z Brunem."

22. The Polish Mother is a legacy of the statelessness that began in 1772, when Poland was partitioned between Austria, Prussia, and Russia, thereby losing independence for 123 years. In 1830, the Romantic poet Adam Mickiewicz wrote the poem "Do Matki Polki" (To a Polish Mother), in which he associates motherhood with sacrificial suffering and the rearing of future patriots willing to fight for independence.

23. Malgorzata Fidelis, *Women, Communism, and Industrialization in Postwar Poland* (Cambridge University Press, 2010), 240.

24. Fidelis, *Women, Communism, and Industrialization*, 238.

25. Fidelis, 241.

26. While present since the 1940s, polio cases peaked in Poland in 1958, with six thousand cases. Vaccination brought numbers down by the beginning of the 1960s. The main fear associated with polio was not mortality, which remained low, but its long-term effects and, equally importantly, the fact that it mostly affected children. See Marcin Stasiak, *Polio w Polsce. Studium z historii niepełnosprawności* [Polio in Poland, 1945–1989: a study in the history of disability] (Universitas, 2021), 6, 81.

27. Stasiak, *Polio w Polsce*, 82, 137, 146.

28. Sarah Phillips, *Disability and Mobile Citizenship in Postsocialist Ukraine* (Indiana University Press, 2011), 61.

29. Wiktor Dega, *Kalekie dziecko* [The impaired child] (Ludowa Spółdzielnia Wydawnicza, 1951), 21–22.

30. See Natalia Pamula, "Maternal Impressions: Disability Memoirs in Socialist Poland," *Aspasia: The International Yearbook of Central, Eastern, and Southeastern European Women's and Gender History* 1, no. 16 (2019): 96.

31. Eugenia Siemaszkiewicz, *Białe Niebo* [White heaven] (Czytelnik, 1967), 12, 75.

32. Maria Dzięgielewska, *Losowi na przekór* [Against fate] (Książka i Wiedza, 1972), 58.

33. Kateřina Kolářová and Martina Winkler, "Introduction: Vision, Promises, Frustrations: Disability and the Socialist Project," in *Re/Imaginations of Disability in State Socialism*, ed. Kateřina Kolářová and Martina Winkler (Campus Verlag, 2021), 16.

34. See Kolářová and Winkler, "Introduction"; and Natalia Pamula, "Precarious Belonging: Blindness, Masculinity, and Work in Polish Young Adult Literature of the 1970s and 1980s," *Canadian Slavonic Papers* 61, no. 2 (2019): 1–18.

35. Kolářová and Winkler, "Introduction," 7.

36. See Natalia Pamula, "Violent Inclusion: Disability and the Nation in Polish 1950s and 1960s Young Adult Literature," *East European Politics and Societies and Cultures* 34, no. 4 (2020): 858–78.

37. This was not the only disability organization under state socialism in Poland. Polskie Towarzystwo do Walki z Kalectwem (Polish Society for the Struggle Against Impairment), one of the most important and influential disability organizations during this period, was created in 1960. Led by experts and doctors, the society's goals included promoting rehabilitation as a complex practice that enabled disabled individuals to rejoin society and the workforce, the prevention of disability, and cooperation with international organizations on disability policies. There were also organizations devoted to blind and deaf people: Founded in 1925, the Polish Society of the Deaf-Mute changed its name to the Polish Society of the Deaf after the war, and the Polish Association of the Blind was established in 1951.

38. Monika Baár, "Informal Networks, International Developments and the Founding of the First-Interest Representing Associations of Disabled People in Hungary in the Late Socialist Period (1970s–1980s)," *Moving the Social—Journal of Social History and the History of Social Movements* 53 (2015): 58.

39. Irena Kowalczyk, *Poza granicą skargi: dzienniki* [Beyond the possibility of grievance: journals] (Wydawnictwo Literackie, 1974), 37.

40. In *Białe niebo* (White heaven), Eugenia Siemaszkiewicz writes about a person who calls herself a "hospital's child" who chooses to live there (12).

41. Pia Schmüsser, "'We as parents must be helped': State-Parent Interactions on Care Facilities for Children with Mental Disabilities in the GDR," in *Re/Imaginations of Disability in State Socialism*, ed. Kateřina Kolářová and Martina Winkler (Campus Verlag, 2021), 220.

42. Magdalena Sokołowska, "Polskie Badania Socjologiczne nad Niepełną Sprawnością: Przeszłość i Stan Obecny" [Polish sociological research on incomplete fitness: past and present], in *Studia z socjologii niepełnej sprawności* [Studies in the sociology of incomplete fitness], ed. Magdalena Sokołowska and Andrzej Rychard (Zakład Narodowy im. Ossolińskich, 1983), 11.

43. Magdalena Grabowska, *Zerwana genealogia: Działalność społeczna i polityczna kobiet po 1945 roku a współczesny polski ruch kobiecy* [A broken genealogy: women's social and political activity after 1945 and the contemporary Polish women's movement] (SCHOLAR, 2018), 111.

44. Kolářová and Winkler, "Introduction," 8.

45. See Dora Vargha, "Missing Pieces: Integrating the Socialist World in Global Health History," *History Compass* 21 (2023): 2.

46. Vargha, "Missing Pieces."

47. Sharon Rotbard, *White City, Black City: Architecture and War in Tel Aviv and Jaffa*, trans. Orit Gat (Pluto, 2015).

48. Merri Lisa Johnson and Robert McRuer, "Cripistemologies. Introduction," *Journal of Literary and Cultural Disability Studies* 8, no. 2 (2014): 127–47.

49. Jess Whatcott, "Crip Collectivity Beyond Neoliberalism in Octavia Butler's *Parable of the Sower*," *Lateral: Journal of the Cultural Studies Association* 10, no. 1 (2021), https://csalateral.org/section/cripistemologies-of-crisis/crip-collectivity-beyond-neoliberalism-octavia-butler-parable-of-the-sower-whatcott/ (accessed December 29, 2025).

50. Whatcott, "Crip Collectivity Beyond Neoliberalism."

Chapter 1. Disrupting History

1. A shortened version of this chapter appeared in *Aspasia: The International Yearbook of Central, Eastern, and Southeastern European Women's and Gender Studies* in 2022 under the title "Ordinary Trauma: Twenty-One Disabled Women Surviving the 1989 Polish Transformation."

2. In *Normy widzialności*, Magdalena Szcześniak writes that "the events of 1989 were dispersed." Magdalena Szcześniak, *Normy widzialności: tożsamość w czasach transformacji* [The visibility norms: identity in times of transformation] (Fundacja Nowej Kultury Bęc Zmiana, Wydawnictwa Uniwersytetu Warszawskiego, 2016), 15.

3. There were major strikes and protests in 1956, 1968, 1970, 1978, and through 1980 and 1981.

4. Igor Rakowski-Kłos, "Nie przeproszę za transformację" [I will not apologize for the transformation], *Gazeta Wyborcza*, January 16, 2021, https://wyborcza.pl/alehistoria/7,121681,26681716,nie-przeprosze-za-transformacje.html.

5. Philipp Ther writes: "In 1989, the International Monetary Fund, the World Bank, the US Ministry of Finances, and high-ranking members of the US Congress passed the Washington Consensus. The agreement was initially intended for Latin American

states that were plagued by high debt and high inflation. . . . The first prescription was an austerity program intended to stabilize the macro-economic situation and fight inflation." See Philipp Ther, "Groping in the Dark: Expectations and Predictions, 1988–1991," in *From Revolution to Uncertainty: The Year 1990 in Central and Eastern Europe*, ed. Joachim von Puttkamer, Włodzimierz Borodziej, and Stanislav Holubec (Routledge, 2020), 1–12.

6. Kateřina Kolářová, *Rehabilitative Postsocialism: Disability, Sex, and Race in Eastern Europe* (University of Michigan Press, 2025), 5–6, 19.

7. Kolářová, *Rehabilitative Postsocialism*, 17.

8. The elections were not entirely free: The Round Table agreement allowed Solidarity "to run candidates in 161 seats—35 percent of the total—in the lower house (the Sejm), and for all 100 seats in the new upper house, the Senate." See Padraic Kenney, *A Carnival of Revolution: Central Europe, 1989* (Princeton University Press, 2002), 258.

9. Maria Chodkowska, ed., *Cierpieniem pisane: pamiętniki kobiet niepełnosprawnych* [Written through suffering: disabled women's memoirs] (Polskie Forum Chrześcijańsko-Demokratyczne, 1991).

10. Adam Michnik, "Nic już nie będzie tak jak dawniej" [Goodbye old, welcome new], *Gazeta Wyborcza* [Electoral Newspaper], June 8, 1989, 2.

11. Lauren Berlant, *Cruel Optimism* (Duke University Press, 2011), 10.

12. Joanna Wawrzyniak and Aleksandra Leyk, *Cięcia: mówiona historia transformacji* [Cuts: an oral history of transformation] (Wydawnictwo Krytyki Politycznej, 2020), 38–39.

13. Kolářová, *Rehabilitative Postsocialism*, 104.

14. A detailed description can be found in Agnieszka Kościańska and Michał Petryk, *Odejdź: rzecz o polskim rasizmie* [Go away: a thing about Polish racism] (Wydawnictwo Krytyki Politycznej, 2022), 143–46.

15. Kościańska and Petryk, *Odejdź*, 148–49.

16. Kościańska and Petryk, 152.

17. Kolářová has described the violence and abandonment suffered by the Roma population of Czechoslovakia after 1989.

18. Kościańska and Petryk, *Odejdź*, 113.

19. Gaile Pohlhaus Jr., "Relational Knowing and Epistemic Injustice: Toward a Theory of Willful Hermeneutical Ignorance," *Hypatia* 27, no. 4 (Fall 2012): 715–35.

20. Grabowska, *Zerwana geneaologia*, 26–27.

21. Dóra Vargha, *Polio Across the Iron Curtain: Hungary's Cold War with an Epidemic* (Cambridge University Press, 2021), 15.

22. Kateřina Kolářová, "The Inarticulate Post-Socialist Crip: On the Cruel Optimism of Neoliberal Transformations in Czech Republic," *Journal of Literary and Cultural Disability Studies* 8, no. 3 (2014): 263, 259.

23. Teresa Torańska, *My* [Us] (Most, 1994), 116.

24. While this name is problematic from a disability studies perspective, it is important to remember that this organization, established in Poland in 1946, was the

first to deal with disability issues. Perhaps the experience of World War II, with its military rhetoric and history of resistance, as well as the views of the pre- and postwar Polish Eugenics Society, informed the choice of name.

25. Maria Chodkowska, ed., *Kobieta niepełnosprawna: socjopedagogiczne problemy postawy* [A disabled woman: sociopedagogical problems of behavior] (Wyd. Uniwersytetu Marii Curie-Skłodowskiej, 1993), 16.

26. Maria Chodkowska did not provide details about specific radio stations and TV channels.

27. Susan Wendell, "Toward a Feminist Theory of Disability," *Hypatia* 4, no. 2 (1989): 120.

28. In email correspondence, the editor of the collection, Maria Chodkowska, told me, "It's been thirty years, I don't remember much from that period" (September 19, 2021).

29. Chodkowska, email.

30. Chodkowska, email.

31. Chodkowska, *Cierpieniem pisane*, 17.

32. Chodkowska, 18.

33. My intersectional analysis is informed by feminist disability studies, particularly Ellen Samuels, *Fantasies of Identification: Disability, Gender, Race* (New York University Press, 2014), 16.

34. Chodkowska, *Cierpieniem pisane*, 44.

35. Chodkowska, 47.

36. Krystyna Wrochno-Stanke, "Niepełnosprawni o swojej sytuacji życiowej" [Disabled people about their living situation], in *Studia z socjologii niepełnej sprawności* [Studies in the sociology of incomplete fitness], ed. Magdalena Sokołowska and Andrzej Rychard (Zakład Narodowy im. Ossolińskich, 1983), 57.

37. Polish Academy of Sciences, *Sytuacja ludzi niepełnosprawnych i stan rehabilitacji w PRL* [The situation of disabled people and the condition of rehabilitation in the Polish People's Republic] (Zakład Narodowy Ossolińskich, 1984), 522.

38. *Constitution of the Polish People's Republic: Adopted by the Legislative Diet on July 22, 1952* (Krajowa Agencja Wydawnicza, 1978), 22.

39. *Sytuacja ludzi niepełnosprawnych*, 82, 89.

40. Sheltered workshops, in which disabled people were employed alongside nondisabled employees, were popular during state socialism. Marcin Stasiak, *Polio w Polsce, 1945–1989: studium z historii niepełnosprawności* [Polio in Poland, 1945–1989: a study of disability history] (Universitas, 2021); Natalia Pamula, "Precarious Belonging: Blindness, Masculinity, and Work in Polish Young Adult Literature of the 1970s and 1980s," *Canadian Slavonic Papers* 61, no. 12 (2019): 186–202.

41. *Sytuacja ludzi niepełnosprawnych*, 94, 116.

42. *Sytuacja ludzi niepełnosprawnych*, 116.

43. Chodkowska, *Cierpieniem pisane*, 42.

44. *Sytuacja ludzi niepełnosprawnych*, 94, 116.

45. Chodkowska, *Cierpieniem pisane*, 110.
46. Wrochno-Stanke, "Niepełnosprawni o swojej sytuacji życiowej," 61–62.
47. Wrochno-Stanke, 103.
48. *Sytuacja ludzi niepełnosprawnych*, 88.
49. *Sytuacja ludzi niepełnosprawnych*, 56.
50. Stasiak, *Polio*, 226–32.
51. Nancy J. Hirschmann and Beth Linker, "Disability, Citizenship, and Belonging: A Critical Introduction," in *Civil Disabilities: Citizenship, Membership, and Belonging*, ed. Nancy J. Hirschmann and Beth Linker (Philadelphia, PA: University of Pennsylvania Press, 2015), 1.
52. Hirschmann and Linker, 10.
53. Hirschmann and Linker, 31.
54. Hirschmann and Linker, 32.
55. Hirschmann and Linker, 99.
56. Hirschmann and Linker, 57.
57. Hirschmann and Linker, 123.
58. *Sytuacja ludzi niepełnosprawnych*, 34.
59. Chodkowska, *Cierpieniem pisane*, 59.
60. *Sytuacja ludzi niepełnosprawnych*, 428.
61. *Sytuacja ludzi niepełnosprawnych*, 168.
62. Chodkowska, *Cierpieniem pisane*, 40.
63. Chodkowska, 40.
64. Chodkowska, 40.
65. Chodkowska, 44.
66. See Maria Cristina Galmarini, *Ambassadors of Social Progress: A History of International Blind Activism in the Cold War* (Northern Illinois University Press, 2024).
67. Zofia Krzemkowska, "International Women's Year 1975," *Review of the European Blind* 3 (1974): 18–22.
68. Krzemkowska, "International Women's Year 1975," 18.
69. Chodkowska, *Cierpieniem pisane*, 77.
70. Chodkowska, 103.
71. Chodkowska.
72. Malgorzata Fidelis, *Women, Communism, and Industrialization in Postwar Poland* (Cambridge University Press, 2010); Padraic Kenney, "The Gender of Resistance in Communist Poland," *American Historical Review* 104, no. 2 (1999): 399–425; Katarzyna Stańczak-Wiślicz, "Od neomatriarchatu do szpitala-pomnika Matki Polki: ideologie macierzyństwa w dyskursach władzy i opozycji w Polsce (1945–1989)" [From neomatriarchy to a Polish Mother hospital-monument: motherhood ideologies in the state and dissidents' discourses (1945–1989)], in *Niebezpieczne związki: macierzyństwo, ojcostwo i polityka* [Dangerous liaisons: motherhood, parenthood, and politics], ed. Renata Hryciuk and Elżbieta Korolczuk (Wydawnictwa Uniwersytetu Warszawskiego, 2015).

73. Stasiak, *Polio*, 175–76.

74. This is a reference to the disability rights movement that originated in the West during the 1960s. In 1990, George H. W. Bush signed the landmark Americans with Disabilities Act, and the first disability pride parade was held in Boston.

75. Chodkowska, *Cierpieniem pisane*, 27.

76. Chodkowska, 29.

77. Chodkowska, 27.

78. In the North American context, Michael Rembis writes that disability offers new ways of envisioning home, care, and family. See Michael Rembis, "Introduction," in *Disabling Domesticity*, ed. Michael Rembis (Palgrave Macmillan, 2016).

79. Wrochno-Stanke, "Niepełnosprawni o swojej sytuacji życiowej," 59.

80. Chodkowska, *Cierpieniem pisane*, 25.

81. Chodkowska, 25.

82. Chodkowska, 22.

83. Chodkowska, 24.

84. Chodkowska, 59.

85. Writing openly about one's faith in God only became permissible after 1989. While authors of disability memoirs published in the 1970s and 1980s refer to the Church as an institution with interest in the disabled population, and some describe their religious experiences and faith, these descriptions are usually short and succinct. See, for example, Anna Domańska, *Los w rękach twoich* [Your destiny is in your hands] (Instytut Wydawniczy PAX, 1975); Eugenia Chajęcka, *Syn! Będzie szczęśliwa* [Son! She will be happy] (Książka i Wiedza, 1988).

86. Chodkowska, *Cierpieniem pisane*, 21.

87. Chodkowska, 24.

88. Chodkowska, 44.

89. Chodkowska, 51.

90. Chodkowska.

91. Chodkowska, 56.

92. Chodkowska.

93. Chodkowska, 21.

94. Arseli Dokumaci, *Activist Affordances: How Disabled People Improvise More Habitable Worlds* (Duke University Press, 2023), 56.

95. Dokumaci, *Activist Affordances*, 98.

96. Dokumaci, 92.

97. Stasiak, *Polio*, 185–89.

98. Stasiak, 189.

99. Chodkowska, *Cierpieniem pisane*, 71.

100. Chodkowska, 136.

101. Chodkowska, 72.

102. Barbara Klich-Kluczewska, *Rodzina, tabu i komunizm w Polsce, 1956–1989* [Family, taboo, and communism in Poland, 1956–1989] (LIBRON, 2015), 215.

103. Klich-Kluczewska, *Rodzina*.

104. Klich-Kluczewska, 220.

105. Jacek Kurczewski, *The Resurrection of Rights in Poland* (Clarendon, 1993).

106. Hirschmann and Linker, "Disability, Citizenship, and Belonging," 2.

107. Theodora Danylevich and Alyson Patsavas, "Introduction: Cripistemologies of Crisis: Emergent Knowledges for the Present," *Lateral: Journal for the Cultural Studies Association* 10, no. 1 (2021), https://csalateral.org/section/cripistemologies-of-crisis/introduction-emergent-knowledges-for-the-present-danylevich-patsavas/ (accessed June 20, 2022).

108. Chodkowska, *Cierpieniem pisane*, 23.

109. Danylevich and Patsavas, "Introduction."

110. Berlant, *Cruel Optimism*, 10.

111. Chodkowska, *Cierpieniem pisane*, 94.

112. Chodkowska, 111.

113. During the late 1970s, disabled people living in Warsaw were asked if they were afraid of the future. Responses included "Can it even get worse?" and "I don't think it can get much worse than this." Wrochno-Stanke, "Niepełnosprawni o swojej sytuacji życiowej," 58–59.

114. The three partitions of 1772, 1793, and 1795 divided the Polish-Lithuanian Commonwealth into the Austrian, Russian, and Prussian Partitions. See Brian Porter-Szücs, *Poland in the Modern World: Beyond Martyrdom* (John Wiley & Sons, 2014).

115. Katherine Lebow, "Autobiography as Complaint: Polish Social Memoir Between the World Wars," *Laboratorium: Russian Review of Social Research* 6, no. 3 (2014): 13.

116. Angela Carter, "When Silence Said Everything: Reconceptualizing Trauma through Critical Disability Studies," *Lateral: Journal for the Cultural Studies Association* 10, no. 1 (2021), https://csalateral.org/section/cripistemologies-of-crisis/when-silence-said-everything-reconceptualizing-trauma-through-critical-disability-studies-carter/ (accessed June 20, 2022).

117. Judith Hermann, *Trauma and Recovery: The Aftermath of Violence—From Domestic Abuse to Political Terror* (Basic Books, 2015), 28.

118. Hermann, *Trauma and Recovery*, 73.

119. Chodkowska, *Cierpieniem pisane*, 112.

120. Steve Matthews, "Anonymity and the Social Self," *American Philosophical Quarterly* 47, no. 4 (2010): 351.

121. Boris Buden, *Strefa przejścia: o końcu komunizmu* [Zone des übergangs: vom ende des postkommunismus/zone of transition: the end of post-communism], trans. Michał Sutowski (Krytyka Polityczna, 2012), 12.

122. Tadeusz Kowalik, *www.PolskaTransformacja.pl* (Muse, 2009), 19.

123. Kenney, *Carnival of Revolution*.

124. Johan Galtung, "Is a Socialist Revolution Under State Capitalism Possible?", *Journal of Peace Research* 17, no. 4 (1980): 281–90.

125. Adam Burakowski, Aleksander Gubrynowicz, and Paweł Ukielski, *1989: jesień narodów* [1989: the fall of nations] (Państwowy Instytut Wydawniczy, 2021), 74.

126. Burakowski, Gubrynowicz, and Ukielski, *1989*, 75.

127. Burakowski, Gubrynowicz, and Ukielski, 76.

128. Burakowski, Gubrynowicz, and Ukielski.

129. Chodkowska, *Cierpieniem pisane*, 131–32.

130. Timothy Garton Ash, *The Magic Lantern: The Revolution of '89 Witnessed in Warsaw, Budapest, Berlin and Prague* (Vintage, 1993); Kenney, *Carnival of Revolution*.

131. Magda Szcześniak has described the difficulty of defining the end of the transformation period. See Szcześniak, *Normy widzialności*.

132. Tomasz Żukowski, "Lewica i PRL w dyskursie głównego nurtu" [The Left and the Polish People's Republic in mainstream public discussion], in *Opowiedzieć PRL* [To narrate the Polish People's Republic], ed. Katarzyna Chmielewska and Grzegorz Wołowiec (Warsaw: Wydawnictwo Instytut Badań Literackich, 2011), 197.

133. Chodkowska, *Cierpieniem pisane*, 43.

134. Chodkowska, 99.

135. Chodkowska, 47.

136. Chodkowska, 118.

137. Chodkowska, 97.

138. Philipp Ther, "Groping in the Dark: Expectations and Predictions, 1988–1991," in *From Revolution to Uncertainty: The Year 1990 in Central and Eastern Europe*, ed. Joachim von Puttkamer, Włodzimierz Borodziej and Stanislav Holubec (Routledge, 2020), 11–12.

139. Ther, "Groping in the Dark," 12.

140. Ther, 15.

141. See Joanna Wawrzyniak, "Transforming Industry: On the Corporate Origins of Post-Socialist Nostalgia in Poland," in *From Revolution to Uncertainty: The Year 1990 in Central and Eastern Europe*, ed. Joachim von Puttkamer, Włodzimierz Borodziej, and Stanislav Holubec (Routledge, 2020), 182–201.

142. Chodkowska, *Cierpieniem pisane*, 47.

143. Chodkowska, 65.

144. Chodkowska, 95.

145. See David Ost, *The Defeat of Solidarity: Anger and Politics in Postcommunist Europe* (Cornell University Press), 2005.

146. Teresa Torańska, *My* [Us] (Warsaw: Most, 1994), 16.

147. Rafał Woś, *Zimna Trzydziestoletnia: nieautoryzowana biografia polskiego kapitalizmu* [A cold thirty-year-old: an unauthorized biography of Polish capitalism] (Mando, 2019), 10–47.

148. Kowalik, *www.PolskaTransformacja.pl*, 73, 63.

149. Chodkowska, *Cierpieniem pisane*, 34.

150. Margaret Price, "Time Harms: Disabled Faculty Navigating the Accommodations Loop," *South Atlantic Quarterly* 120, no. 2 (2021): 257–77.

151. Katherine Verdery, *What Was Socialism and What Comes Next* (Princeton University Press, 1996), 46.

152. Verdery, *What Was Socialism*, 40.

153. Rosemarie Garland Thomson, "Misfits: A Feminist Materialist Disability Concept," *Hypatia* 26, no. 3 (2011): 591–609.

154. G. Thomas Couser, *Signifying Bodies: Disability in Contemporary Life Writing* (University of Michigan Press, 2009), 31.

155. Remi Yergeau has described the difficulties that neurodiverse subjects can face when composing a text. See Melanie Yergeau, *Authoring Autism: On Rhetoric and Neurological Queerness* (Duke University Press, 2018).

156. Chodkowska, *Cierpieniem pisane*, 82.

157. Chodkowska, 67.

158. Chodkowska.

159. Chodkowska, 112.

160. Chodkowska.

161. Piotr Sztompka, "The Ambivalence of Social Change in Post-Communist Societies," in *Czy koniec socjalizmu? Polska transformacja w teoriach socjologicznych* [Polish transformation through the lens of sociological theories], ed. Anna Śliz and Marek S. Szczepański (Scholar, 2008), 36.

162. Kościańska and Petryk, *Odejdź*, 204.

163. "Przymusowe wysiedlenie i zniszczenie mienia Romów rumuńskich w Gdańsku" [Forced displacement and destruction of property belonging to Romanian Roma in Gdańsk], Amnesty International, August 7, 2014, https://www.amnesty.org.pl/przymusowe-wysiedlenie-i-zniszczenie-mienia-romów-rumuńskich-w-gdańsku/; Marcin Żółtowski, "Miasto nierówności: jak Gdańsk wyklucza Romów" [The city of inequality: how Gdańsk excludes Roma people], *Krytyka Polityczna* [Political Critique], December 11, 2019, https://krytykapolityczna.pl/kraj/gdansk-romowie-dyskryminacja-dulkiewicz/.

164. Kościańska and Petryk, *Odejdź*, 196–98.

165. Magda Szcześniak, "Od chłopa do rolnika: socjalistyczne opowieści awansu na polskiej wsi w latach sześćdziesiątych" [From peasant to farmer: socialist tales of advancement in the Polish countryside in the 1960s], *Kultura i Społeczeństwo* 2 (2022): 106.

166. Krystyna Kersten and Tomasz Szarota, "Znaczenie masowych materiałów pamiętnikarskich w badaniach historycznych oraz aktualne możliwości ich wykorzystania" [The significance of mass diary materials in historical research and current possibilities for their use], *Dzieje Najnowsze* 1 (1979): 162.

Chapter 2. Violent Intimacy

1. See Jennifer Natalya Fink, *All Our Families: Disability Lineage and the Future of Kinship* (Beacon, 2022), xvi.

2. Although my focus is Polish narratives, the text that best illustrates my analysis in this chapter is Renu Addlakha, "Kinship Destabilized! Disability and the Micropolitics of Care in Urban India," *Current Anthropology* 61, no. S21(2020): S46–54. Addlakha starts her article by stating: "Historically, the biological family is most germane to

care. It is families that continue to matter as a critical source of survival for disabled people particularly in low-income countries; and in many instances, they also play the dual role of being oppressive toward the disabled family member(s) to whom they provide support. Gender is a critical structuring principle in the organization of care throughout the life cycle, given women's centrality in procreation, childcare, and the larger domestic sphere." Addlakha's analysis resonates closely with my discussion of disability, gender, and care in post-socialist Poland.

3. Akemi Nishida, *Just Care: Messy Entanglements of Disability, Dependency, and Desire* (Temple University Press, 2022), 9.

4. Nancy Fraser, "Contradictions of Capital and Care," *New Left Review* 100 (2016): 101.

5. Raj Patel and Jason W. Moore, *A History of the World in Seven Cheap Things: A Guide to Capitalism, Nature, and the Future of Our Planet* (Black, 2018), 124.

6. Many Ukrainians currently work in the Polish care industry, either in institutions for the elderly and disabled or as live-in care workers.

7. For an extended discussion on coercion and care work, see Evelyn Nakano Glenn, *Forced to Care: Coercion and Caregiving in America* (Harvard University Press, 2010).

8. This is not to say that disabled subjects never take on broadly defined caregiving roles. For example, adult disabled children might be able to offer help and support, including emotionally. Disabled children might provide care to their younger siblings and pets.

9. See Elżbieta Korolczuk and Renata Hryciak, "Wstęp" [Introduction], in *Pożegnanie z Matką Polką: dyskursy, praktyki i reprezentacje macierzyństwa we współczesnej Polsce* [Farewell to the Polish Mother: discourses, practices, and representations of motherhood in modern Poland] (Wydawnictwa Uniwersytetu Warszawskiego, 2012), 7.

10. Urszula Bartnikowska, Katarzyna Ćwirynkało, *Rodziny adopcyjne i zastępcze dziecka z niepełnosprawnością* [Adoptive and foster families of a disabled child] (Oficyna Wydawnicza Impuls, 2013), 9.

11. Sandra Sufian, *Familial Fitness: Disability, Adoption, and Family in Modern America* (University of Chicago Press, 2022), 8.

12. Małgorzata Kościelska, *Odpowiedzialni rodzice: z doświadczeń psychologa* [Responsible parents: from the experience of a psychologist] (Oficyna Wydawnicza Impuls, 2011), 75; Urszula Bartnikowska and Katarzyna Ćwirynkało, *Rodziny adopcyjne i zastępcze dziecka z niepełnosprawnością* [Adoptive and foster families of a disabled child] (Oficyna Wydawnicza Impuls, 2013); Magdalena Chrzszczonowicz, "Polskie dzieci tylko dla Polaków: nieludzka decyzja Ministerstwa Rodziny. 'Taką mamy teraz rzeczywistość'" [Polish children only for Poles: an inhumane decision by the Ministry of Family Affairs. "This is our reality now"], OKO.press, January 24, 2017, https://oko.press/polskie-dzieci-dla-polakow-nieludzka-decyzja-ministerstwa-rodziny-taka-teraz-rzeczywistosc.

13. Addlakha, "Kinship Destabilized!," 46.

14. Poland is not unique in its lack of deinstitutionalization. As Eastern European scholars have shown, despite legal commitments to deinstitutionalization the Czech

Republic, Bulgaria, Latvia, and Lithuania have failed to implement adequate solutions. Slovenia introduced a Personal Assistance Act in 2019, which has enabled many disabled people to avoid institutionalization. However, as Slovenian scholars Darja Zaviršek and Svenja Fischbach have noted, this has strengthened familial care, as it is mostly women who have become paid personal assistants to relatives with a disability, thereby limiting the self-determination of individuals with disabilities. Darja Zaviršek and Svenja Fischbach, "Independent Living in Post-Socialist Countries: Between Familialism, Deinstitutionalisation, and Reinstitutionalisation," *International Journal of Disability and Social Justice* 3.1(2023): 96–113.

15. Dorota Szelewa, "Polityka rodzinna w Polsce po 1989 roku: od familalizmu prywatnego do publicznego?" [Family policy in Poland after 1989: from private to public familism?], in *Niebezpieczne związki: macierzyństwo, ojcostwo i polityka* [Dangerous relationships: motherhood, fatherhood, and Politics] (Wydawnictwa Uniwersytetu Warszawskiego, 2015), 107, 111.

16. Szelewa, "Polityka rodzinna w Polsce," 106.

17. See Natalia Pamula, "Maternal Impressions: Disability Memoirs in Socialist Poland," *Aspasia: The International Yearbook of Central, Eastern, and Southeastern European Women's and Gender History* 1, no. 13 (2019): 95–112.

18. There have been books authored by people with disabilities that have gained popularity, and many are analyzed in this book. However, the leading texts that shape public imaginaries of disability have been written by nondisabled people. There is also a robust disability presence on social media, such as Life on Wheels and Pełnoprawna on Instagram.

19. Nishida, *Just Care*, 127.

20. Szelewa, "Polityka rodzinna w Polsce."

21. Szelewa, 113.

22. A number of homes from six to ten inhabitants with their own room and bathroom have been established. There is a community home for autistic people in Gdansk, and one for people with intellectual disabilities in Sopot.

23. Jacek Hołub, *Żeby umarło przede mną: opowieści matek niepełnosprawnych dzieci* [Hoping my child dies before I do: stories of mothers of disabled children] (Wydawnictwo Czarne, 2018), 14.

24. In 2016, the Polish Parliament passed the law entitled "Za życiem" to provide support for pregnant women and families with children with a disability. The law was at least partially a response to the 2014 People with Disabilities' Protest and the 2015 attempt to restrict abortion law and ban abortion based on disability status. A one-time payment of 4,000 PLN (around $1,000) is available for women who give birth to a severely disabled child, making this more a form of compensation than systemic support. Moreover, the new law promised shorter waiting times for doctor visits as well as easier and cheaper access to a number of products and medicines. Yet, as revealed in Hołub's collection of interviews, accessing the resources promised by this law is extremely difficult. Although waiting times should be less than a week, one mother—after a long argument in which she reminded the scheduling nurse about

the law—managed to schedule an examination at a medical clinic six months in advance. Hołub summarizes by claiming that "mothers of disabled children are seen as overly demanding; we need to fight for everything" (Hołub, *Żeby umarło przede mną*, 94). According to the news website OKO.Press, an official report by the Supreme Audit Office in August 2021 concluded that the program has failed to reach the majority of its goals. Agata Szczęśniak, "Klęska programu 'Za Życiem': ujawniamy miażdżący raport NIK" [The failure of the "In Support of Life" program: we reveal a damning report by the Supreme Audit Office (NIK)], OKO.Press, November 4, 2021, https://oko.press/kleska-programu-za-zyciem-ujawniamy-miazdzacy-raport-nik-tylko-w-oko-press/?u=true#comment-105482.

25. In some cases that I describe below, husbands are involved to a certain degree.

26. Maria Chodkowska, ed., *Mieć dziecko z porażeniem mózgowym: pamiętniki matek* (Pracownia Wydawn. Fundacji "Masz Szansę," 1995), 7.

27. Chodkowska, *Mieć dziecko z porażeniem mózgowym*, 15.

28. Chodkowska, 13.

29. Korolczuk and Hruciak, *Pożegnanie z Matką Polką*, 11.

30. Korolczuk and Hruciak, 7.

31. Chodkowska, *Mieć dziecko*, 140.

32. Chodkowska, 103.

33. Chodkowska, 97.

34. The book was commented on by journalists in weekly magazines such as *Newsweek* (Polish edition) and *Polityka*, as well as bloggers and disabled people themselves on various media sites. @OutLet, "Do przeczytania w jeden dzień—do zapamiętania na zawsze" [Read it in one day—remember it forever],nakanapie.pl, May 3, 2020, https://nakanapie.pl/recenzje/do-przeczytania-w-jeden-dzien-do-zapamietania-na-z-zeby-umarlo-przede-mna-opowiesci-matek-niepelnosprawnych-dzieci; Karolina Kucharczyk, "Żeby umarło przede mną—recenzja" [*Hoping My Child Dies Before I Do*: a review], Xiegarnia.pl, September 25, 2018, https://xiegarnia.pl/recenzje/zeby-umarlo-przede-mna-recenzja/; Krytycznym okiem, "W imię miłości" [In the name of love], Krytycznym okiem, August 15, 2018, http://krytycznymokiem.blogspot.com/2018/08/zeby-umaro-przede-mna-opowiesci-matek.html.

35. Staged under the same title at a theater in Koszalin by a young female director, Daria Wiktoria Kopiec, the play was based on one of the interviews. Jacek Hołub was not involved.

36. Klaudia Muca, *Opowiedzieć niepełnosprawność: wybrane problemy kulturowych reprezentacji niepełnsoprawności* [To narrate a disability] (fundacja terytoria książki, 2024), 370.

37. "Żeby umarło przede mną—rozmowa z Jackiem Hołubem" [*Hoping My Child Dies Before I Do*—a conversation with Jacek Hołub], YouTube video, 1:16:33, March 6, 2019, https://www.youtube.com/watch?v=ruT40MTD2WY.

38. Klaudia Muca has described the book as having "an advocacy aspect" (*Opowiedzieć niepełnosprawność*, 371).

39. Nonfiction became increasingly popular in post-1989 Poland, particularly during the 2000s. There are a number of large and prestigious publishing houses specializing in nonfiction, including Czarne and Dowody na Istnienie, and nonfiction literary awards, such as the Ryszard Kapuscinski Award. Since the largest literary award in Poland, NIKE, was established in 1997, nominations have usually included works of nonfiction.

40. Chodkowska, *Mieć dziecko*, 140.

41. Hołub, *Żeby umarło*, 157–58.

42. Hołub, *Żeby umarło*, 11.

43. Chodkowska, *Mieć dziecko*, 156, 145, 170, 170.

44. Hołub, 70.

45. Hołub, *Żeby umarło*, 70, 25.

46. The number of private community and nursing homes is increasing due to an aging society. In 2020, there were almost seven hundred private institutions for elderly and disabled people. These private institutions comprise around 33 percent of all institutions for senior citizens. "Wzrasta liczba prywatnych domów opieki nad seniorami" [The number of private nursing homes for seniors is increasing], *Medycyna Prywatna*, March 8, 2020, https://medycynaprywatna.pl/wzrasta-liczba-prywatnych-domow-opieki-nad-seniorami-w-polsce/.

47. In April 2020, the Supreme Audit Office released a report on state oversight of private facilities for the elderly and disabled. It listed 108 private institutions that had been operating without any legal permission for between ten and eighteen years. Usually, the owners had not applied for permission due to buildings that did not meet requirements, opting to pay any potential fines if an extremely rare check was conducted. Additionally, the report revealed that in many private and public institutions, patient rights had been violated, particularly in regard to health, life, and dignity. "Pozorny nadzór państwa nad placówkami świadczącymi opiekę całodobową" [Apparent state supervision of facilities providing round-the-clock care], Najwyższa Izba Kontroli, April 22, 2020, https://www.nik.gov.pl/aktualnosci/nadzor-nad-placowkami-opieki-calodobowej.html.

48. Chodkowska, *Mieć dziecko*, 88.

49. Chodkowska, 99.

50. Hołub, *Żeby umarło*, 22.

51. Chodkowska, *Mieć dziecko*, 159.

52. Hołub, *Żeby umarło*, 144.

53. A third edition of *Poczwarka* [The pupa] was published in 2014, and the book has been translated into three languages: German, Lithuanian, and Vietnamese.

54. Dorota Terakowska, *Poczwarka* (Wydawnictwo Literackie, 2001), 123.

55. Terakowska, *Poczwarka*, 112.

56. Eunjung Kim, *Curative Violence: Rehabilitating Disability, Gender, and Sexuality in Modern Korea* (Duke University Press, 2017), 193.

57. Kim, *Curative Violence*, 169.

58. Kim, 192–93.

59. Przemysław Czapliński, *Efekt bierności: literatura w czasie normalnym* [The effect of passivity: literature in normal times] (Wydawnictwo Literackie, 2004), 90.

60. Czapliński claims "*The Pupa* shows that impairment forms an impenetrable closed world which does not give us a chance to establish normal contact" (*Efekt bierności*, 86), as a person with intellectual disabilities "does not share a common language with us" (90).

61. Czapliński, *Efekt bierności*, 86.

62. Terakowska, *Poczwarka*, 316.

63. While some scholars claim to have identified Pippi's disability, I prefer to resist the cultural imperative to diagnose people with disabilities.

64. For more information on discussions and processes relating to institutionalization and deinstitutionalization in Poland, see Zbigniew Głąb, *Między ideologią a utopia: deinstytucjonalizacja wybranych usług dla osób z niepełnosprawnościami w Polsce. Perspektywa socjologii wiedzy* [Between ideology and utopia: deinstitutionalization of selected services for people with disabilities in Poland. The perspective of the sociology of knowledge] (Wydawnictwo Uniwersytetu Łódzkiego, 2024).

65. "Włączenie społeczne" [Social inclusion], Włączenie Społeczne, accessed January 5, 2026, https://wlaczeniespoleczne.pl.

66. Katarzyna Ryrych, *Wyspa mojej siostry* (Wydawnictwo Stentor, 2011), 109.

67. Ryrych, *Wyspa mojej siostry*, 114–15.

68. Ryrych, 115.

69. Ryrych, 11.

70. Alicja Fidowicz, *Niepełnosprawność w polskiej literaturze XX i XXI wieku dla dzieci i młodzieży* [Disability in twentieth- and twenty-first-century Polish literature for children and young adults] (Wydawnictwo Uniwersytetu Jagiellońskiego, 2020), 228.

71. Fidowicz, *Niepełnosprawność w polskiej literaturze*, 233–36.

72. Czapliński, *Efekt bierności*, 92, 90, 86.

73. Przemysław Czapliński, "Nadnaturalny dar ułomności" [The supernatural gift of impairment], *Polityka*, April 7, 2001, https://www.polityka.pl/archiwumpolityki/1834492,1,nadnaturalny-dar-ulomnosci.read; "Poczwarka Dorota Terakowska—recenzja" [*The Pupa* by Dorota Terakowska: a review], Lekturia, accessed January 5, 2026, http://lekturia.blogspot.com/p/10-poczwarka.html; Pożeraczka Książek, "Recenzja książki—*Poczwarka*, Dorota Terakowska" [A review of a book—*The Pupa*, Dorota Terakowska], Pożeraczka książek, December 3, 2014, http://wer-pozeraczkaksiazek.blogspot.com/2014/12/recenzja-ksiazki-poczwarka-dorota.html.

74. "Bestsellery 2003" [The 2003 bestsellers], *Gazeta Wyborcza*, January 18, 2004, https://krakow.wyborcza.pl/krakow/7,35796,1871476.html.

75. Rayna Rapp and Faye D. Ginsburg, "Enabling Disability: Rewriting Kinship, Reimagining Citizenship," *Public Culture* 13, no. 3(2002): 537.

76. Krwawa Siekiera, "Monolog podwójnie niszowy (*Emil i my: monolog wielodzietnej matki*)" [A doubly niche monologue (*Emil and us: a monologue of a mother of three*)], Na

ostrzu siekiery, January 9, 20022, https://siekierka.home.blog/2022/01/09/monolog-podwojnie-niszowy-magdalena-moskal-emil-i-my-monolog-wielodzietnej-matki/; Mariola, "Książka o niepełnosprawności—*Emil i my: monolog wielodzietnej matki*" [A book about disability—*Emil and us: a monologue of a mother of three*], Lamarida, August 23, 2022, http://lamarida.pl/2022/08/23/emil-i-my/; Maria Bator, "Rozmowa o macierzyństwie z Magdą Moskal" [A conversation about motherhood with Magda Moskal], October 31, 2021, https://ladnebebe.pl/rozmowa-o-macierzynstwie-z-magda-moskal/; Katarzyna Kubisiowska, "Emil nie jest inny" [Emil is not different], *Tygodnik Powszechny*, September 13, 2021, https://www.tygodnikpowszechny.pl/emil-nie-jest-inny-169004.

77. Rapp and Ginsburg, "Enabling Disability," 552.

78. Magdalena Moskal, *Emil i my* [Emil and us] (Wydawnictwo Karakter, 2021), 5.

79. Moskal, *Emil i my*, 54.

80. Moskal, 37.

81. Moskal, 46.

82. Moskal, 138.

83. Moskal, 76.

84. Moskal, 9.

85. Małgorzata Nocuń, "My to każdy z nas" [We are each of us], Znak, December 2021 https://www.miesiecznik.znak.com.pl/my-to-kazdy-z-nas/?fbclid=IwAR2pKB2E56DwK1UEJ5bcmEqiAXaE_NSKqzAjISAlzxJKG62V5hOZjoRtMhA (accessed February 2, 2026).

86. Moskal, *Emil i my*, 55.

87. Moskal, 107.

88. Moskal, 18.

89. Moskal, 64, 34.

90. Agnieszka Szpila, "Gdzie są te dzieci? W dupie!," Krytyka Polityczna, September 11, 2022, https://krytykapolityczna.pl/kraj/swiadczenie-pielegnacyjne-dla-opiekunow-osob-z-niepelnosprawnoscia/.

91. See Nishida, *Just Care*, 59.

92. In 2022 this was 2119 PLN, equating to around $566. By 2025, it had been raised to 3287 PLN, around $879.

93. Szpila "Gdzie są te dzieci? W dupie!" [Where are these children? They are fucked!], *Krytyka Polityczna*, September 12, 2022, https://krytykapolityczna.pl/kraj/swiadczenie-pielegnacyjne-dla-opiekunow-osob-z-niepelnosprawnoscia/,

94. Szpila, "Gdzie są te dzieci."

95. Justyna Nagłoswska, "Tota, która mówi dość," accessed December 29, 2025, https://open.spotify.com/episode/2KsKm6KpG498HjAzbUAla3.

96. Szpila, "Gdzie są te dzieci."

97. Nagłowska, "Tota."

98. Nishida, *Just Care*, 100.

99. Szpila, "Gdzie są te dzieci."

100. Szpila.

101. Oktawia Kromer, "Karolina Kosecka: protest rodzin osób z niepełnosprawnościami" [Karolina Kosecka: protest by families of people with disabilities], *Vogue .pl*, December 31, 2022, https://www.vogue.pl/a/karolina-kosecka-wywiad-ze-wspolorganizatorka-protestu-rodzin-ozn-ktore-walcza-o-prawo-do-pracy.

102. Szpila does raise the issue of independent living in a number of interviews.

103. Rather than arguing that the proper definition of work should include care labor, I am simply highlighting Szpila's normative and capitalist understanding of work.

104. Szpila discusses the social marginalization of mothers as care laborers, not of people with disabilities.

105. Szpila believes she could earn two or three times the state benefit.

106. Szpila, "Gdzie są te dzieci," accessed December 29, 2025, https://krytykapolityczna.pl/kraj/swiadczenie-pielegnacyjne-dla-opiekunow-osob-z-niepelnosprawnoscia/.

107. Szpila, "Gdzie są te dzieci."

108. Szpila.

109. Nagłowska, "Tota."

110. Szpila, "Gdzie są te dzieci."

111. Monika Tutak-Goll, "Agnieszka Szpila: mie mamy w domu kontaktów. Biurko połamane przez Milenkę. Piszę pod kołdrą. Piszę, żeby żyć" [Agnieszka Szpila: We don't have any outlets at home. Milenka broke the desk. I'm writing under the covers. I write to live], *Wysokie Obcasy*, October 6, 2022, https://www.wysokieobcasy.pl/wysokie-obcasy/7,173910,28982538,agnieszka-szpila-nie-pozwalaja-mi-pracowac-bo-pobieram-swiadczenie.html?utm_source=facebook.com&utm_medium=SM&utm_campaign=FB_wysokieobcasy&fbclid=IwAR0_23rh35EOe01HSzvxOgq_k-1fCuDBT5OARlZAWAg9e6qgFBTeryTocD4.

112. Agnieszka Szpila, *Łebki od szpilki* [Pinheads] (Wydawnictwo W. A. B., 2015), 146.

113. Szpila, "Gdzie są te dzieci."

114. Szpila.

Chapter 3. Disability Confessions

1. Maria Chodkowska, ed., *Cierpieniem pisane: Pamiętniki kobiet niepełnosprawnych* [Written through suffering: Disabled women's memoirs] (Polskie Forum Chrześcijańsko-Demokratyczne, 1991), 47.

2. For more information on this protest, see Magdalena Zdrodowska, "I'm Angry! Disability Protests in Post-Communist Poland," *Problems of Post-Communism*, (2023): 1–12.

3. Agnieszka Król, *Reprodukcja a reżimy sprawności* [Reproduction vs. fitness regimes] (NOMOS, 2022), 11.

4. Aimi Hamraie and Kelly Fritsch, "Crip Technoscience Manifesto," *Catalyst: Feminism, Theory, Technoscience* 5, no. 1 (2019): 7.

5. I want to thank Svetlana Borodina for this comment.

6. Sigmund Freud and Joseph Bauer, *Studies in Hysteria*, trans. Nicola Luckhurst (Penguin, 2004), 34.

7. Michel Foucault, *The History of Sexuality. Volume 1: An Introduction*, trans. Robert Hurley (Vintage, 1990), 61.

8. Mel Y. Chen, Alison Kafer, Eunjung Kim, and Julie Avril Minich, eds., *Crip Geneaologies* (Duke University Press, 2023), 3.

9. See Chen et al., *Crip Geneaologies*.

10. See Kateřina Kolářová, "Crip Genealogies from the Postsocialist East," in *Crip Genealogies*, eds. Mel Y. Chen et al. (Duke University Press, 2023), 217–38; and Kateřina Kolářová, *Rehabilitative Postsocialism: Disability, Sex, and Race in Eastern Europe* (University of Michigan Press, 2025).

11. Nancy Fraser, "Rethinking the Public Sphere: A Contribution to the Critique of Actually Existing Democracy," *Social Text* nos. 25–26 (1990): 67.

12. Magdalena Zdrodowska compared Polish disability protests to the disability protests in the UK and the US in the 1980s and 1990s and characterized them as "far less effective." See Zdrodowska, "I'm Angry!," 1.

13. "Rodzice niepełnosprawnych dzieci okupują Sejm" [Disabled children's parents occupy the Parliament], *Gazeta Prawna*, March 21, 2014, https://www.gazetaprawna.pl/wiadomosci/artykuly/785566,rodzice-niepelnosprawnych-dzieci-okupuja-sejm.html.

14. See Paweł Kubicki, Rafał Bakalarczyk, and Mackiewicz-Ziccardi, "Protests of People with Disabilities as Examples of Fledgling Disability Activism in Poland," *Canadian Journal of Disability Studies* 8, no. 5 (October 2019): 141–61.

15. Marta Sałkowska, "Sejmowe protesty opiekunów osób z niepełnosprawnościami—wybrane wątki analityczne artykułów prasowych" [Parliamentary protests of caregivers for people with disabilities—selected analytical themes of newspaper articles], *Societas/Communitas* 26, no. 2 (2018): 233–46.

16. Sałkowska, "Sejmowe protesty," 243.

17. Kubicki et al., "Protests of People with Disabilities," 144.

18. "Kolejny protest: tym razem opiekunów osób dorosłych" [Another protest: this time caregivers of adults], https://archiwum.niepelnosprawni.pl/ledge/x/181182 (no longer available).

19. There is no official record and the various people I spoke to, who had observed and supported the protest inside Parliament, were unsure when the outside protest ended.

20. "Stop dyskryminacji niepełnosprawnych" [Stop discrimination against the disabled], YouTube video, 4:41, January 23, 2014, https://www.youtube.com/watch?v=cViehtzJb6U.

21. "Zdesperowani rodzice niepełnosprawnych dzieci okupują Sejm" [Desperate parents of disabled children occupy the Parliament], YouTube video, 3:29, March 20, 2014, https://www.youtube.com/watch?v=VCWacQn3M9M.

22. "Sorry, ale jest pan kłamcą! Tusk spotkał się z protestującymi" [Sorry, but you're a liar! Tusk met with protesters], YouTube video, 5:23, March 22, 2014, https://www.youtube.com/watch?v=Rf9wXrQA3XM.

23. "Protest rodziców dzieci niepełnosprawnych" [Protest by parents of disabled children], YouTube video, 3:47, March 26, 2014, https://www.youtube.com/watch?v=q_N6-DIEpz4.

24. "Protest w Sejmie trwa" [The protest in the Parliament continues], YouTube video, 1:22, March 23, 2014, https://www.youtube.com/watch?v=azLvF40gRSQ.

25. "Protest w Sejmie trwa."

26. There were also Solidarity demonstrations elsewhere, including Konin and Słupsk.

27. "Ostrołęka: protest rodziców dzieci niepełnosprawnych" [Ostrołęka: protest by parents of disabled children], YouTube video, 10:32, March 27, 2014, https://www.youtube.com/watch?v=wHvh5wo1SIU.

28. "Iwona Hartwich do Tuska: Głosowałam na Pana! Protest niepełnosprawnych 2014 r" [Iwona Hartwich to Tusk: I voted for you! Protest by people with disabilities, 2014], YouTube video, 1:04:53, May 25, 2018, https://www.youtube.com/watch?v=ooh4DTEn6yk.

29. "Opiekunowie osób niepełnosprawnych nadal protestują" [The caregivers of disabled people continue to protest], YouTube video, 1:20, April 15, 2014, https://www.youtube.com/watch?v=B_jSeB1ZAp8.

30. "Iwona Hartwich do Tuska."

31. "Zdesperowani rodzice niepełnosprawnych dzieci okupują Sejm."

32. Tusk was regularly accused of this when prime minister between 2007 and 2014, and since regaining the post in 2023. See, for example,"Kaczyński: Premier Tusk świadomie działa na szkodę Polski" [Kaczyński: prime minister Tusk knowingly acts to the detriment of Poland], Onet.pl, March 2, 2012, https://wiadomosci.onet.pl/kraj/kaczynski-premier-tusk-swiadomie-dziala-na-szkode-polski/66z9c; "Tusk działa na szkodę polskich interesów i polskiego bezpieczeństwa dogadując się z Niemcami" [Tusk acts to the detriment of Polish interests and Polish security by making a deal with Germany], wPolityce, February 11, 2024, https://wpolityce.pl/polityka/681485-romanowski-tusk-dziala-na-szkode-polskich-interesow.

33. "Stop dyskryminacji niepełnosprawnych" [Stop discrimination against the disabled], YouTube video, 4:41, January 23, 2014, https://www.youtube.com/watch?v=cViehtzJb6U.

34. "Zdaniem Seniora TV: Protest opiekunów dorosłych niepełnosprawnych pod sejmem" [According to Senior TV: Protest by caregivers of disabled adults outside the Parliament], YouTube video, 5:20, April 5, 2014, https://www.youtube.com/watch?v=5Me4crXV47c.

35. See Bolaji Balogun and Margaret Amaka Ohia-Nowak, "Geographies of Race in Poland and Central and Eastern Europe," *Ethnic and Racial Studies* 49, no. 1 (2024): 1–20.

36. See Margaret Ohia-Nowak, *Antyczarny rasizm: język—dyskurs—komunikacja* [Anti-Black racism: language—discourse—communication] (Wydawnictwo UMCS 2025); Agnieszka Kościańska and Michał Petryk, *Odejdź! Rzecz o polskim rasizmie* [Go away! A thing about Polish racism] (Wydawnictwo Krytyki Politycznej, 2022); Łukasz Zaremba, "Słowiański blackface: z archiwum wizualnego kompleksu kolonialnego międzywojnia" [Slavic blackface: excerpts from the visual archive of the interwar colonial complex], *Konteksty: Polska Sztuka Ludowa* 338, no. 3 (2022): 44–55; Magdalena Gawin, *Rasa i nowoczesność: historia polskiego ruchu eugenicznego* [Race and modernity: the history of the Polish eugenics movement] (Instytut Historii PAN, 2003).

37. Kolářová, "Crip Genealogies from the Post-Socialist East," 224.

38. "Zasiłki dla opiekunów niepełnosprawnych jak węzeł gordyjski: nowy protest, stare zaszłości" [Benefits for disabled caregivers like a Gordian knot: a new protest, old pasts], tvn24, April 19, 2018, https://tvn24.pl/polska/protest-opiekunow-niepelnosprawnych-w-sejmie-postulaty-ra830809-2360987; "OKO.press przedstawia: Protest osób z niepełnosprawnością w Sejmie 5 maja" [OKO.press presents: Protest by people with disabilities in the Parliament on May 5], YouTube video, 3:32, May 5, 2018, https://www.youtube.com/watch?v=Ox9uk7yT69o&t=10s.

39. "Protest w Sejmie zawieszony" [Protest in parliament suspended], dziennik.pl, May 27, 2018, https://wiadomosci.dziennik.pl/wydarzenia/artykuly/575181,protest-w-sejmie-zawieszony-iwona-hartwich-niepelnosprawni-koniec.html.

40. Karolina Nowakowska, "Rok po proteście niepełnosprawnych w Sejmie: żaden z 21 postulatów nie został w całości zrealizowany" [One year after the protest for the disabled in the Sejm: none of the twenty-one demands has been fully implemented], *Gazeta Prawna*, May 7, 2019, https://praca.gazetaprawna.pl/artykuly/1410843,rok-po-protescie-niepelnosprawnych-w-sejmie-zaden-z-21-postulatow-nie-zostal-w-calosci-zrealizowany.html.

41. "Protest w Sejmie zawieszony."

42. Kubicki et al., "Protests of People with Disabilities," 152.

43. See Maciej Wieczorek and Katarzyna Ojrzyńska, "Disability, Dis(sensual) Art, and the Politics of Participation," in *Disability and Dissensus: Strategies of Disability Representation and Inclusion in Contemporary Culture*, ed. Maciej Wieczorek and Katarzyna Ojrzyńska (Leiden: Brill, 2020).

44. "Zasiłki dla opiekunów."

45. "OKO.press przedstawia: Protest osób z niepełnosprawnością w Sejmie 5 maja."

46. Natalia Pamula and Magda Szarota, "Symbiotic Citizenship and a Struggle for the Right to Life as Frames for Interpreting the Forty-Day Disability Protest in the Polish Parliament," in *Rethinking Disability and Human Rights: Participation, Equality, and Citizenship*, ed. Inger Marie Lid, Edward Steinfeld and Michael Rembis (London: Routledge, 2023), 95.

47. "Protest osób niepełnosprawnych we Włocławku" [Disabled people's protest in Włocławek], YouTube video, 17:30, May 8, 2018, https://www.youtube.com/watch?v=huTY9nN3lYk.

48. Galina Goncharova, "The Generation of the Transition in Bulgaria and the Sentimental Narrative of Disability," *Critique and Humanism: Journal for Human and Social Studies* 55, no. 3 (2021): 87, 91.

49. There was also a smaller protest, centered on the issue of inaccessible housing, in the Czech Republic.

50. Goncharova, "Generation of the Transition," 85.

51. Goncharova, 87.

52. See Wieczorek, "Disability, Dis(sensual) Art, and the Politics of Participation"; Kubicki et al., "Protests of People with Disabilities"; Zdrodowska, "I'm Angry!"; Szarota, "Symbiotic Citizenship"; and Julia Kubisa and Katarzyna Rakowska, "Was It a Strike? Notes on the Polish Women's Strike and the Strike of Parents of Persons with Disabilities," *Praktyka Teoretyczna* 30, no. 4 (2018): 15–50.

53. Theatre 21 is a Warsaw-based professional theatrical group in which most actors and actresses have Down syndrome or autism. They have been active for more than twenty years and presented their plays both in Poland and abroad. The founder is the theater director Justyna Sobczyk.

54. *Niepełnosprawność i społeczeństwo: performatywna siła protestu* [Disability and society: the performative power of protest], edited by Ewelina Godlewska-Byliniak, Justyna Lipko-Konieczna (Fundacja Teatr 21, 2018).

55. "Łamistrajki! Protest rodziców osób niepełnosprawnych" [Strike breakers! Protest by parents of disabled people], YouTube video, 4:05, April 25, 2018, https://www.youtube.com/watch?v=soZFpYFyGfU.

56. Katarzyna Żeglicka, Facebook, https://www.facebook.com/StowarzyszenieStrefaWenusZMilo/videos/2083766198551961 (no longer available).

57. Żeglicka.

58. Żeglicka.

59. Żeglicka.

60. Żeglicka.

61. Żeglicka.

62. Agnieszka Jędrzejczyk, "Ogniowkurw na media: za sposób mówienia o niepełnosprawności" [Firecracker at the media: for the way they talk about disability], OKO.press, March 24, 2023, https://oko.press/ogniowkurw-o-mowieniu-o-niepelnosprawnosci.

63. Two social campaigns took place in 2021, one to promote disabled sport, the other to defend the right of disabled people to be in romantic relationships, form families, and have children. The former was entitled "First, I Am a Sportsman," the latter "Able-Bodied in Love." These titles erase disability and sustain the ableist norm: The former campaign emphasizes the identity of a sportsman, while the latter posits able-bodiedness as good and claims that love makes everyone nondisabled. Nowhere in these campaigns is disability represented as a legitimate identity that can be celebrated. Conversely to this cultural erasure of disability identity, Zasadzki thinks of himself as disabled and, highlighting the relational aspect of disability, comments on

the crucial role the disability community has in the formation of a disability identity. It is important to remember that the Kraków rally as well as the Parliament occupation were enabled by the disability community and a shared identity.

64. Piotr Zasadzki, Facebook, https://www.facebook.com/Stowarzyszenie StrefaWenusZMilo/videos/2083766198551961 (no longer available).

65. "Majówka2018 #8: Brak serca Polski—emigracja przyjaciela" [May Day 2018 #8: Poland lacks a heart—a friend's emigration], YouTube video, 3:20, May 2, 2018, https://www.youtube.com/watch?v=-1Ps5Nb50sQ&list=PLoHHRVts-QZyaAoXf8x UpclvxY6VjHCtk&index=8.

66. " Majówka2018 #12.5: zmienić system" [May Day 2018 #12.5: change the system], YouTube video, 7:01, May 3, 2018, https://www.youtube.com/watch?v=fYnwq N2DaXQ&list=PLoHHRVts-QZyaAoXf8xUpclvxY6VjHCtk&index=13.

67. "Majówka2018 #1: rachunki za cały dzień stałej opieki" [May Day 2018 #1: bills for a full day of nonstop care], YouTube video, 4:56, May 2, 2018, https://www.youtube .com/watch?v=8afVqVksoso&list=PLoHHRVts-QZyaAoXf8xUpclvxY6VjHCtk &index=1.

68. Kamil Siałkowski and Zuzanna Bukłaha, "Protest pod Sejmem wsparciem dla strajku okupacyjnego RON. 'Rząd mówi, że jesteśmy roszczeniowi'" [Protest outside Parliament in support of RON occupation strike. "The government says we are demanding"], *Gazeta Wyborcza*, May 5, 2018, https://warszawa.wyborcza.pl/warszawa/7,54420 ,23359191,protestuja-pod-sejmem-wspierajac-strajk-okupacyjny-ron-rzad.html.

69. Anna J. Dudek, "Jan Paweł II o niepełnosprawnych: 'Uczą świat, czym jest miłość.' Abp Hoser o proteście: 'Kościół nie jest stroną sporu'" [John Paul II on the disabled: "They teach the world what love is." Archbishop Hoser on the protest: "The Church is not a party to this dispute"], *Wysokie Obcasy*, May 9, 2018, https://www.wysokieobcasy .pl/wysokie-obcasy/7,100865,23371500,jan-pawel-ii-o-niepelnosprawnych-ucza -swiat-czym-jest-milosc.html.

70. Archbishop Hoser deemed the protest illegitimate due to support and/or involvement by the government's political opposition.

71. "Jan Paweł II o niepełnosprawnych."

72. Agata Szczerbiak, "Nie odsyłajmy protestujących niepełnosprawnych z Sejmu" [Let's not send disabled protesters out of Parliament], Polityka, May 7, 2018, https://www.polityka.pl/tygodnikpolityka/spoleczenstwo/1747666,1,nie-odsylajmy -protestujacych-niepelnosprawnych-z-sejmu.read.

73. Szczerbiak, "Nie odsyłajmy protestujących niepełnosprawnych z Sejmu."

74. Zdrodowska, "I'm Angry!," 1.

75. Rafał Detlaff, "O Godności ludzi z upośledzeniem umysłowym w nauczania Jana Pawła II" [About the dignity of people with mental impairment in the teaching of John Paul II], *Studia Gdańskie* 14 (2001): 298.

76. Marta Sałkowska, *Lista (nie)obecności: niepełnosprawność w podręcznikach szkolnych* [List of (dis)attendance: disability in textbooks] (Collegium Civitas, 2021), 57.

77. Sałkowska, *Lista (nie)obecności*, 70.

78. Anna Maliszewska, "W pełni ludzie: osoby z głęboką niepełnosprawnością intelektualną przez prymat nauczania Kościoła Katolickiego" [Fully human: people with profound intellectual disabilities through the primacy of Catholic Church teachings], *Studia Bobolanum* 29, no. 2 (2018): 47–48.

79. Malgorzata Fidelis, *Women, Communism, and Industrialization in Postwar Poland* (Cambridge University Press, 2010), 201.

80. Agata Chełstowska, "Stigmatisation and Commercialisation of Abortion Services in Poland: Turning Sin into Gold," *Reproductive Health Matters* 19, no. 37 (2011): 100.

81. Fidelis, *Women, Communism, and Industrialization in Postwar Poland*, 201.

82. *1993*, dir. Magda Mosiewicz, Magda Lipska, and Łukasz Ronduda, Museum of Modern Art in Warsaw, 2022.

83. Kazimiera Szczuka, *Milczenie owieczek: rzecz o aborcji* [The silence of the lambs: on abortion] (WAB, 2004), 228.

84. Szczuka, *Milczenie owieczek*, 216.

85. Marcin Kościelniak, *Aborcja i demokracja. Przeciw-historia Polski, 1956–1993* [Abortion and democracy: counterhistory of Poland, 1956–1993] (Wydawnictwo Krytyki Politycznej, 2024).

86. Chełstowska, *Stigmatization and Commercialization*, 100–101.

87. Katherine Verdery, *What Was Socialism and What Comes Next* (Princeton University Press, 1996), 79.

88. There had been very little use of the term "disabled fetus" in public discourse prior to the CT ruling.

89. Of course, it is unclear to what extent the demonstrators supported unrestricted access to abortion or even a return to the previous legal situation.

90. Król, *Reprodukcja a reżimy sprawności*, 114.

91. Katarzyna Bierzanowska, "'Nadszedł czas na walkę': Kobiety z niepełnosprawnością przeciw 'kapłanom' i 'faszystom'" ["It's time to fight back": Women with disabilities against "priests and fascists"], OKO.press, November 3, 2020, https://oko.press/nadszedl-czas-na-walke-kobiety-z-niepelnosprawnoscia-przeciw-kaplanom-i-faszystom.

92. Bierzanowska, "'Nadszedł czas na walkę.'"

93. Bierzanowska.

94. Bierzanowska.

95. In this sense, her confession echoes feminist disability studies and discussions about the silencing of pain during the 1990s. A very nuanced and complex analysis of the trajectory of feminist disability studies in the UK and US is presented in Magda Szarota, "Niepełnosprawność, aktywizm i feminizm, czyli (feministyczne) studia o niepełnosprawności w pigułce" [Disability, activism, and feminism, or (feminist) disability studies in a nutshell], in *Zespół Turnera: głosy i doświadczenia* [Turner syndrome: voices and experiences], ed. Ewa Maciejewska-Mroczek, Magdalena Radkowska-Walkowicz, and Maria Reimann (Oficyna Naukowa, 2019).

96. Courtney W. Bailey, "On the Impossible: Disability Studies, Queer Theory, and the Surviving Queer," *Disability Studies Quarterly* 39, no. 4 (2019), https://dsq-sds.org/article/id/1436/.

97. Bailey, "On the Impossible."

98. Bierzanowska, "Nadszedł czas na walkę."

99. Bierzanowska.

100. Magda Szarota, "Niepełnosprawność, aktywizm i feminizm, czyli (feministyczne) studia o niepełnosprawności w pigułce" [Disability, activism, and feminism, or (feminist) disability studies in a nutshell], in *Zespół Turnera: głosy i doświadczenia* [Turner syndrome: voices and experiences], ed. Ewa Maciejewska-Mroczek, Magdalena Radkowska-Walkowicz, and Maria Reimann (Oficyna Naukowa, 2019), 211.

101. Patrycja Polczyk, "Nie jestem matką, nie chcę nią być" [I'm not a mother, I don't want to be one], *Wysokie Obcasy*, October 28, 2020, https://www.wysokieobcasy.pl/wysokie-obcasy/7,163229,26443655,nie-jestem-matka-nie-chca-nia-byc-moja-niepelnosprawnosc-wynika.html.

102. Polczyk, "Nie jestem matką."

103. Szarota, "Niepełnosprawność, aktywizm i feminizm," 207.

104. Szarota.

105. Szarota.

106. Szarota.

107. Szarota.

108. Szarota.

109. " . . . by mieć wybór!" [. . . to have a choice!], YouTube video, 12:38, October 29, 2020, https://www.youtube.com/watch?v=mPUpQDLthZg&t=140s.

110. " . . . by mieć wybór!"

111. See Magdalena Waligórska, *Cross Purposes: Catholicism and the Political Imagination in Poland* (Cambridge: Cambridge University Press, 2024).

112. Waligórska, *Cross Purposes*, 201.

113. Waligórska, 2.

114. Waligórska.

115. Monika Tutak-Goll, "'Ja też chcę mieć prawo wyboru': Film niepełnosprawnej Bogumiły Siedleckiej zobaczyło już prawie 300 tys. osób" ["I also want to have the right to choose": the film by disabled Bogumiła Siedlecka has already been seen by nearly 300,000 people], *Wysokie Obcasy*, November 4, 2020, https://www.wysokieobcasy.pl/wysokie-obcasy/7,163229,26477727,mama-zajmowala-sie-mna-przez-18-lat-tylko-dlatego-ze-poszla.html.

116. Tutak-Goll, "'Ja też chcę mieć prawo wyboru.'"

117. Although there has been a movement to support and expand the rights of caregivers since at least 2017, including the right to work while keeping the state benefit, it has not attained the visibility of the protests described here. See "Inspiracja" [Inspiration], Chcemy Całego Życia, https://chcemycalegozycia.pl/o-nas/inspiracja/; and Dorota Próchniewicz, "Chcemy całego życia! Pozwólcie nam pracować!" [We want

the whole of life! Let us work!], Niepełnosprawni.pl, October 11, 2017, http://www.niepelnosprawni.pl/ledge/x/587808.

118. "Protest niepełnosprawnych w Katowicach 25.11.2022" [Disabled people's protest in Katowice on November 25, 2022," YouTube video, 1:52, November 25, 2022,]https://www.youtube.com/watch?v=dekmsq4VyoE.

119. "Żyją za 2119 zł i nie mogą dorobić, bo stracą świadczenie: to los opiekunów osób niepełnosprawnych" [They live on PLN 2,119 and cannot earn extra money because they would lose their benefits: this is the fate of caregivers of people with disabilities], YouTube video, 1:45, November 19, 2022, https://www.youtube.com/watch?v=IY_w_eWOSJc.

120. Ina Dimitrova, "Impasses of Disability Alliance Building in Bulgaria," *Research in Social Science and Disability* 12 (2021): 79.

121. Oktawia Kromer, "Karolina Kosecka: protest rodzin osób z niepełnosprawnościami" [Karolina Kosecka: protest by families of people with disabilities], *Vogue.pl*, December 31, 2022, https://www.vogue.pl/a/karolina-kosecka-wywiad-ze-wspolorganizatorka-protestu-rodzin-ozn-ktore-walcza-o-prawo-do-pracy.

122. Kromer, "Karolina Kosecka."

123. Magdalena Karst-Adamczyk, "Powiedziałam, że muszę się zobaczyć z psychiatrą: dostałam potrójną diagnozę" ["I said I needed to see a psychiatrist: I got a triple diagnosis"], *Wysokie Obcasy*, December 16, 2022, https://www.wysokieobcasy.pl/wysokie-obcasy/7,173910,29255492,maz-powiedzial-ze-diagnoza-naszego-syna-polozy-cieniem-na-zyciu.html.

124. Kromer, "Karolina Kosecka."

125. Kromer.

126. Kromer.

127. See Sarah Phillips, *Disability and Mobile Citizenship in Postsocialist Ukraine* (Indiana University Press, 2011).

Chapter 4. Autistic Disavowals

1. Other examples include Dawn Prince Hughes's *Songs of the Gorilla Nation* and Simon Baron-Cohen's *The Science of Evil.*

2. See Cameron Awkward-Rich, *The Terrible We: Thinking with Trans Maladjustment* (Duke University Press, 2022), 4.

3. Awkward-Rich, *Terrible We*, 16.

4. Anne McGuire, *War on Autism: On the Cultural Logic of Normative Violence* (University of Michigan Press, 2016), 9.

5. Although autistic and neurodivergent subjects as well as their caregivers are also on various online forums and social media, these are beyond the scope of my investigation.

6. See McGuire, *War on Autism.*

7. Joanna Grochowska, http://badabada.pl/.

8. Agata Bujnik, http://badabada.pl/.

9. The foundation has since revisited its philosophy statement. See "Nasza filozofia" [Our philosophy], Prodeste, https://prodeste.pl/filozofia/.

10. "Nasza filozofia."

11. See Tom Shakespeare, "The Social Model of Disability," in *The Disability Studies Reader*, 4th ed. (Routledge, 2013), 215.

12. The main tenets of what is now known as the social model of disability were articulated in 1975 by the Union of the Impaired Against Segregation, a UK-based "small, hardcore group of disabled people, inspired by Marxism": that "it is society which disabled physically impaired people. Disability is something imposed on top of our impairments, by the way we are unnecessarily isolated and excluded from full participation in society. Disabled people are therefore an oppressed group in society." See Shakespeare, "Social Model of Disability," 215.

13. "Nasza filozofia."

14. "Czy autyzm jest niepełnosprawnością" [Is autism a disability?], Prodeste, https://prodeste.pl/dzialania/autyzm.

15. "Definicja" [Definition], Synapsis.org, https://synapsis.org.pl/autyzm/czym-jest-autyzm/definicja-autyzmu/.

16. https://synasis.org.pl/o-nas/fundacja/misja-i-cele/ (no longer available).

17. https://synapsis.org.pl/o-nas/fundacja/misja-i-cele/ (no longer available).

18. https://synapsis.org.pl/o-nas/fundacja/misja-i-cele/ (no longer available).

19. Agata Szczerbiak, "Pięć krótkich zdań" [Five short sentences], Polityka, February 11, 2020, https://www.polityka.pl/tygodnikpolityka/kultura/ksiazki/1941528,1,recenzja-ksiazki-jacek-holub-niegrzeczne-historie-dzieci-z-adhd-autyzmem-i-zespolem-aspergera.read; Paulina Małochleb, "W słusznej sprawie" (For a just cause), *Przekrój*, February 17, 2020, https://przekroj.pl/artykuly/recenzje/w-slusznej-sprawie; Wojciech Szot, "Książka tygodnia—*Niegrzeczne: historie dzieci z ADHD, autyzmem i zespołem Aspergera*. Recenzja" (Book of the week: *Rude: Stories of Children with ADHD, Autism, and Asperger's Syndrome*. Review), Empik, January 23, 2020, https://www.empik.com/pasje/ksiazka-tygodnia-niegrzeczne-historie-dzieci-z-adhd-autyzmem-i-zespolem-aspergera-recenzja,110949.

20. Małochleb, "W słusznej sprawie"; Szot, "Książka tygodnia."

21. Krytycznym Okiem, "Niegrzeczne: historie dzieci z ADHD, autyzmem i zespołem Aspergera" Jacek Hołub" (Rude: stories of Children with ADHD, Autism, and Asperger's Syndrome), Krytycznym Okiem, February 14, 2020, http://krytycznymokiem.blogspot.com/2020/02/niegrzecne-historie-dzieci-z-adhd.html.

22. Fink, *All Our Families*, 6.

23. Jacek Hołub, *Niegrzeczne: Historie dzieci z ADHD, autyzmem i zespołem Aspergera* [Rude: stories of children with ADHD, autism, and Asperger's syndrome] (Wydawnictwo Czarne, 2020), 14.

24. Hołub, *Niegrzeczne*, 43.

25. Hołub, 153.

26. Hołub, 61, 164.

27. Remi M. Yargeau, *Authoring Autism: On Rhetoric and Neurological Queerness* (Duke University Press, 2018), 124.

28. Łukasz Pilip, "Geniusz z autyzmem: 'Moje ciało to kula u nogi.' Zna sześć języków, skończył prawo. Dopiero uczy się mówić" [A genius with autism: "My body is a ball and chain." He knows six languages and has a law degree. He is just learning to speak], *Duży Format*, March 20, 2017, https://wyborcza.pl/duzyformat/7,127290,21510116,geniusz-z-autyzmem-moje-cialo-to-kula-u-nogi-zna-szesc.html; Jan Pelczar, "Autystyczny syn, zdesperowany ojciec. Rodzice: Zrezygnować z terapeutyzowania własnego dziecka, żeby się wyspać?" [An autistic son, a desperate father. Parents: Give up therapy for your child so you can get some sleep?], *Duży Format*, March 4, 2020, https://wyborcza.pl/duzyformat/7,127290,24499835,autystyczny-syn-zdesperowany-ojciec-rodzic-staje-przed.html; Kamila Kołęda, "Mama chorego na autyzm Kuby: Jestem gotowa do walki" (Mother of Kuba, who is ill with autism: I am ready to fight), *Duży Format*, October 13, 2016, https://wyborcza.pl/duzyformat/7,127290,20825984,mama-chorego-na-autyzm-kuby-jestem-gotowa-do-walki.html.

29. Fink, *All Our Families*, 17.

30. Yargeau, *Authoring Autism*, 3.

31. Ewa Furgał, *Dziewczyna w spektrum* (Biała Plama, 2022), 101.

32. Dorota Kotas, *Cukry* (Wydawnictwo Cyranka, 2021), 36.

33. Furgał, *Dziewczyna*, 149–60.

34. Kotas, *Cukry*, 26.

35. Awkward-Rich, *Terrible We*, 16.

36. Alison Kafer, *Feminist Queer Crip* (Indiana University Press, 2013), 152.

37. José Esteban Muñoz, *Disidentifications: Queers of Color and the Performance of Politics* (University of Minnesota Press, 1999), 8.

38. See Kafer on coalitions: "Coalitions as a process in which the interests and identities themselves are always open to contestation and debate. How does 'disabled' shift, expand, or contract in these various movements and theories? In other words, part of what excites me about the coalitions I examine here is that they often trouble the boundaries of the constituencies involved" (*Feminist Queer Crip*, 150–51).

39. Kotas, *Cukry*, 11.

40. Furgał, *Dziewczyna*, 16, 8.

41. Basia Czyżewska, "Joanna Musiał: Spektrum autyzmu to nie choroba" (Joanna Musiał: The autism spectrum is not an illness), *Vogue.pl*, April 2, 2022, https://www.vogue.pl/a/joanna-musial-spektrum-autyzmu-to-nie-choroba.

42. Kotas, *Cukry*, 12, 14.

43. Furgał, *Dziewczyna*, 30.

44. Furgał, 30–31.

45. Kotas, *Cukry*, 10.

46. Kotas, 10.

47. David T. Mitchell, "Body Solitaire: The Singular Subject of Disability Autobiography," *American Quarterly* 52, no. 2 (2000): 312.
48. Kotas, *Cukry*, 37.
49. Kotas, 15.
50. Yergeau, *Authoring Autism*, 3–4.
51. Kotas, *Cukry*, 14.
52. Furgał, *Dziewczyna*, 7.
53. Furgał, 7.
54. See Magda Szarota, "Niepełnosprawność, aktywizm i feminizm, czyli (feministyczne) studia o niepełnosprawności w pigułce" [Disability, activism, and feminism, or (feminist) disability studies in a nutshell], in *Zespół Turnera: Głosy i doświadczenia* [Turner syndrome: voices and experiences], ed. Ewa Maciejewska-Mroczek, Magdalena Radkowska-Walkowicz, and Maria Reimann (Warszawa: Oficyna Naukowa, 2019).
55. Szarota, "Niepełnosprawność, aktywizm i feminizm," 33.
56. Szarota, 8.
57. Szarota, 10–16.
58. Szarota, 8.
59. Szarota, 29.
60. Szarota, 63.
61. Szarota, 59; emphasis mine.
62. Szarota, 140.
63. Karolina Dec, *Aspergerka, czyli życie na obcej planecie* (Rozpisani.pl, 2020), 11, 10.
64. Weronika Janiak, "Recenzja: Karolina Dec, *Aspergerka, czyli życie na obcej planecie*" [Review: Karolina Dec, *The Asperger Woman, or Life on a Distant Planet*], *Niebieska-Fala*, May 27, 2020, http://fundacja-furia.pl/niebieska-fala/2020/05/27/recenzja-karolina-dec-aspergerka-czyli-zycie-na-obcej-planecie-wyd-rozpisani-pl/, http://goodbuk.pl/2020/07/20/aspergerka-czyli-zycie-na-obcej-planecie-k-dec/ (no longer available).
65. Dec, *Aspergerka*, 14.
66. Dec, 15.
67. Dec, *Aspergerka*, 104–5.
68. Kotas, *Cukry*, 14.
69. Alexander Kondakov, "Crip Kinship: A Political Strategy of People Who Were Deemed Contagious by the Shirtless Putin," *Feminist Formations* 30, no. 1 (2018): 76–77.
70. Kondakov, "Crip Kinship."
71. Kotas, *Cukry*, 37.
72. Kotas, 105.
73. Kotas, *Cukry*, 154.
74. "Lubimy czytać: *Cukry*" (We like to read: *Sugars*), *Sugars* review site, https://lubimyczytac.pl/ksiazka/4964939/cukry.

75. *Sugars* review site.
76. Kotas, *Cukry,* 38.
77. Kotas, 38.
78. Philippe Lejeune, *On Autobiography* (University of Minnesota Press, 1989).
79. See Mary L. Gray, Colin R. Johnson, and Brian Joseph Gilley, eds., *Queering the Countryside: New Frontiers in Rural Queer Studies* (New York University Press, 2016).
80. Jack Halberstam, *In a Queer Time and Place* (New York University Press, 2005).
81. Kotas, *Cukry,* 144.
82. Kotas, 106.
83. Kotas, 155.
84. Kotas, 156.
85. Kotas, 97.
86. Kotas, 109.
87. In 2020, Dorota Kotas received a Conrad Award for the best debut novel published in 2019.
88. Kotas, *Cukry,* 140.
89. Kotas, 39.
90. Furgał, *Dziewczyna,* 21.
91. Furgał, 158.
92. Furgał, 56.
93. Furgał, 55.
94. Furgał, 54.
95. See Fink, *All Our Families.*
96. Dec, *Aspergerka,* 5.
97. Dec, 5.
98. Dec, 5.
99. Dec, 6.
100. Dec, 8.
101. Dec, 11.
102. Dec, 11.
103. Dec, 8.
104. Dec, 50.
105. Dec, 12.
106. Dorota Próchniewicz, "Hejt na autyzm" [Hate toward autism], *Niepełnosprawni,* March 31, 2021, http://www.niepelnosprawni.pl/ledge/x/1775715.
107. Girl on the Spectrum Foundation, https://dziewczynywspektrum.pl/.
108. Kotas collaborated, for example, with the Warsaw theatre, TR Warszawa, and the Museum of Modern Art in Warsaw.
109. Tomasz Kwaśniewski, "Dzieci z cechami ADHD i spektrum autyzmu są wtłaczane przez dorosłych w schematy, w których po prostu się nie mieszczą" [Children with ADHD and autism spectrum disorder are forced by adults into patterns that they simply do not fit into], *Duży Format,* July 11, 2022, https://wyborcza.pl/duzyformat/

7,127290,28667695,psychiatra-o-neuroroznorodnosci-te-dzieci-takie-sa-ze-robia.html#commentsAnchor.

110. Dorota Próchniewicz, "Autyzm jest problemem" [Autism is a problem], *Niepełnosprawni*, August 12, 2022, http://www.niepelnosprawni.pl/ledge/x/2025460?fbclid=IwAR2tBWFnl9YI9bAGqENAZ33R-ojmk483GbGV9IzUDuTtuR-oEXeK8yjs8CU.

111. Próchniewicz, "Autyzm jest problemem."

112. Such a criticism has been made against both Ewa Furgał and Dorota Kotas.

Epilogue

1. "Pierwszy przypadek koronawirusa w Polsce" [First case of coronavirus in Poland], Ministerstwo Zdrowia, March 4, 2020, https://www.gov.pl/web/zdrowie/pierwszy-przypadek-koronawirusa-w-polsce.

2. Thalia Schaffer, *Communities of Care: The Social Ethics of Victorian Fiction* (Princeton University Press, 2021), 5.

3. Around the time I was finishing this book, in 2025, Jędrzej Dudkiewicz published with a large, mainstream publishing house a book about the residential institutions in Poland. This is probably one of the most popular texts about this topic in post-1989 Poland released by a popular publishing house. See Jędrzej Dudkiewicz, *Inny dom: ludzie, system i granice wsparcia w polskich DPS* [Another home: people, the system, and the limits of support in Polish nursing homes] (Znak, 2025).

4. Rafał Bakalarczyk, "Wirus w domach pomocy społecznej" [Virus in nursing homes], Krytyka Polityczna, April 10, 2020, https://krytykapolityczna.pl/kraj/domy-opieki-spolecznej-koronawirus-rafal-bakalarczyk/.

5. Agnieszka Jędrzejczyk, "Koronawirus: testy i sprzęt ochronny dla domów opieki to teraz kwestia życia i śmierci. RPO do premiera" [Coronavirus: testing and protective equipment for nursing homes is now a matter of life and death. The Commissioner for Human Rights writes to the prime minister], *Biuletyn Informacji Publicznej RPO*, April 7, 2020, https://bip.brpo.gov.pl/pl/content/koronawirus-testy-i-ochrona-dla-domow-opieki-rpo-do-premiera.

6. For example, Bakalarczyk, "Wirus w domach opieki społecznej"; "Koronawirus w DPS-ie w Drzewicy: kolejne zachorowania na COVID-19 i śmierć podopiecznej" [Coronavirus in the residential institution in Drzewica: more cases of COVID-19 and the death of a ward], Nam!, https://tomaszowmazowiecki.naszemiasto.pl/blednyadres (no longer available); "Śmierć w DPS-ach: statystki mówią, że zgonów z powodu koronawirusa nie było tak dużo, ale rzeczywistość może być inna" [Deaths in the residential institutions: statistics say coronavirus deaths were not that many, but reality may be different], Głosu Wielkopolskiego, https://plus.gloswielkopolski.pl/smierc-w-dpsach-statystki-mowia-ze-zgonow-z-powodu-koronawirusa-nie-bylo-tak-duzo-ale-rzeczywistosc-moze-byc-inna/ar/c1-14987744 (no longer available).

7. Paulina Nowosielska and Klara Klinger, "COVID-eutanazji nie było, ale prokuratura przygląda się DPS-om: zawinił system?" [COVID euthanasia didn't hap-

pen, but prosecutors are looking at the institutions: was the system at fault?], Forsal, May 19, 2020, https://forsal.pl/artykuly/1477485,prokuratura-przyglada-sie-dps-om-koronawirus-covid-eutanazja.html.

8. "Prokuratura bada sprawę śmierci piętnastu pensjonariuszy domu opieki przy Bobrowieckiej" [Prosecutor's office investigates death of fifteen residents of Bobrowiecka nursing home], TVN24 Warszawa, June 1, 2020, https://tvn24.pl/tvnwarszawa/najnowsze/koronawirus-w-warszawie-dps-przy-bobrowieckiej-nie-zyje-pietnastu-pensjonariuszy-prokuratura-bada-sprawe-4599685.

9. "Dramatyczna sytuacja w DPS w Kaliszu: zmarło 7 pensjonariuszy, brakuje kadry" [Dramatic situation at a residential institution in Kalisz: 7 residents died, staff is missing], *Gazeta Prawna,* April 17, 2020, https://www.gazetaprawna.pl/wiadomosci/artykuly/1469995,koronawirus-kalisz-dps-smierc-7-osob.html.

10. Monika Stelmach, "Chaos i dezorganizacja przyczyniły się do śmierci pensjonariuszy DPS-u w Kaliszu" [Chaos and disorganization contributed to death of an institution's residents in Kalisz], *Termedia,* May 7, 2020, https://www.termedia.pl/koronawirus/NSZZ-Solidarnosc-Chaos-i-dezorganizacja-przyczynily-sie-do-smierci-pensjonariuszy-DPS-u-w-Kaliszu,37777.html.

11. "Koronawirus w Zakładzie Opiekuńczo-Leczniczym: niepełnosprawne dzieci zostały bez opieki" [Coronavirus in a care facility: Disabled children were left unattended], *Gazeta.pl,* https://www.gazeta.pl/0,0.html?404.

12. Sebastian Klauziński, "'Nie ma kto dać jeść, przewinąć pieluch. Nie wytrzymamy dłużej': koronawirus zaatakował już 8 DPS-ów" ["There is no one to give food, change diapers. We can't hold out much longer': coronavirus has already attacked 8 residential institutions], OKO.press, April 4, 2020, https://oko.press/nie-ma-kto-dac-jesc-przewinac-pieluch-nie-wytrzymamy-dluzej-koronawirus-zaatakowal-juz-8-dps-ow.

13. Mieczysław Rudy, "Minister zdrowia zabiera głos w sprawie trudnej sytuacji w DPS-ach" [Health minister speaks out on difficult situation in residential institutions], Bankier, April 15, 2020, https://www.bankier.pl/wiadomosc/Minister-zdrowia-zabiera-glos-w-sprawie-trudnej-sytuacji-w-DPS-ach-7863863.html.

14. "Nowe ogniska COVID-19; Szumowski zapowiada zmiany w pracy personelu medycznego" [New COVID-19 outbreaks; Szumowski announces changes to medical staff], RadioZet, https://wiadomosci.radiozet.pl/tag/kategoria/koronawirus (no longer available).

15. "Dramat w DPS-ach: miały być bezpieczną przystanią, a stały się śmiertelną pułapką" [Drama in the residential institutions: they were supposed to be a safe haven, but became a death trap], Fakt, April 16, 2020, https://www.fakt.pl/wydarzenia/polska/koronawirus-w-polsce-ewakuacja-domow-pomocy-spolecznej/9xdc2lg.

16. Marta K. Nowak, "W placówkach opiekuńczych nawet 969 zakażonych: Ziobro chce ścigać uciekający wycieńczony personel" [Up to 969 infected in care facilities: Ziobro wants to prosecute fleeing and exhausted staff], OKO.press, April 18, 2020, https://oko.press/w-placowkach-opiekunczych-nawet-969-zakazonych-ziobro-chce-scigac-uciekajacy-personel.

17. "Maląg: O osoby starsze i potrzebujące dbamy codziennie, nie tylko incydentalnie" [Maląg: We take care of the elderly and needy every day, not just incidentally], TVP Parlament, April 16, 2020, https://www.tvpparlament.pl/47596517/malag-o-osoby-starsze-i-potrzebujace-dbamy-codziennie-nie-tylko-incydentalnie.

18. "Pomoc dla osób niepełnosprawnych w dobie koronawirusa" [Help for people with disabilities in the times of coronavirus], *Miejsko Gminny Ośrodek Pomocy Społecznej w Gniewie*, April 9, 2020, https://www.mgops.gniew.pl/pomoc-dla-osob-niepelnosprawnych-w-dobie-koronawirusa/.

19. Mateusz Różański, "Jak uniknąć tragedii w domach pomocy społecznej?" [How to avoid tragedies in nursing homes?], *Niepełnosprawni*, April 9, 2020, http://www.niepelnosprawni.pl/ledge/x/960902.

20. Różański, "Jak uniknąć tragedii w domach pomocy społecznej?"

21. Katarzyna Nowak, "Lekarze pozostawili w mieszkaniu niepełnosprawną 80-latkę" [Doctors left a disabled 80-year-old in the apartment], *Gazeta.pl*, November 14, 2020, https://wiadomosci.gazeta.pl/wiadomosci/7,114883,26510817,plock-lekarze-pozostawili-w-mieszkaniu-niepelnosprawna-80-latke.html.

22. Rafał Bakalarczyk, "Opiekunowie osób wymagających stałego wsparcia bez priorytetu w szczepieniach: to błąd" [Caregivers of people requiring ongoing support without prioritizing vaccinations: this is a mistake], OKO.press, January 6, 2021, https://oko.press/opiekunowie-bez-priorytetu-w-szczepieniach-to-blad.

23. Vaccination started in late 2020 and continued throughout 2021. The elderly were a prioritized group. Beata Dązbłaż, "Chcesz wyjść z DPS-u? Powiedz: po co, z kim, dlaczego. Weekendy bez odwiedzin" [Do you want to leave the institution? Tell us: why, with whom, why. Weekends without visits], *Niepełnosprawni*, August 6, 2021, http://www.niepelnosprawni.pl/ledge/x/1837278;jsessionid=B715B2A88BCEC539AE86A8429FB79FCD; Karolina Nowakowska, "Mieszkańcy DPS-ów umierają w samotności. Szczepienia miały to zmienić. Sprawdzamy, jak jest w rzeczywistości" [Residents at the institutions are dying alone. Vaccination was supposed to change that. We check how it is in reality], *Gazeta Prawna*, February 27, 2021, https://www.gazetaprawna.pl/wiadomosci/kraj/artykuly/8106693,dps-szczepienia-wychodzenie-odwiedziny-przepisy.html; Przmysław Wilczyński, "Uwięzieni w DPS-ach: na wszelki wypadek" [Trapped at the institutions: just in case], *Tygodnik Powszechny*, March 29, 2021, https://www.tygodnikpowszechny.pl/uwiezieni-w-dps-ach-na-wszelki-wypadek-166963.

24. Dązbłaż "Chcesz wyjść z DPS-u?"

25. "List do Premiera ws. trudnej sytuacji mieszkanek i mieszkańców DPS-ów" [Letter to the prime minister on the plight of the residents of the insitutions], Fundacja Instytut Rozwoju Regionalnego, March 24, 2021, https://firr.org.pl/list-do-premiera-ws-trudnej-sytuacji-mieszkanek-i-mieszkancow-dps-ow/.

26. Zbigniew Głąb and Magdalena Kocejko, "Between Safety and Isolation: The Governmental-Ministerial Approach to Care Homes in Poland During the COVID-19 Pandemic," *Disability & Society* 39, no. 6 (2022): 15.

27. Liat Ben-Moshe, *Decarcerating Disability: Desinstitutionalization and Prison Abolition* (University of Minnesota Press, 2020), 1–2.

28. Ben-Moshe, *Decarcerating Disability*, 15.

29. For example, "To jest igranie z ludzkim życiem—koronawirus w domach pomocy Społecznej" [This is playing with people's lives—coronavirus in nursing homes], Tokfm, October 1, 2020, https://audycje.tokfm.pl/podcast/96223,-To-jest-igranie-z-ludzkim-zyciem-koronawirus-w-Domach-Pomocy-Spolecznej.

30. Magdalena Kocejko, "Sytuacja dzieci z niepełnosprawnościami w czasie pandemii COVID-19—analiza intersekcjonalna" [The situation of children with disabilities during the COVID-19 pandemic—an intersectional analysis], *Dziecko Krzywdzone: Teoria, badania, praktyka* 20, no. 2 (2021): 84–85.

31. Paulina Siegień, "Uwięzieni w czterech ścianach? Dla wielu z nas to codzienność" [Trapped in four walls? For many of us, this is our daily reality], *Krytyka Polityczna*, May 1, 2020, https://krytykapolityczna.pl/kraj/anna-duniewicz-chcemy-calego-zycia-koronawirus-autyzm-niepelnosprawnosc/.

32. Jakub Mirowski and Anna Mikulska, "Izolacja na co dzień: dzieci w spektrum autyzmu w dobie koronawirusa" [Isolation every day: children on the autism spectrum in the age of coronavirus], Krytyka Polityczna, June 20, 2020, https://krytykapolityczna.pl/kraj/izolacja-na-co-dzien-dzieci-w-spektrum-autyzmu-w-dobie-koronawirusa-mikulska-mirowski/.

33. Kocejko, "Sytuacja dzieci z niepełnosprawnościami w czasie pandemii COVID-19," 86.

34. "Uwięzieni w czterech ścianach?"

35. Bakalarczyk, "Opiekunowie osób wymagających stałego wsparcia."

36. Monika Tutak-Goll, "Agnieszka Szpila: Nie mamy w domu kontaktów. Biurko połamane przez Milenkę. Piszę pod kołdrą. Piszę, żeby żyć" [We have don't have any outlets at home. Milenka broke the desk. I'm writing under the covers. I write to live], *Wysokie Obcasy*, October 6, 2022, https://www.wysokieobcasy.pl/wysokie-obcasy/7,173910,28982538,agnieszka-szpila-nie-pozwalaja-mi-pracowac-bo-pobieram-swiadczenie.html?utm_source=facebook.com&utm_medium=SM&utm_campaign=FB_wysokieobcasy&fbclid=IwAR0_23rh35EOe01HSzvxOgq_k-1fCuDBT5OARlZAWAg9e6qgFBTeryTocD4.

37. Głąb and Kocejko, "Between Safety and Isolation," 10–11.

38. Barbara Gburzyńska, "W jakiej kolejności będą szczepieni opiekunowie osób niepełnosprawnych?" [In what order will caregivers of people with disabilities be vaccinated?], *Gazeta Wyborcza*, January 11, 2021, https://wyborcza.pl/7,162657,26675181,w-jakiej-kolejnosci-beda-szczepieni-opiekunowie-osob-niepelnosprawnych.html.

39. "Dramatyczny apel ojca dziecka z niepełnosprawnością: Bez szczepienia będziemy więźniami we własnych domach" [Dramatic plea from the father of a child with disabilities: Without vaccination, we will be prisoners in our own homes], *Gazeta Wyborcza*, March 24, 2021, https://wroclaw.wyborcza.pl/wroclaw/7,35771,26913208,dramatyczny-apel-ojca-dziecka-z-niepelnosprawnoscia-bez-szczepienia.html.

40. Marta K. Nowak, "Rząd nie szczepi szybciej osób z niepełnosprawnościami" [Government fails to vaccinate people with disabilities faster], OKO.press, April 22, 2021, https://oko.press/rzad-nie-szczepi-szybciej-osob-z-niepelnosprawnosciami.

41. Nowak, "Rząd zadrwił z osób z niepełnosprawnościami?"

42. Nowak.

43. Bednarek, "Od miesięcy nie wyszli z domu."

44. Bednarek and Ewa Furtak, "Niepełnosprawni wciąż bez szczepień."

45. Bakalarczyk, "Opiekunowie osób wymagających stałego wsparcia."

46. Bednarek and Furtak, "Niepełnosprawni wciąż bez szczepień."

47. Nowak, "Rząd nie szczepi szybciej osób z niepełnosprawnościami."

48. Agnieszka Jędrzejczyk, "Rodzice dzieci z niepełnosprawnościami—niewolnicy polscy" [Parents of children with disabilities—Polish slaves], OKO.press, February 17, 2023, https://oko.press/rodzice-dzieci-z-niepelnosprawnosciami-niewolnicy-polscy-temat-5-7-agnieszki-szpili.

49. Magdalena Kocejko, "Nic o nas bez nas? Zaangażowanie ruchu osób z niepełnosprawnościami w monitoring wdrażania Konwencji ONZ o prawach osób niepełnosprawnych w Polsce. Studium przypadku [Nothing about us without us? Involvement of the movement of persons with disabilities in the monitoring of the implementation of the UN Convention on the Rights of Persons with Disabilities in Poland: a case study]," *Studia z Polityki Publicznej* 20, no. 4 (2018): 10.

50. "Koronawirus w Polsce. Maląg o osobach w kwarantannie: Nikt nie będzie pozostawiony sam sobie" [Coronavirus in Poland. Maląg on people in quarantine: No one will be left alone], *Gazeta Prawna,* March 18, 2020, https://www.gazetaprawna.pl/wiadomosci/artykuly/1461373,koronawirus-w-polsce-malag-osoba-w-kwarantannie.html.

51. Grażyna J. Leśniak, "MRPiPS pracuje nad planem działań przed drugą falą COVID-19" [The Ministry of Family and Labor is working on an action plan ahead of the second wave of COVID-19], *Prawo.pl,* August 3, 2020, https://www.prawo.pl/kadry/kogo-planuje-chronic-przed-druga-fala-covid-19-resort-pracy,502116.html.

52. Paulina Nowosielska and Klara Klinger, "Nie ma winnych śmierci w DPS-ach w czasie COVID-19—były doniesienia, są umorzenia" [No culprits in the residential institutions' deaths during Covid-19—there were reports, there are write-offs], *Gazeta Prawna,* January 17, 2023, https://www.gazetaprawna.pl/wiadomosci/kraj/artykuly/8638202,pandemia-covid-19-koronawirus-smierc-seniorow-w-dps-spoleczenstwo.html.

53. "Na koronawirusa w Polsce zmarło już ponad 100 tys. osób: Marcin Wiącek pisze do Ministra Zdrowia" [More than 100,000 people have already died from coronavirus in Poland: Marcin Wiącek writes to the minister of health], *Biuletyn Informacji Publicznej RPO,* January 17, 2022, https://bip.brpo.gov.pl/pl/content/rpo-mz-koronawirus-alarmujaco-duzo-zgonow.

54. Jina B. Kim, *Care at the End of the World: Dreaming of Infrastructure in Crip-of-Color Writing* (Duke University Press, 2025), 11.

BIBLIOGRAPHY

Addlakha, Renu. "Kinship Destabilized! Disability in the Micropolitics of Care in Urban India." *Current Anthropology* 61, S21 (2020): 46–54.

Awkward-Rich, Cameron. *The Terrible We: Thinking with Trans Maladjustment*. Duke University Press, 2022.

Baár, Monika. "Informal Networks, International Developments, and the Founding of the First-Interest Representing Associations of Disabled People in Hungary in the Late Socialist Period (1970s–1980s)." *Moving the Social—Journal of Social History and the History of Social Movements* 53 (2015): 39–62.

Balogun, Bolaji, and Margaret Amaka Ohia-Nowak. "Geographies of Race in Poland and Central and Eastern Europe." *Ethnic and Racial Studies* 49, no. 1 (2024): 1–20.

Bartnikowska, Urszula, and Katarzyna Ćwirynkało. *Rodziny adopcyjne i zastępcze dziecka z niepełnosprawnością* [Adoptive and foster families of a disabled child]. Oficyna Wydawnicza Impuls, 2013.

Ben-Moshe, Liat. *Decarcerating Disability: Desinstitutionalization and Prison Abolition*. Minnesota University Press, 2020.

Berlant, Lauren. *Cruel Optimism*. Duke University Press, 2011.

Biehl, Joao. *Vita: Life in a Zone of Social Abandonment*. University of California Press, 2013.

Buden, Boris. *Strefa przejścia: o końcu komunizmu* [Zone of transition: the end of post-communism]. Translated by Michał Sutowski. Krytyka Polityczna, 2012.

Burakowski, Adam, Aleksander Gubrynowicz, and Paweł Ukielski. *1989: Jesień narodów* [1989: the fall of nations]. Państwowy Instytut Wydawniczy, 2021.

Carter, Angela. "When Silence Said Everything: Reconceptualizing Trauma through Critical Disability Studies." *Lateral: Journal for the Cultural Studies Association* 10, no. 1 (2021). https://doi.org/10.25158/L10.1.8.

Chajęcka, Eugenia. *Syn! Będzie szczęśliwa* [Son! She will be happy]. Książka i Wiedza, 1988.

Chełstowska, Agata. "Stigmatisation and Commercialisation of Abortion Services in Poland: Turning Sin into Gold." *Reproductive Health Matters* 19, no. 37 (2011): 98–106.

Chen, Mel Y., Alison Kafer, Eunjung Kim, and Julie Avril Minich, eds. *Crip Geneaologies*. Duke University Press, 2023.

Chodkowska, Maria. *Kobieta niepełnosprawna: socjopedagogiczne problemy postawy* [A disabled woman: sociopedagogical problems of behavior]. Wyd. Uniwersytetu Marii Curie-Skłodowskiej, 1993.

Chodkowska, Maria, ed. *Mieć dziecko z porażeniem mózgowym: pamiętniki matek* [To have a child with cerebral palsy: mothers' memoirs]. Pracownia Wydawnicza Fundacji "Masz Szansę," 1995.

Cierpieniem pisane: pamiętniki kobiet niepełnosprawnych [Written through suffering: disabled women's memoirs]. Polskie Forum Chrześcijańsko-Demokratyczne, 1991.

Constitution of the Polish People's Republic. Adopted by the Legislative Diet on July 22, 1952. Krajowa Agencja Wydawnicza, 1978.

Couser, G. Thomas. *Signifying Bodies: Disability in Contemporary Life Writing*. University of Michigan Press, 2009.

Czapliński, Przemysław. *Efekt bierności: literatura w czasie normalnym* [The passivity effect: literature in normal time]. Wydawnictwo Literackie, 2004.

Danylevich, Theodora, and Alyson Patsavas. "Introduction: Cripistemologies of Crisis: Emergent Knowledges for the Present." *Lateral: Journal for the Cultural Studies Association* 10, no. 1 (2021). https://doi.org/10.25158/L10.1.7.

Dec, Karolina. *Aspergerka, czyli życie na obcej planecie* [The Asperger woman, or life on a distant planet]. Rozpisani.pl, 2020.

Dega, Wiktor. *Kalekie dziecko* [The impaired child]. Ludowa Spółdzielnia Wydawnicza, 1951.

Detlaff, Rafał. "O Godności ludzi z upośledzeniem umysłowym w nauczania Jana Pawła II" [About the dignity of people with mental impairment in the teaching of John Paul II]. *Studia Gdańskie* 14 (2001): 297–311.

Dimitrova, Ina. "Impasses of Disability Alliance Building in Bulgaria." *Research in Social Science and Disability* 12 (2021): 67–85.

Dokumaci, Arseli. *Activist Affordances: How Disabled People Improvise More Habitable Worlds*. Duke University Press, 2023.

Domańska, Anna. *Los w rękach twoich* [Your destiny is in your hands]. Instytut Wydawniczy PAX, 1975.

Douglas, Jennifer. "Toward More Honest Description." *American Archivist* 79, no. 1 (2016): 26–55.

Dzięgielewska, Maria. *Losowi na przekór* [Against fate]. Książka i Wiedza, 1972.

Fidelis, Malgorzata. *Women, Communism, and Industrialization in Postwar Poland*. Cambridge University Press, 2010.

Fidowicz, Alicja. *Niepełnosprawność w polskiej literaturze XX i XXI wieku dla dzieci i młodzieży* [Disability in twentieth and twenty-first-century Polish literature for children and young people]. Wydawnictwo Uniwersytetu Jagiellońskiego, 2020.

Fink, Jennifer Natalya. *All Our Families: Disability Lineage and the Future of Kinship.* Beacon, 2022.

Foucault, Michel. *The History of Sexuality, Volume 1: An Introduction.* Translated by Robert Hurley. Vintage, 1990.

Fraser, Nancy. "Contradictions of Capital and Care." *New Left Review*, no. 100 (2016): 99–117.

Fraser, Nancy. "Rethinking the Public Sphere: A Contribution to the Critique of Actually Existing Democracy." *Social Text*, nos. 25–26 (1990): 56–80.

Freud, Sigmund, and Joseph Bauer. *Studies in Hysteria.* Translated by Nicola Luckhurst. Penguin, 2004.

Furgał, Ewa. *Dziewczyna w spektrum* [Girl on the spectrum]. Biała Plama, 2022.

Galmarini, Maria Cristina. *Ambassadors of Social Progress: A History of International Blind Activism in the Cold War.* Northern Illinois University Press, 2024.

Galtung, Johan. "Is a Socialist Revolution Under State Capitalism Possible?" *Journal of Peace Research* 17, no. 4 (1980): 281–90.

Garland Thomson, Rosemarie. "Misfits: A Feminist Materialist Disability Concept." *Hypatia* 26, no. 3 (2011): 591–609.

Garton Ash, Timothy. *The Magic Lantern: The Revolution of '89 Witnessed in Warsaw, Budapest, Berlin, and Prague.* Vintage, 1993.

Gawin, Magdalena. *Rasa i nowoczesność: historia polskiego ruchu eugenicznego* [Race and modernity: the history of the Polish eugenics movement]. Instytut Historii PAN, 2003.

Głąb, Zbigniew, and Magdalena Kocejko. "Between Safety and Isolation: The Governmental-Ministerial Approach to Care Homes in Poland During the COVID-19 Pandemic." *Disability & Society* 39, no. 6 (2022): 1–23.

Godlewska-Byliniak, Ewelina, and Justyna Lipko-Konieczna, eds. *Niepełnosprawność i społeczeństwo: performatywna siła protestu* [Disability and society: the performative power of protest]. Fundacja Teatr 21, 2018.

Goncharova, Galina. "The Generation of the Transition in Bulgaria and the Sentimental Narrative of Disability." *Critique and Humanism: Journal for Human and Social Studies* 55, no. 3 (2021): 83–101.

Grabowska, Magdalena. *Zerwana genealogia: Działalność społeczna i polityczna kobiet po 1945 roku a współczesny polski ruch kobiecy* [A broken genealogy: women's social and political activity after 1945 and the contemporary polish women's movement]. SCHOLAR, 2018.

Gray, Mary L., Colin R. Johnson, and Brian Joseph Gilley, eds. *Queering the Countryside: New Frontiers in Rural Queer Studies.* New York University Press, 2016.

Halberstam, Jack. *In a Queer Time and Place.* New York University Press, 2005.

Hamraie, Aimi, and Kelly Fritsch. "Crip Technoscience Manifesto." *Catalyst: Feminism, Theory, Technoscience* 5, no. 1 (2019): 1–33.

Hermann, Judith. *Trauma and Recovery: The Aftermath of Violence—From Domestic Abuse to Political Terror.* Basic Books, 2015.

Hirschmann, Nancy J., and Beth Linker. "Disability, Citizenship, and Belonging: A Critical Introduction." In *Civil Disabilities: Citizenship, Membership, and Belonging*, edited by Nancy J. Hirschmann and Beth Linker. University of Pennsylvania Press, 2015.

Hołub, Jacek. *Niegrzeczne: historie dzieci z ADHD, autyzmem i zespołem Aspergera* [Rude: stories of children with ADHD, autism, and Asperger's syndrome]. Wydawnictwo Czarne, 2020.

Hołub, Jacek. *Żeby umarło przede mną: opowieści matek niepełnosprawnych dzieci* [Hoping my child dies before I do: memoirs from mothers of disabled children]. Wydawnictwo Czarne, 2018.

Johnson, Merri Lisa, and Robert McRuer. "Cripistemologies: Introduction." *Journal of Literary and Cultural Disability Studies* 8, no. 2 (2014): 127–47.

Kafer, Alison. *Feminist Queer Crip.* Indiana University Press, 2013.

Kenney, Padraic. *A Carnival of Revolution: Central Europe, 1989.* Princeton University Press, 2002.

Kenney, Padraic. "The Gender of Resistance in Communist Poland." *American Historical Review* 104, no. 2 (1999): 399–425.

Kersten, Krystyna, and Tomasz Szarota. "Znaczenie masowych materiałów pamiętnikarskich w badaniach historycznych oraz aktualne możliwości ich wykorzystania" [The significance of mass diary materials in historical research and current possibilities of their use]. *Dzieje Najnowsze* 1 (1979): 159–66.

Kim, Eunjung. *Curative Violence: Rehabilitating Disability, Gender, and Sexuality in Modern Korea.* Duke University Press, 2017.

Kim, Jina B. *Care at the End of the World: Dreaming of Infrastructure in Crip-of-Color Writing.* Duke University Press, 2025.

Klich-Kluczewska, Barbara. *Rodzina, tabu i komunizm w Polsce, 1956–1989* [Family, taboo, and communism in Poland, 1956–1989]. LIBRON, 2015.

Kocejko, Magdalena. "Sytuacja dzieci z niepełnosprawnościami w czasie pandemii COVID-19—analiza intersekcjonalna [The situation of children with disabilities during the COVID-19 pandemic—an intersectional analysis]." *Dziecko Krzywdzone: Teoria, badania, praktyka* 20, no. 2 (2021): 76–91.

Kolářová, Kateřina. "Crip Genealogies from the Postsocialist East." In *Crip Genealogies*, edited by Mel Y. Chen, Alison Kafer, Eunjung Kim, and Julie Avril Minich. Duke University Press, 2023.

Kolářová, Kateřina. "The Inarticulate Post-Socialist Crip: On the Cruel Optimism of Neoliberal Transformations in Czech Republic." *Journal of Literary and Cultural Disability Studies* 8, no. 3 (2014): 257–74.

Kolářová, Kateřina. *Rehabilitative Postsocialism: Disability, Sex, and Race in Eastern Europe.* University of Michigan Press, 2025.

Kolářová, Kateřina, and Martina Winkler. "Introduction: Vision, Promises, Frustrations: Disability and the Socialist Project." In *Re/Imaginations of Disability in State Socialism*, edited by Kateřina Kolářová and Martina Winkler. Campus Verlag, 2021.

Kondakov, Alexander. "Crip Kinship: A Political Strategy of People Who Were Deemed Contagious by the Shirtless Putin." *Feminist Formations* 30, no. 1 (2018): 71–90.

Kotas, Dorota. *Cukry* [Sugars]. Wydawnictwo Cyranka, 2021.

Korolczuk, Elzbieta, and Renata Hryciak. "Wstęp" [Introduction]. In *Pożegnanie z Matką Polką: dyskursy, praktyki i reprezentacje macierzyństwa we współczesnej Polsce* [Farewell to the Polish mother: discourses, practices and representations of motherhood in modern poland], edited by Elżbieta Korolczuk and Renata Hryciuk. Wydawnictwa Uniwersytetu Warszawskiego, 2012.

Kościańska, Agnieszka, Michał Petryk. *Odejdź: rzecz o polskim rasizmie* [Go away: a thing about Polish racism]. Wydawnictwo Krytyki Politycznej, 2022.

Kościelska, Małgorzata. *Odpowiedzialni rodzice: z doświadczeń psychologa* [Responsible parents: from the experience of a psychologist]. Oficyna Wydawnicza Impuls, 2011.

Kowalik, Tadeusz. *www.PolskaTransformacja.pl* [www.PolishTransformation.pl]. Muza, 2009.

Król, Agnieszka. *Reprodukcja a reżimy sprawności* [Reproduction vs. fitness regimes]. NOMOS, 2022.

Krzemkowska, Zofia. "International Women's Year 1975." *Review of the European Blind* 3 (1974): 18–22.

Kubicki, Paweł, Rafał Bakalarczyk, and Marek Mackiewicz-Ziccardi. "Protests of People with Disabilities as Examples of Fledgling Disability Activism in Poland." *Canadian Journal of Disability Studies* 8, no. 5 (October 2019): 141–61.

Kubisa, Julia, and Katarzyna Rakowska. "Was It a Strike? Notes on the Polish Women's Strike and the Strike of Parents of Persons with Disabilities." *Praktyka Teoretyczna* 30, no. 4 (2018): 15–50.

Kurczewski, Jacek. *The Resurrection of Rights in Poland.* Clarendon, 1993.

Lebow, Katherine. "Autobiography as Complaint: Polish Social Memoir Between the World Wars." *Laboratorium: Russian Review of Social Research* 6, no. 3 (2014): 13–25.

Lejeune, Philippe. *On Autobiography*. University of Minnesota Press, 1989.

Maliszewska, Anna. "W pełni ludzie: osoby z głęboką niepełnosprawnością intelektualną przez prymat nauczania Kościoła Katolickiego" [Fully human: people with profound intellectual disabilities through the primacy of Catholic Church teachings]. *Studia Bobolanum* 29, no. 2 (2018): 45–76.

Matthews, Steve. "Anonymity and the Social Self." *American Philosophical Quarterly* 47, no. 4 (2010): 351–63.

McGuire, Anne. *War on Autism: On the Cultural Logic of Normative Violence*. University of Michigan Press, 2016.

McRuer, Robert. *Crip Times: Disability, Globalization, Resistance*. New York University Press, 2018.

Michalczak, Katarzyna. *Gdzie zgłosić dzikie zwierzę* [Where to report a wild animal]. Wydawnictwo Cyranka, 2024.

Mitchell, David T. "Body Solitaire: The Singular Subject of Disability Autobiography." *American Quarterly* 52, no. 2 (2000): 311–15.

Moskal, Magdalena. *Emil i my: monolog wielodzietnej matki* [Emil and us: a monologue of a mother of three]. Wydawnictwo Karakter, 2021.

Muca, Klaudia. *Opowiedzieć niepełnosprawność: wybrane problemy kulturowych reprezentacji niepełnsoprawności* [To narrate a disability: selected issues of cultural representations of disability]. fundacja terytoria książki, 2024.

Muñoz, José Esteban. *Disidentifications: Queers of Color and the Performance of Politics*. University of Minnesota Press, 1999.

Nishida, Akemi. *Just Care: Messy Entanglements of Disability, Dependency, and Desire*. Temple University Press, 2022.

Nowak, Margaret Ohia. Antyczarny rasizm: język—dyskurs—komunikacja [Anti-Black racism: language—discourse—communication]. Wydawnictwo UMCS, 2025.

Ost, David. *The Defeat of Solidarity: Anger and Politics in Postcommunist Europe*. Cornell University Press, 2005.

Pamula, Natalia. "Maternal Impressions: Disability Memoirs in Socialist Poland." *Aspasia: The International Yearbook of Central, Eastern, and Southeastern European Women's and Gender History* 1, no. 13 (2019): 95–112.

Pamula, Natalia. "Ordinary Trauma: Twenty-One Disabled Women Surviving the 1989 Polish Transformation." *Aspasia: The International Yearbook of Central, Eastern, and Southeastern European Women's and Gender Studies* 1, no. 16 (2022): 130–48.

Pamula, Natalia. "Precarious Belonging: Blindness, Masculinity, and Work in Polish Young Adult Literature of the 1970s and 1980s." *Canadian Slavonic Papers* 61, no. 12 (2019): 186–202.

Pamula, Natalia. "Violent Inclusion: Disability and the Nation in Polish 1950s and 1960s Young Adult Literature." *East European Politics and Societies and Cultures* 34, no. 4 (2020): 858–78.

Pamula, Natalia, and Magda Szarota. "Symbiotic Citizenship and a Struggle for the Right to Life as Frames for Interpreting the 40-Day Disability Protest in the Polish Parliament." In *Rethinking Disability and Human Rights: Participation, Equality, and Citizenship*, edited by Inger Marie Lid, Edward Steinfeld, and Michael Rembis. Routledge, 2023.

Phillips, Sarah. *Disability and Mobile Citizenship in Postsocialist Ukraine*. Indiana University Press, 2011.

Pohlhaus, Gail, Jr. "Relational Knowing and Epistemic Injustice: Toward a Theory of Willful Hermeneutical Ignorance." *Hypatia* 27, no. 4 (2012): 715–35.

Porter-Szücs, Brian. *Poland in the Modern World: Beyond Martyrdom*. John Wiley & Sons, 2014.

Price, Margaret. "Time Harms: Disabled Faculty Navigating the Accommodations Loop." *South Atlantic Quarterly* 120, no. 2 (2021): 257–77.

Rapp, Rayna, and Faye Ginsburg. "Enabling Disability: Rewriting Kinship, Reimagining Disability." *Public Culture* 13, no. 3 (2001): 533–56.

Rembis, Michael. "Introduction." In *Disabling Domesticity*, edited by Michael Rembis. Palgrave Macmillan, 2016.

Rotbard, Sharon. *White City, Black City: Architecture and War in Tel Aviv and Jaffa*. Translated by Orit Gat. Pluto, 2015.

Ryrych, Katarzyna. *Wyspa mojej siostry* [My sister's island]. Wydawnictwo Stentor, 2011.

Sałkowska, Marta. "Sejmowe protesty opiekunów osób z niepełnosprawnościami—wybrane wątki analityczne artykułów prasowych" [Parliamentary protests of caregivers for people with disabilities—selected analytical themes of newspaper articles]. *Societas/Communitas* 26, no. 2 (2018): 233–46.

Sałkowska, Marta et al. *Lista (nie)obecności: niepełnosprawność w podręcznikach szkolnych* [List of (dis)attendance: disability in textbooks]. Collegium Civitas, 2021.

Samuels, Ellen. *Fantasies of Identification: Disability, Gender, Race.* New York University Press, 2014.

Schaffer, Talia. *Communities of Care: The Social Ethics of Victorian Fiction.* Princeton University Press, 2021.

Schmüsser, Pia. "'We as parents must be helped': State-Parent Interactions on Care Facilities for Children with Mental Disabilities in the GDR." In *Re/Imaginations of Disability in State Socialism*, edited by Kateřina Kolářová and Martina Winkler. Campus Verlag, 2021.

Schwartz, Joan M., and Terry Cook. "Archives, Records, and Power: The Making of Modern Memory." *Archival Science* 2 (2002): 1–19.

Shakespeare, Tom. "The Social Model of Disability." In *The Disability Studies Reader, Fourth Edition*, edited by Lennard J. Davis. Routledge, 2013.

Siemaszkiewicz, Eugenia. *Białe niebo* [White heaven]. Czytelnik, 1967.

Sokołowska, Magdalena. "Polskie badania socjologiczne nad niepełną sprawnością: przeszłość i stan obecny" [Polish sociological research on incomplete fitness: past and present]. In *Studia z socjologii niepełnej sprawności* [Studies in the sociology of incomplete fitness], edited by Magdalena Sokołowska and Andrzej Rychard. Zakład Narodowy im. Ossolińskich, 1983.

Stańczak-Wiślicz, Katarzyna. "Od neomatriarchatu do szpitala-pomnika Matki Polki: ideologie macierzyństwa w dyskursach władzy i opozycji w Polsce (1945–1989)" [From neomatriarchy to a Polish Mother hospital-monument: motherhood ideologies in the state and dissidents' discourses (1945–1989)]. In *Niebezpieczne związki: macierzyństwo, ojcostwo i polityka* [Dangerous relationships: motherhood, parenthood, and politics], edited by Renata Hryciuk and Elżbieta Korolczuk. Wydawnictwa Uniwersytetu Warszawskiego, 2015.

Stasiak, Marcin. *Polio w Polsce, 1945–1989: studium z historii niepełnosprawności* [Polio in Poland, 1945–1989: a study of disability history]. Universitas, 2021.

Sufian, Sandra. *Familial Fitness: Disability, Adoption, and Family in Modern America.* University of Chicago Press, 2022.

Szarota, Magda. "Niepełnosprawność, aktywizm i feminizm, czyli (feministyczne) studia o niepełnosprawności w pigułce," [Disability, activism, and feminism, or (feminist) disability studies in a nutshell]. In *Zespół Turnera: głosy i doświadczenia* [Turner syndrome: voices and experiences], edited by Ewa Maciejewska-Mroczek, Magdalena Radkowska-Walkowicz, and Maria Reimann. Oficyna Naukowa, 2019.

Szcześniak, Magda. *Normy widzialności: tożsamość w czasie transformacji* [Norms of visibility: identity in the times of transformation]. Fundacja Nowej Kultury Bęc Zmiana, 2016.

Szcześniak, Magda. "Od chłopa do rolnika: socjalistyczne opowieści awansu na polskiej wsi w latach sześćdziesiątych"[From peasant to farmer: socialist tales of advancement in the Polish countryside in the 1960s]. *Kultura i Społeczeństwo* 2 (2022): 99–124.

Szczuka, Kazimiera. *Milczenie owieczek: rzecz o aborcji* [The silence of the lambs: on abortion]. WAB, 2004.

Szelewa, Dorota. "Polityka rodzinna w Polsce po 1989 roku: od familalizmu prywatnego do publicznego?" [Family policy in Poland after 1989: from private to public familism?]. In *Niebezpieczne związki: macierzyństwo, ojcostwo i polityka* [Dangerous relationships: motherhood, fatherhood and politics], edited by Renata Hryciuk and Elżbieta Korolczuk. Wydawnictwa Uniwersytetu Warszawskiego, 2015. Szpila, Agnieszka. *Łebki od szpilki* [Pinheads]. WAB, 2015.

Sztompka, Paweł. "The Ambivalence of Social Change in Post-Communist Societies." In *Czy koniec socjalizmu? Polska transformacja w teoriach socjologicznych* [Polish transformation through the lens of sociological theories], edited by Anna Śliz and Marek S. Szczepański. Scholar, 2008.

Sytuacja ludzi niepełnosprawnych i stan rehabilitacji w PRL [The situation of disabled people and the condition of rehabilitation in the Polish People's Republic]. Zakład Narodowy Ossolińskich, 1984.

Terakowska, Dorota. *Poczwarka* [The pupa]. Wydawnictwo Literackie, 2001.

Ther, Philipp. "Groping in the Dark: Expectations and Predictions, 1988–1991." In *From Revolution to Uncertainty: The Year 1990 in Central and Eastern Europe*, edited by Joachim von Puttkamer, Włodzimierz Borodziej, and Stanislav Holubec. Routledge, 2020.

Torańska, Teresa. *My* [Us]. Most, 1994.

Vargha, Dora. "Missing Pieces: Integrating the Socialist World in Global Health History." *History Compass* 21 (2023): 1–8.

Vargha, Dora. *Polio Across the Iron Curtain: Hungary's Cold War with an Epidemic.* Cambridge University Press, 2021.

Verdery, Katherine. *What Was Socialism and What Comes Next*. Princeton University Press, 1996.

Waligórska, Magdalena. *Cross Purposes: Catholicism and the Political Imagination in Poland.* Cambridge University Press, 2024.

Wawrzyniak, Joanna. "Transforming Industry: On the Corporate Origins of Post-Socialist Nostalgia in Poland." In *From Revolution to Uncertainty: The Year 1990 in Central and Eastern Europe*, edited by Joachim von Puttkamer, Włodzimierz Borodziej, and Stanislav Holubec. Routledge, 2020.

Wawrzyniak, Joanna, and Aleksandra Leyk. *Cięcia: mówiona historia transformacji* [Cuts: an oral history of transformation]. Wydawnictwo Krytyki Politycznej, 2020.

Wendell, Susan. "Toward a Feminist Theory of Disability." *Hypatia* 4, no. 2 (1989): 104–24.

Whatcott, Jess. "Crip Collectivity Beyond Neoliberalism in Octavia Butler's *Parable of the Sower*." *Lateral: Journal of the Cultural Studies Association* 10, no. 1 (2021). https://csalateral.org/section/cripistemologies-of-crisis/crip-collectivity-beyond-neoliberalism-octavia-butler-parable-of-the-sower-whatcott/.

Wieczorek, Maciej, and Katarzyna Ojrzyńska. "Disability, Dis(sensual) Art, and the Politics of Participation." In *Disability and Dissensus: Strategies of Disability Representation and Inclusion in Contemporary Culture*, edited by Katarzyna Ojrzyńska and Maciej Wieczorek. Brill, 2020.

Woś, Rafał. *Zimna Trzydziestoletnia: nieautoryzowana biografia polskiego kapitalizmu* [A cold thirty-year-old: an unauthorized biography of Polish capitalism]. Mando, 2019.

Wrochno-Stanke, Krystyna. "Niepełnosprawni o swojej sytuacji życiowej" [Disabled people about their living situation]. In *Studia z socjologii niepełnej sprawności* [Studies in the sociology of incomplete fitness], edited by Magdalena Sokołowska and Andrzej Rychard. Zakład Narodowy im. Ossolińskich, 1983.

Yergeau, Remi M. *Authoring Autism: On Rhetoric and Neurological Queerness.* Duke University Press, 2018.

Zaremba, Łukasz. "Słowiański blackface: z archiwum wizualnego kompleksu kolonialnego międzywojnia" [Slavic blackface: excerpts from the visual archive of the interwar colonial complex]. *Konteksty: Polska Sztuka Ludowa* 338, no. 3 (2022): 44–55.

Zavirŝek, Darja. and Svenja Fischbach. "Independent Living in Post-Socialist Countries: Between Familialism, Deinstitutionalisation, and Reinstitutionalisation." *International Journal of Disability and Social Justice* 3, no. 1(2023): 96–113.

Zdrodowska, Magdalena. "I'm Angry! Disability Protests in Post-Communist Poland." *Problems of Post-Communism* 72, no. 3 (2023): 1–12.

Żukowski, Tomasz. "Lewica i PRL w dyskursie głównego nurtu" [The Left and the Polish People's Republic in mainstream public discussion]. In *Opowiedzieć PRL* [To narrate the Polish People's Republic], edited by Katarzyna Chmielewska and Grzegorz Wołowiec. Wydawnictwo Instytut Badań Literackich, 2011.

News and Online Articles

"Andrzej Duda o LGBT" [Andrzej Duda on LGBT]. *Rzeczpospolita*, June 16, 2020. https://www.rp.pl/wydarzenia/art8909311-andrzej-duda-o-lgbt-probuja-wmowic-ze-to-ludzie-to-ideologia.

Badabada. http://badabada.pl.

Bakalarczyk, Rafał. "Opiekunowie osób wymagających stałego wsparcia bez priorytetu w szczepieniach: to błąd" [Caregivers of people requiring ongoing support without prioritizing vaccinations: this is a mistake]. OKO.press, January 6, 2021. https://oko.press/opiekunowie-bez-priorytetu-w-szczepieniach-to-blad.

Bakalarczyk, Rafał. "Wirus w domach pomocy społecznej" [Virus in nursing homes]. *Krytyka Polityczna*, April 10, 2020. https://krytykapolityczna.pl/kraj/domy-opieki-spolecznej-koronawirus-rafal-bakalarczyk/.

Bednarek, Michalina, and Ewa Furtak. "Niepełnosprawni wciąż bez szczepień i umierają na COVID-19" [Disabled still without vaccinations and dying of COVID-19]. *Wyborcza.pl-Katowice*, April 3, 2021. https://katowice.wyborcza.pl/katowice/7,35063,26936614,najbardziej-narazeni-wciaz-bez-szczepien-umieraja-na-covid-19.html.

Bednarek, Michalina. "Od miesięcy nie wyszli z domu, proszą o szczepionki: 'To eutanazja w białych rękawiczkach'" [They haven't left home for months, asking for vaccines: 'It's euthanasia in white gloves']. *Wyborcza.pl-Katowice*, January 20, 2021. https://katowice.wyborcza.pl/katowice/7,35063,26700013,od-miesiecy-nie-wyszli-z-domu-bo-dla-nich-wirus-rowna-sie-smierc.html.

"Bestselly 2003" [2003 bestsellers]. *Wyborcza.pl-Kraków*, January 18, 2004. https://krakow.wyborcza.pl/krakow/7,35796,1871476.html.

Bierzanowska, Katarzyna. "'Nadszedł czas na walkę': Kobiety z niepełnosprawnością przeciw 'kapłanom' i 'faszystom'" ["It's time to fight back": Women with disabilities against "priests" and "fascists"]. OKO.press, November 3, 2020. https://oko.press/nadszedl-czas-na-walke-kobiety-z-niepelnosprawnoscia-przeciw-kaplanom-i-faszystom.

Chrzszczonowicz, Magdalena. "Polskie dzieci tylko dla Polaków: nieludzka decyzja Ministerstwa Rodziny. "Taką mamy teraz rzeczywistość" [Polish children only for Poles: inhuman decision of the Ministry of Family. "This is the reality we have now"]. OKO.press, January 24, 2021. https://oko.press/polskie-dzieci-dla-polakow-nieludzka-decyzja-ministerstwa-rodziny-taka-teraz-rzeczywistosc.

Czapliński, Przemysław. "Nadnaturalny dar ułomności" [The supernatural gift of defect]. *Polityka*, April 7, 2001. https://www.polityka.pl/archiwumpolityki/1834492,1,nadnaturalny-dar-ulomnosci.read.

Czechowicz, Jarosław. "*Niegrzeczne: historie dzieci z ADHD, autyzmem i zespołem Aspergera*" [*Rude: Stories of Children with ADHD, Autism, and Asperger's Syndrome*]. *Krytycznym okiem*, January 22, 2020. http://krytycznymokiem.blogspot.com/2020/02/niegrzeczne-historie-dzieci-z-adhd.html.

"Cukry" [Sugars]. *Lubimy czytać*. https://lubimyczytac.pl/ksiazka/4964939/cukry.

Czyżewska, Basia. "Joanna Musiał: Spektrum autyzmu to nie choroba" [Joanna Musiał: Autism spectrum is not a disease]. *Vogue.pl*, April 2, 2022. https://www.vogue.pl/a/joanna-musial-spektrum-autyzmu-to-nie-choroba.

Danielewicz, Marta. "Śmierć w DPS-ach: statystki mówią, że zgonów z powodu koronawirusa nie było tak dużo, ale rzeczywistość może być inna" [Deaths in the residential institutions: statistics say coronavirus deaths were not that many, but reality may be different]. *Głos Wielkopolski*, May 26, 2020. https://plus.gloswielkopolski.pl/smierc-w-dpsach-statystki-mowia-ze-zgonow-z-powodu-koronawirusa-nie-bylo-tak-duzo-ale-rzeczywistosc-moze-byc-inna/ar/c1-14987744.

Dazbłąż, Beata. "Chcesz wyjść z DPS-u? Powiedz: po co, z kim, dlaczego. Weekendy bez odwiedzin" [Do you want to leave the institution? Tell us: why, with whom, why. Weekends without visits]. *Niepełnosprawni.pl*, August 6, 2021. http://www.niepelnosprawni.pl/ledge/x/1837278;jsessionid=B715B2A88BCEC539AE86A8429FB79FCD.

"Definicja" [Definition]. Synapsis.org, January 8, 2026. https://synapsis.org.pl/autyzm/czym-jest-autyzm/definicja-autyzmu/.

"Dramatyczny apel ojca dziecka z niepełnosprawnością: Bez szczepienia będziemy więźniami we własnych domach" [Dramatic plea from the father of a child with disabilities: Without vaccination, we will be prisoners in our own homes]. *Wyborcza.pl-Wrocław*, March 24, 2021. https://wroclaw.wyborcza.pl/wroclaw/7,35771,26913208,dramatyczny-apel-ojca-dziecka-z-niepelnosprawnoscia-bez-szczepienia.html.

"Dramatyczna sytuacja w DPS w Kaliszu: zmarło 7 pensjonariuszy, brakuje kadry" [Dramatic situation at a residential institution in Kalisz: 7 residents died, staff is missing]. *Gazeta Prawna*, April 17, 2020. https://www.gazetaprawna.pl/wiadomosci/artykuly/1469995,koronawirus-kalisz-dps-smierc-7-osob.html.

Dobrzyńska, Beata. "Koronawirus w DPS-ie w Drzewicy: kolejne zachorowania na COVID-19 i śmierć podopiecznej" [Coronavirus in the residential institution in Drzewica: more cases of COVID-19 and the death of a ward]. *Tomaszów Mazowiecki NaszeMiasto*, April 12, 2020. https://tomaszowmazowiecki.naszemiasto.pl/koronawirus-w-dps-ie-w-drzewicy-kolejne-zachorowania-na/ar/c1-7650619.

"Dramat w DPS-ach: miały być bezpieczną przystanią, a stały się śmiertelną pułapką" [Drama in the residential institutions: they were supposed to be a safe haven, but became a death trap]. Fakt, April 16, 2020. https://www.fakt.pl/wydarzenia/polska/koronawirus-w-polsce-ewakuacja-domow-pomocy-spolecznej/9xdc2lg.

Dudek, Anna J. "Jan Paweł II o niepełnosprawnych: 'Uczą świat, czym jest miłość.' Abp Hoser o proteście: 'Kościół nie jest stroną sporu'" [John Paul II on the disabled: "They teach the world what love is." Archbishop Hoser on the protest: "The Church is not a party to this dispute."]. *Wysokie Obcasy*, May 9, 2018. https://www.wysokieobcasy.pl/wysokie-obcasy/7,100865,23371500,jan-pawel-ii-o-niepelnosprawnych-ucza-swiat-czym-jest-milosc.html.

Gołdyn, Dominik. "Nowe ogniska COVID-19. Szumowski zapowiada zmiany w pracy personelu medycznego" [New COVID-19 outbreaks; Szumowski announces changes to medical staff]. Radio Zet Wiadomości, April 20, 2024. https://wiadomosci.radiozet.pl/Koronawirus/Nowe-ogniska-koronawirusa.-Szumowski-zapowiada-zmiany-w-pracy-personelu-medycznego.

Janiak, Monika. "Aspergerka, czyli życie na obcej planecie" [An Asperger woman, or life on a distant planet]. Goodbuk.pl, July 20, 2020. http://goodbuk.pl/2020/07/20/aspergerka-czyli-zycie-na-obcej-planecie-k-dec/.

Janiak, Weronika. "Recenzja: Karolina Dec, *Aspergerka, czyli życie na obcej planecie*" [A review: Karolina Dec, An Asperger woman, or life on a distant planet]. *Niebieska-Fala*, May 5, 2020. http://fundacja-furia.pl/niebieska-fala/2020/05/27/recenzja-karolina-dec-aspergerka-czyli-zycie-na-obcej-planecie-wyd-rozpisani-pl//.

Jędrzejczyk, Agnieszka. "Ogniowkurw na media: za sposób mówienia o niepełnosprawności" [Firecracker at the media: for the way they talk about disability]. OKO.press, March 24, 2023. https://oko.press/ogniowkurw-o-mowieniu-o-niepelnosprawnosci.

"Kaczyński: Premier Tusk świadomie działa na szkodę Polski" [Kaczyński: Prime minister Tusk knowingly acts to the detriment of Poland]. Onet, March 2, 2012. https://wiadomosci.onet.pl/kraj/kaczynski-premier-tusk-swiadomie-dziala-na-szkode-polski/66z9c

Karst-Adamczyk, Magdalena. "Powiedziałam, że muszę się zobaczyć z psychiatrą: Dostałam potrójną diagnozę" ["I said I needed to see a psychiatrist: I got a triple diagnosis"]. *Wysokie Obcasy*, December 16, 2022. https://www.wysokieobcasy.pl/wysokie-obcasy/7,173910,29255492,maz-powiedzial-ze-diagnoza-naszego-syna-polozy-cieniem-na-zyciu.html.

Klauziński, Sebastian. "'Nie ma kto dać jeść, przewinąć pieluch. Nie wytrzymamy dłużej'. Koronawirus zaatakował już 8 DPS-ów" ["There is no one to give food, change diapers. We can't hold out much longer." Coronavirus has already attacked 8 residential institutions]. OKO.press, April 4, 2020. https://oko.press/nie-ma-kto-dac-jesc-przewinac-pieluch-nie-wytrzymamy-dluzej-koronawirus-zaatakowal-juz-8-dps-ow.

Kolęda, Kamila. "Mama chorego na autyzm Kuby: Jestem gotowa do walki" [Mom of Kuba who is ill with autism: I'm ready to fight]. *Duży Format*, October 13, 2016. https://wyborcza.pl/duzyformat/7,127290,20825984,mama-chorego-na-autyzm-kuby-jestem-gotowa-do-walki.html.

"Koronawirus w Polsce—Maląg o osobach w kwarantannie: Nikt nie będzie pozostawiony sam sobie" [Coronavirus in Poland—Maląg on people in quarantine: No one will be left alone]. *Gazeta Prawna*, March 18, 2020. https://www.gazetaprawna.pl/wiadomosci/artykuly/1461373,koronawirus-w-polsce-malag-osoba-w-kwarantannie.html.

"Koronawirus w Zakładzie Opiekuńczo-Leczniczym: niepełnosprawne dzieci zostały bez opieki" [Coronavirus in a care facility: disabled children were left unattended]. *eDziecko*, October 14, 2020. https://www.edziecko.pl/zdrowie_dziecka/7,173990,26395385,koronawirus-u-pielegniarek-i-opiekunow-w-zakladzie-opiekunczo-leczniczym.html.

Kromer, Oktawia. "Karolina Kosecka: Protest rodzin osób z niepełnosprawnościami" [Karolina Kosecka: Protest by families of people with disabilities]. *Vogue.pl*, December 31, 2022. https://www.vogue.pl/a/karolina-kosecka-wywiad-ze-wspolorganizatorka-protestu-rodzin-ozn-ktore-walcza-o-prawo-do-pracy.

Kwaśniewski, Tomasz. "Dzieci z cechami ADHD i spektrum autyzmu są wtłaczane przez dorosłych w schematy, w których po prostu się nie mieszczą" [Children with

ADHD and autism spectrum traits are forced by adults into patterns in which they simply do not fit]. *Duży Format*, July 11, 2022. https://wyborcza.pl/duzyformat/7,127290,28667695,psychiatra-o-neuroroznorodnosci-te-dzieci-takie-sa-ze-robia.html#commentsAnchor.

Leśniak, Grażyna J. "MRPiPS pracuje nad planem działań przed drugą falą COVID-19" [The Ministry of Family and Labor is working on an action plan ahead of the second wave of COVID-19]. *Prawo.pl*, August 3, 2020. https://www.prawo.pl/kadry/kogo-planuje-chronic-przed-druga-fala-covid-19-resort-pracy,502116.html.

Lichnerowicz, Agnieszka. "'To jest igranie z ludzkim życiem'—koronawirus w domach pomocy społecznej" ["This is playing with people's lives"—coronavirus in nursing homes]. TokFM, October 1, 2020. https://audycje.tokfm.pl/podcast/96223,-To-jest-igranie-z-ludzkim-zyciem-koronawirus-w-Domach-Pomocy-Spolecznej.

"List do Premiera ws. trudnej sytuacji mieszkanek i mieszkańców DPS-ów" [Letter to the prime minister on the plight of the residents of the institutions]. FIRR, March 24, 2021. https://firr.org.pl/list-do-premiera-ws-trudnej-sytuacji-mieszkanek-i-mieszkancow-dps-ow/.

"Maląg: O osoby starsze i potrzebujące dbamy codziennie, nie tylko incydentalnie" [Malag: We take care of the elderly and needy every day, not just incidentally]. TVPParlament, April 16, 2020. https://www.tvpparlament.pl/47596517/malag-o-osoby-starsze-i-potrzebujace-dbamy-codziennie-nie-tylko-incydentalnie.

"Minister zdrowia zabiera głos w sprawie trudnej sytuacji w DPS-ach" [Health minister speaks out on difficult situation in residential institutions]. *Bankier*, April 15, 2020. https://www.bankier.pl/wiadomosc/Minister-zdrowia-zabiera-glos-w-sprawie-trudnej-sytuacji-w-DPS-ach-7863863.html.

Mirowski, Jakub, and Anna Mikulska. "Izolacja na co dzień: dzieci w spektrum autyzmu w dobie koronawirusa" [Isolation every day: children on the autism spectrum in the age of coronavirus]. *Krytyka Polityczna*, June 20, 2020. https://krytykapolityczna.pl/kraj/izolacja-na-co-dzien-dzieci-w-spektrum-autyzmu-w-dobie-koronawirusa-mikulska-mirowski/.

"Misja i cele" [Mission and goals]. Synapsis.org, https://synapsis.org.pl/o-nas/fundacja/misja-i-cele/ (no longer available).

Nocuń, Małgorzata. "*My* to każdy z nas" ["We" is each of us]. *Znak*, December 2021, https://www.miesiecznik.znak.com.pl/my-to-kazdy-z-nas/?fbclid=IwAR2pKB2E56DwK1UEJ5bcmEqiAXaE_NSKqzAjISAlzxJKG62V5hOZjoRtMhA.

Nowak, Katarzyna, ed. "Lekarze pozostawili w mieszkaniu niepełnosprawną 80-latkę" [Doctors left a disabled 80-year-old in an apartment]. *Gazeta.pl Wiadomości*, November 14, 2020. https://wiadomosci.gazeta.pl/wiadomosci/7,114883,26510817,plock-lekarze-pozostawili-w-mieszkaniu-niepelnosprawna-80-latke.html.

Nowak, Marta K. "Rząd nie szczepi szybciej osób z niepełnosprawnościami" [Government fails to vaccinate people with disabilities faster]. OKO.press, April 22, 2021. https://oko.press/rzad-nie-szczepi-szybciej-osob-z-niepelnosprawnosciami.

Nowak, Marta K. "Rząd zadrwił z osób z niepełnosprawnościami? Dla wielu szczepionek brak, ale za to bez kolejki" [The government has made a mockery of people with disabilities? For many, vaccines are in short supply, but without a queue]. OKO.press, May 13, 2021. https://oko.press/rzad-zadrwil-z-osob-z-niepelnosprawnosciami-szczepionek-dla-nich-brak.

Nowak, Marta K. "W placówkach opiekuńczych nawet 969 zakażonych: Ziobro chce ścigać uciekający wycieńczony personel" [Up to 969 infected in care facilities: Ziobro wants to prosecute fleeing and exhausted staff]. OKO.press, April 18, 2020. https://oko.press/w-placowkach-opiekunczych-nawet-969-zakazonych-ziobro-chce-scigac-uciekajacy-personel.

Nowakowska, Karolina. "Mieszkańcy DPS-ów umierają w samotności: szczepienia miały to zmienić. Sprawdzamy, jak jest w rzeczywistości" [Residents at the institutions are dying alone: vaccination was supposed to change that. We check how it is in reality]. *Gazeta Prawna*, February 27, 2021. https://www.gazetaprawna.pl/wiadomosci/kraj/artykuly/8106693,dps-szczepienia-wychodzenie-odwiedziny-przepisy.html.

Nowakowska, Karolina. "Rok po proteście niepełnosprawnych w Sejmie: żaden z 21 postulatów nie został w całości zrealizowany" [One year after the protest for the disabled in the Sejm: none of the 21 demands has been fully implemented]. *Gazeta Prawna*, May 7, 2019. https://www.gazetaprawna.pl/praca/artykuly/1410843,rok-po-protescie-niepelnosprawnych-w-sejmie-zaden-z-21-postulatow-nie-zostal-w-calosci-zrealizowany.html.

Nowosielska, Paulina, and Klara Klinger. "COVID-eutanazji nie było, ale prokuratura przygląda się DPS-om: Zawinił system?" [COVID-euthanasia didn't happen, but prosecutors are looking at the institutions: Was the system at fault?]. *Forsal.pl*, May 19, 2020. https://forsal.pl/artykuly/1477485,prokuratura-przyglada-sie-dps-om-koronawirus-covid-eutanazja.html.

Nowosielska, Paulina, and Klara Klinger. "Nie ma winnych śmierci w DPS-ach w czasie Covid-19—były doniesienia, są umorzenia" [No culprits in the residential institutions' deaths during COVID-19—there were reports, there are write-offs]. *Gazeta Prawna*, January 17, 2023. https://www.gazetaprawna.pl/wiadomosci/kraj/artykuly/8638202,pandemia-covid-19-koronawirus-smierc-seniorow-w-dps-spoleczenstwo.html.

Pelczar, Jan. "Autystyczny syn, zdesperowany ojciec: Rodzice: Zrezygnować z terapeutyzowania własnego dziecka, żeby się wyspać? [Autistic son, desperate father. Parents: giving up therapizing your own child to get some sleep?]. *Duży Format*, March 4, 2020. https://wyborcza.pl/duzyformat/7,127290,24499835,autystyczny-syn-zdesperowany-ojciec-rodzic-staje-przed.html.

"Pierwszy przypadek koronawirusa w Polsce [First case of coronavirus in Poland]. Ministerstwo Zdrowia, March 4, 2020. https://www.gov.pl/web/zdrowie/pierwszy-przypadek-koronawirusa-w-polsce.

Pilip, Łukasz. "Geniusz z autyzmem: 'Moje ciało to kula u nogi.' Zna sześć języków, skończył prawo. Dopiero uczy się mówić" [A genius with autism: "My body is a crutch." He speaks six languages and graduated from law school. He is just learning to speak]. *Duży Format*, March 20, 2017. https://wyborcza.pl/duzyformat/7,127290,21510116,geniusz-z-autyzmem-moje-cialo-to-kula-u-nogi-zna-szesc.html.

"Poczwarka" [The pupa]. Biblionetka.pl, December 25, 2005. https://www.biblionetka.pl/art.aspx?id=23247.

"Poczwarka—recenzja" [The pupa—a review]. Lekturia. http://lekturia.blogspot.com/p/10-poczwarka.html.

Polczyk, Patrycja. "Nie jestem matką, nie chcę nią być" [I'm not a mother, I don't want to be one]. *Wysokie Obcasy*, October 28, 2020. https://www.wysokieobcasy.pl/wysokie-obcasy/7,163229,26443655,nie-jestem-matka-nie-chca-nia-byc-moja-niepelnosprawnosc-wynika.html.

"Pozorny nadzór państwa nad placówkami świadczącymi opiekę całodobową" [Apparent state supervision of twenty-four-hour care facilities]. *Najwyższa Izba Kontroli*, April 22, 2020. https://www.nik.gov.pl/aktualnosci/nadzor-nad-placowkami-opieki-calodobowej.html.

Pożeraczka książek. "Recenzja książki—*Poczwarka*" [A review of a book—*The pupa*]. *Pożeraczka książek*, December, 3, 2014. http://wer-pozeraczkaksiazek.blogspot.com/2014/12/recenzja-ksiazki-poczwarka-dorota.html.

"Prokuratura bada sprawę śmierci piętnastu pensjonariuszy domu opieki przy Bobrowieckiej" [Prosecutor's office investigates death of fifteen residents of Bobrowiecka nursing home]. Tvn24, June 1, 2020. https://tvn24.pl/tvnwarszawa/najnowsze/koronawirus-w-warszawie-dps-przy-bobrowieckiej-nie-zyje-pietnastu-pensjonariuszy-prokuratura-bada-sprawe-st4599685.

"Protest w Sejmie zawieszony" [Protest in parliament suspended]. *Dziennik.pl*, May 27, 2018. https://wiadomosci.dziennik.pl/wydarzenia/artykuly/575181,protest-w-sejmie-zawieszony-iwona-hartwich-niepelnosprawni-koniec.html.

Próchniewicz, Dorota. "Autyzm jest problemem" [Autism is a problem]. *Niepełnosprawni.pl*, August 12, 2022. http://www.niepelnosprawni.pl/ledge/x/2025460?fbclid=IwAR2tBWFnl9YI9bAGqENAZ33R-ojmk483GbGV9IzUDuTtuR-oEXeK8yjs8CU.

Próchniewicz, Dorota. "Chcemy całego życia! Pozwólcie nam pracować!" [We want all the life! Let us work!]. *Niepelnosprawni.pl*, October 11, 2017. http://www.niepelnosprawni.pl/ledge/x/587808.

Próchniewicz, Dorota. "Hejt na autyzm" [Hating autism]. *Niepełnosprawni.pl*, March 31, 2021. http://www.niepelnosprawni.pl/ledge/x/1775715.

"Przymusowe wysiedlenie i zniszczenie mienia Romów rumuńskich w Gdańsku" [Forced displacement and destruction of property belonging to Romanian Roma in Gdańsk]. Amnesty International, August 7, 2014. https://www.amnesty.org.pl/przymusowe-wysiedlenie-i-zniszczenie-mienia-rom%C3%B3w-rumu%C5%84skich-w-gda%C5%84sku/.

Rakowski-Kłos, Igor. "Nie przeproszę za transformację" [I will not apologize for the transformation]. *Gazeta Wyborcza*, January 16, 2021. https://wyborcza.pl/alehistoria/7,121681,26681716,nie-przeprosze-za-transformacje.html.

"Rodzice niepełnosprawnych dzieci okupują Sejm" [Disabled children's parents occupy the Parliament]. *Gazeta Prawna*, March 21, 2014. https://www.gazetaprawna.pl/wiadomosci/artykuly/785566,rodzice-niepelnosprawnych-dzieci-okupuja-sejm.html.

Różański, Mateusz. "Jak uniknąć tragedii w domach pomocy społecznej?" [How to avoid tragedies in nursing homes?]. *Niepełnosprawni.pl*, April 9, 2020. http://www.niepelnosprawni.pl/ledge/x/960902.

Różański, Mateusz. "Kolejny protest: tym razem opiekunów osób dorosłych" [Another protest: this time caregivers of adults]. *Niepełnosprawni.pl*, March 27, 2014. http://www.niepelnosprawni.pl/ledge/x/181182.

Siałkowski, Kamil, and Zuzanna Bukłaha. "Protest pod Sejmem wsparciem dla strajku okupacyjnego RON" [Protest outside Parliament in support of RON occupation strike]. *Wyborcza.pl—Warszawa*, May 5, 2018. https://warszawa.wyborcza.pl/warszawa/7,54420,23359191,protestuja-pod-sejmem-wspierajac-strajk-okupacyjny-ron-rzad.html.

Siegień, Paulina. "Uwięzieni w czterech ścianach? Dla wielu z nas to codzienność" [Trapped in four walls? For many of us, this is our daily reality]. *Krytyka Polityczna*, May 1, 2020. https://krytykapolityczna.pl/kraj/anna-duniewicz-chcemy-calego-zycia-koronawirus-autyzm-niepelnosprawnosc/.

Stelmach, Monika. "Chaos i dezorganizacja przyczyniły się do śmierci pensjonariuszy DPS-u w Kaliszu" [Chaos and disorganization contributed to death of an institution's residents in Kalisz]. Termedia, May 7, 2020. https://www.termedia.pl/koronawirus/NSZZ-Solidarnosc-Chaos-i-dezorganizacja-przyczynily-sie-do-smierci-pensjonariuszy-DPS-u-w-Kaliszu,37777.html.

Szczerbiak, Agata. "Nie odsyłajmy protestujących niepełnosprawnych z Sejmu" [Let's not send disabled protesters out of Parliament]. *Polityka*, May 7, 2018. https://www.polityka.pl/tygodnikpolityka/spoleczenstwo/1747666,1,nie-odsylajmy-protestujacych-niepelnosprawnych-z-sejmu.read.

Szczęśniak, Agata. "Klęska programu 'Za Życiem': ujawniamy miażdżący raport NIK" [The disaster of the "In Support of Life" program: we reveal the crushing NIK report]. OKO.press, November 4, 2021. https://oko.press/kleska-programu-za-zyciem-ujawniamy-miazdzacy-raport-nik-tylko-w-oko-press?u=true#comment-105482.

Szpila, Agnieszka. "Gdzie są te dzieci? W dupie" [Where are these children? They are fucked!]. *Krytyka Polityczna*, September 12, 2022. https://krytykapolityczna.pl/kraj/swiadczenie-pielegnacyjne-dla-opiekunow-osob-z-niepelnosprawnoscia/.

Szpila, Agnieszka. "Rodzice dzieci z niepełnosprawnościami—niewolnicy polscy" [Parents of children with disabilities—Polish slaves]. OKO.press, https://oko.press/rodzice-dzieci-z-niepelnosprawnosciami-niewolnicy-polscy-temat-5-7-agnieszki-szpili.

"Tusk działa na szkodę polskich interesów i polskiego bezpieczeństwa dogadując się z Niemcami" [Tusk acts to the detriment of Polish interests and Polish security by making a deal with Germany]. *WPolityce*, February 11, 2024. https://wpolityce.pl/polityka/681485-romanowski-tusk-dziala-na-szkode-polskich-interesow.

Tutak-Goll, Monika. "Agnieszka Szpila: Nie mamy w domu kontaktów. Biurko połamane przez Milenkę. Piszę pod kołdrą. Piszę, żeby żyć" [We have no outlets at home.

Desk is broken by Milenka. I write under the covers. I write to live]. *Wysokie Obcasy*, October 6, 2022. https://www.wysokieobcasy.pl/wysokie-obcasy/7,173910,28982538,agnieszka-szpila-nie-pozwalaja-mi-pracowac-bo-pobieram-swiadczenie.html?utm_source=facebook.com&utm_medium=SM&utm_campaign=FB_wysokieobcasy&fbclid=IwAR0_23rh35EOe01HSzvxOgq_k-1fCuDBT5OARlZAWAg9e6qgFBTeryTocD4&disableRedirects=true.

Tutak-Goll, Monika. "'Ja też chcę mieć prawo wyboru.' Film niepełnosprawnej Bogumiły Siedleckiej zobaczyło już prawie 300 tys. osób" ["I also want to have the right to choose." The film by disabled Bogumiła Siedlecka has already been seen by nearly 300,000 people]. *Wysokie Obcasy*, November 4, 2020. https://www.wysokieobcasy.pl/wysokie-obcasy/7,163229,26477727,mama-zajmowala-sie-mna-przez-18-lat-tylko-dlatego-ze-poszla.html.

"W jakiej kolejności będą szczepieni opiekunowie osób niepełnosprawnych?" [In what order will caregivers of people with disabilities be vaccinated?]. *Wyborcza.pl*, January 11, 2021. https://wyborcza.pl/7,162657,26675181,w-jakiej-kolejnosci-beda-szczepieni-opiekunowie-osob-niepelnosprawnych.html.

Wilczyński, Przemysław. "Uwięzieni w DPS-ach: na wszelki wypadek" [Trapped at the institutions: just in case]. *Tygodnik Powszedni*, March 29, 2021. https://www.tygodnikpowszechny.pl/uwiezieni-w-dps-ach-na-wszelki-wypadek-166963.

"Wsparcie dla rodzin to nie łaska, a obowiązek państwa" [Support for families is not a favor, but a duty of the state]. *Gazeta Prawna*. https://www.gazetaprawna.pl/wiadomosci/kraj/artykuly/8733737,minister-marlena-malag-wsparcie-dla-rodzin-to-nie-laska-a-obowiazek-panstwa.html.

"Wzrasta liczba prywatnych domów opieki nad seniorami" [Number of private care homes for seniors on the rise]. *Medycyna prywatna*, March 8, 2020. https://medycynaprywatna.pl/wzrasta-liczba-prywatnych-domow-opieki-nad-seniorami-w-polsce/.

Zagórski, Sławomir. "My z Brunem jesteśmy naczyniami połączonymi. Matka OzN prosi o rozszerzoną eutanazję [Bruno and I are connected vessels. A mother of a disabled child asks for an extended euthanasia]." OKO.press, April 21, 2024. https://oko.press/osoba-z-niepelnosprawnoscia-matka-rozmowa?fbclid=IwZXhobgNhZW0CMTEAAR3ygm6Mo7qnNX94hSvzU1CPT8sxwHd1H_wr13rzZ2sa31hVozi_m8gpBJ4_aem_ATq308ZEFX71lr3OhRacLSx-ezTmVhPRb_2fskDeSVY_4mcil66q74pMmcUqRown6O3dlzRuPYO13G8ZGzs5vxJx.

"Zasiłki dla opiekunów niepełnosprawnych jak węzeł gordyjski: nowy protest, stare zaszłości" [Benefits for disabled caregivers like a Gordian knot: a new protest, old pasts]. Tvn24, April 18, 2018. https://tvn24.pl/polska/protest-opiekunow-niepelnosprawnych-w-sejmie-postulaty-ra830809-ls2360987.

Żółtowski, Mateusz. "Miasto Nierówności. Jak Gdańsk wyklucza Romów." *Krytyka Polityczna*, December 11, 2019. https://krytykapolityczna.pl/kraj/gdansk-romowie-dyskryminacja-dulkiewicz/.

Government Communiqués

"Koronawirus: Testy i sprzęt ochronny dla domów opieki to teraz kwestia życia i śmierci. RPO do premiera" [Coronavirus: testing and protective equipment for nursing homes is now a matter of life and death. The Commissioner for Human Rights writes to the prime minister]. *Biuletyn Informacji Publicznej RPO*, April 7, 2020. https://bip.brpo.gov.pl/pl/content/koronawirus-testy-i-ochrona-dla-domow-opieki-rpo-do-premiera.

"Pierwszy przypadek koronawirusa w Polsce [First case of coronavirus in Poland]. *Ministerstwo Zdrowia*, March 4, 2020. https://www.gov.pl/web/zdrowie/pierwszy-przypadek-koronawirusa-w-polsce.

"Pomoc dla osób niepełnosprawnych w dobie koronawirusa" [Help for people with disabilities in the times of coronavirus]. *Miejsko-Gminny Ośrodek Pomocy Społecznej w Gniewie*, April 9, 2020. https://www.mgops.gniew.pl/pomoc-dla-osob-niepelnosprawnych-w-dobie-koronawirusa/.

"Na koronawirusa w Polsce zmarło już ponad 100 tys. osób: Marcin Wiącek pisze do Ministra Zdrowia" [More than 100,000 people have already died from coronavirus in Poland: Marcin Wiącek writes to the Minister of Health]. *Biuletyn Informacji Publicznej RPO*, January 17, 2022. https://bip.brpo.gov.pl/pl/content/rpo-mz-koronawirus-alarmujaco-duzo-zgonow.

INDEX

NATALIA PAMUŁA is an assistant professor at the American Studies Center at the University of Warsaw.

The University of Illinois Press
is a founding member of the
Association of University Presses.

Composed in 10.25/13 Marat Pro
with Archer and Amboy displays
by Lisa Connery
at the University of Illinois Press

University of Illinois Press
1325 South Oak Street
Champaign, IL 61820–6903
www.press.uillinois.edu